Rose Growing Complete

Rose Growing Complete

E. B. LE GRICE

FABER AND FABER
3 Queen Square
London

First published in 1965
New and revised edition 1976
First published in this edition 1976
3 Queen Square London WC1
Printed in Great Britain by
Latimer Trend & Company Ltd Plymouth
All rights reserved

ISBN 0 571 10911 X (Faber Paperbacks)
ISBN 0 571 04906 0 (hardbound edition)

To my Mother
who taught me to love roses
and to my Wife
for whom I grow them

 CONTENTS

 ILLUSTRATIONS

Between pages 160 and 161

Acknowledgements for the photographs are made to the following: Jarrold & Sons Ltd. for plates 1, 2, 4, 7, 8, 9; The Ministry of Agriculture for plate 10; Messrs. Boots for plates 11, 13 and 14; Frederick Mace, M.M.P.A., for plates 5, 15 and 16; plate 12, Crown copyright, reproduced by permission of Controller, H.M.S.O.

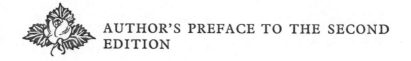 AUTHOR'S PREFACE TO THE SECOND EDITION

In preparing this new edition I have been dismayed by the many alterations made necessary by changes during the last eleven years. Metrication has made many changes inevitable and at this transitional stage actual measurements have been based on the old form.

Again I am indebted to many willing helpers and would like to thank Mr. and Mrs. R. E. R. Ling who helped my wife and myself classify new roses for perfume; Mr. A. G. Brown of the John Innes Institute for rechecking the chapter on genetics. Especially would I thank Mr. Turner, Secretary of the Royal National Rose Society for his corrections and suggestions for my chapter, 'One Hundred Years of the Royal National Rose Society'; Mr. Alex Dickson and Mr. Sam McGredy for notes of their firms' histories, also Mr. R. F. N. Wood of the Ministry of Agriculture for his help on modern sprays and Dr. D. P. de Vries of the Wageningen Institute of Plant Breeding for confirming my statement on early roses found in use in Holland.

I would like to express my thanks to Miss E. D. Brooksbank and Mrs. G. F. Renwick for their help and advice in the production of this edition, and especially to the latter for putting all the alterations into readable form for the printers.

If I have omitted anyone please accept my apologies. It has been a great pleasure to meet many readers in many parts of the world and I thank them for their encouragement and correspondence.

E. B. Le Grice
1975

Before the book goes to press I must record with great regret the deaths of Mr. Alex Dickson and Mr. R. E. R. Ling.

December 1975

AUTHOR'S FOREWORD TO THE FIRST EDITION

When the production of this book was first mooted I undertook the task readily, little realizing how much was involved.

Its inception was typical of its production, for the synopsis was prepared as I was driven from my home in Norfolk to the National Trial Grounds at St. Albans. Since then, odd chapters have been written on holiday, at home and abroad, as information has been sought and found. The railway train, the waiting-room, the British Museum Library, The Royal Horticultural Society Library have afforded places for adding to my store of knowledge or putting it down on paper.

I have been bewildered by the conflicting evidence, often from a common source of error, which has persisted uncorrected. While I have tried to verify my facts it has not always been possible to sift what is factual from what is traditional. In such a case I have tried to give reasons for my conclusions. Possibly further information may be obtainable and if so I hope it may be possible to add such knowledge in later editions.

Whatever the reception of this book may be, I, at least, have learned much during its production; if only, 'The more one learns, the less one knows, one knows.'

One of the pleasing features of this attempt to write *Rose Growing Complete* has been the willing co-operation of authorities in their specialist departments and the friendly help I have received on every hand.

Especially would I like to thank Mr. Richard de la Mare of Messrs. Faber & Faber for his encouragement and help at all times; Dr. R. H. Cammack for his help and information on virus in roses; and Her Majesty's Stationery Office for permission to use Crown Copyright photographs of these diseases; Miss Agar of the Burlingham Horticultural Station for her help in preparing the section on the genetics of the rose, especially for her original diagrams on cell division; Messrs. Boots, through Mr. Tom Fletcher, for advice and help on black spot, and for the loan of photographs.

I am particularly indebted to Mr. Neville F. Miller of Palmerston, U.S.A., for helping me with the chapter on perfume and reading the script and making suggestions; also to Mr. H. Fessel of Universal Rose Selection for obtaining specimens of the rose 'Rose de Mai', and for other help. Thanks are due, too, to Mr. Spek for his help on early Dutch Roses and to Monsieur J. Gaujard for his painstaking and lengthy correspondence on the history of hybridizing.

My thanks also to the Secretaries of the Royal National and American Rose Societies for their help. I have greatly appreciated the assistance given by the Librarian Mr. P. F. M. Stageman and staff of the Lindley Library of the Royal Horticultural Society and for the opportunity of reading books in the British Museum Library.

Eastern Electricity supplied information on glass-house heating; and for information and literature on sludge disposal and composting I am indebted to Mr. E. A. Blyth. I am grateful to *Chambers's Encyclopaedia* for the help of their Research and Information Bureau, and to Mr. Ralph M. Dasher, Executive Secretary Treasurer of the All America Rose Selection, for information.

For practical help from their experience I am indebted to Mrs. Toogood, Mrs. J. Steward, Mr. R. J. Hicks, and Mr. J. Mattock who introduced me to the finest work on roses so far produced in England, namely William Paul's *The Rose Garden*.

If I have omitted to thank any whom I should where thanks are due forgive my lapse and be assured that I have been most grateful for the help and kindness shown.

My aim has been to give as complete a work on the practical side of rose growing as possible. Every section might well be extended with advantage, but I have neither time nor ability to do so. My hope is that the pleasure of more than forty years of practical rose growing, now shared with you, may prove of help and encouragement to the very many who love the rose.

Since going to press, it has been announced that Her Majesty the Queen has graciously commanded that the National Rose Society be known as the Royal National Rose Society.

E. B. Le Grice
1965

PART I

GROWING ROSES

 CHAPTER I

Why Grow Roses?

To grow roses is easy. To grow roses well is not hard, but to grow the best roses demands and repays all the care and skill we can lavish upon them. Rose growing, like all else, is a question of practical application, and of experience which increases in range with successful achievement. There is added pleasure in the fellowship of sharing and comparing what we have done with what others have accomplished.

Once we have achieved a measure of success we want to know all we can about the rose: its past history stretching back into the earliest beginnings of gardening; the welding of distant families, drawn from the Far and Near East, with the roses of Europe, into new strains bearing the best qualities of their forebears; why some of these qualities are so hard to obtain and why others hold tenaciously to what we consider weaknesses wedded to their desirable assets; how colours combine to give depth, variety, and purity with unfading strength; how far does a perfume denote a colour, and how is the scent made? Why does this perfume vary in strength at different times of the day, and why does it change sometimes in type, as the bloom matures? The more we seek to know, the more there will be to discover. There are still great contributions to be made to our knowledge, not least the simple explanation of a complicated process, hitherto obscured by the scientific terminology so frightening to the bewildered layman.

It is the adaptability of the rose which makes its appeal so wide. Whether it be the tired business man seeking relaxation; the week-end owner of the cottage demanding quick results with little work; the not-so-young wishing to reduce labour; the wild-garden enthusiast, wanting specimen bushes with maximum appeal and minimum trouble; or the formal gardener, with a colour scheme and a set design; all can find their answer and many another too, in the great adaptability and wide variety to be found among roses.

To glance briefly at the opportunity for selection: take, for instance, height. Supported, a climber will clamber to the eaves of a house 7·6 m (25 ft) up. There are, however, in this same class of supported types, perpetual-flowering or once-flowering forms from 1·8 m (6 ft) coverage upwards. Nor need these claim upright support only. Drooping over a high bank, festooning a wire fence, wandering through the boughs of an ancient apple tree, they are a delight to the eye and can form a discreet covering for an unsightly object.

Today considerable areas need ground cover. It is impossible to keep large areas between shrubs or specimen roses hoed and planted. New roses are being bred and old cultivars adapted to cover such areas with spreading types of growth so that their foliage and flowers turn a problem into a blessing while a dressing of Simazine will solve the problem of annual weeds.

Shrub roses present an almost bewildering choice in height, colour, time and type of flowering. Some will flower profusely from early May. Many of the most beautiful are once-flowering, but their tracery of frond-like foliage, arching branches, or translucent thorns, with the added autumn attraction of differing hips, give a long season of charm, culminating in golden, red, copper, or russet foliage as they prepare for their winter's rest.

These are one branch only of the shrub roses. Many varieties will flower intermittently or perpetually. A few will have red hips nestling against the white flowers of autumn. Others will flaunt bold trusses of bloom until the autumn gales or early frost bring their season's delight to an end. Among such specimens are to be found a few with aromatic foliage, an added attraction.

There are the so-called 'old garden' varieties, some with the sanctity of age, many seen through the sentimental rose-coloured spectacles we use for viewing the past. There are many beauties not to be passed by. However, it was not for nothing that our forebears grew many of these roses in their kitchen gardens. There, the transient beauty of the flowers passed in a few days, leaving the petals to be gathered for potpourri, which would give lingering memories of warm June days in bleak December.

In the heady atmosphere of romance engendered by the enthusiast, the beginner should tread warily, lest he clutter his small garden with barren bushes for all but ten days of the year. With discretion and knowledge the old may give its best on equal terms with the new. It is when we turn to the present crowded century of progress that we are most bewildered by the choice presented to us.

Bush forms from 2 m (7 ft) downwards present their attractions. We may choose the large specimen flower with perfect reflexed petals building up to the pointed centre. We may prefer the clustered flower. These may be small and double, small and single, or larger still until they merge into the specimen flower on one stem in summer or as candelabras of bloom in the autumn. But what is more lovely than the perfection of a five-petalled flower, whether carried singly or in clusters? Braving rain as the more 'full' roses seldom do, they reveal the perfection of their golden or brown anthers, and are a revelation of the beauty which nature at her best, aided by man, can produce.

It is in the colouring that these more modern types excel. Pure golden yellow, the flame shades, the bicolours, the red lead, the mauve and lilac and now the browns and purple are all of recent introduction. Unknown before the 1900s, many of these owe their origin to the patient work of the French raiser, Pernet-Ducher. The fascinating story of how these changes came demands a chapter to itself (Chapter XIV).

With such a wide field reviewed so briefly, it would be small wonder if a novice, seeking to choose his first half-dozen varieties, foundered. Fortunately, there are simple means of breaking up this vast collection of many thousand varieties into groups, and from these groups choosing outstanding sorts which have the particular virtues for which we seek.

Rose growing calls forth so many varied and unexpected qualities. The skill of the craftsman, the creative vision of the artist, the persistence of the lover, the trained eye of constant observation. Of one thing we may be certain, the joys of rose growing strengthen with practice. The qualities fostered in the quiet country garden or the small suburban patch bring a friendly rivalry tempered with a sympathy born of experience. Whether it is from strolling in the cool of the evening, or better still, in the early dews of the morning, among our roses, or from taking a few blooms to a sick friend, or from exhibiting at some show, the pleasure of achievement is enhanced by sharing one's pleasure.

Some may feel that these statements are like an angler dangling bait to catch an unwary fish. Rather are they an invitation to share in the pleasure which fifty years of hard work in the production of roses have increased immeasurably. It is in the sharing of experience that one's knowledge grows. The object of this book will be, not to issue a rule-of-thumb guide but to explain 'the reason why'. If the reason for an action can be explained, then it can be adapted to the variable conditions of soil, climate, and finance which we all experience.

If there is one fact to be stressed above all else, it is that the rose plant is a living organism. It breathes, it feeds, it excretes. It differs, however, from the animal kingdom in the basic fact that it builds simple compounds into complex substances. Where the animal breaks down the plant builds up. As we apply this principle, we shall in future as soon leave an unprotected rose root to the biting wind as expose a naked baby to the winter's cold.

The fact that the plant is living is perhaps better realized than the fact that the soil too is a medium made usable to the plant because it is vitally alive, crowded with active bacteria, many good, some harmful, but each contributing to the health or otherwise of the plant. To maintain a satisfactory balance in this ceaseless war, our knowledge may tip the scales in favour of the plant.

When we are growing plants certain demands must be met. The four urgent needs are for air, water, warmth, and food. These must be applied in the right amount at the right time. This is easy to state but difficult to achieve. Fortunately, like all healthy humans, the plant is very adaptable, and although the best may not be possible, the necessary can be.

The rose as we know it is not a weakling to be sheltered and cosseted. It has had to contend with wide ranges of temperatures, with arid heat and bitter cold. It has survived the windswept wastes of sand dunes by the sea or open prairie, it has climbed perseveringly in forest glades to seek the sun. Because of this spartan upbringing it flourishes where air abounds and for this reason air is important for good health. This seems a simple demand but in practice it is not so easy. The confined site in a small garden may lead to diseases, such as mildew; to pests such as the leaf-rolling sawfly and to weakly, spindly growth. The nurseryman with his field-grown trees, buffeted by the winds of heaven, is seldom troubled by aphis or other pests, they prefer more comfortable quarters. This fact may help us to estimate the need of the roses. Abounding air, moving naturally, not as a cutting draught, is an important rule of health. We can strive for the maximum of air with the minimum of draught.

Although our conditions may not be ideal, if we realize the limitation of the site, we may mitigate the worst effects by the wise selection of surroundings within our choice. We can use a non-conductive material for our fences. Nothing will produce mildew more easily than a corrugated-iron fence. Temperature changes are rapid and devasting, giving a wide range on a hot day followed by a cool night, the ideal way to breed such trouble. A wooden fence of split chestnut or even a woven fence is preferable. If this is not possible and room can be spared, a hedge with limited root-run or even a post and plastic-covered wire fence will serve the purpose. We can avoid overplanting both by limiting the number of our bushes, and even more important, avoiding enclosing our plot with too many quick-growing shrubs and trees. When we come to the needs of the individual plant we can ensure the maximum of air by thoughtful pruning.

Water in its ideal form is warm rain. How often we get the chilly flood, reducing the earth to a quagmire when planting is to be done, or a heavy, brief downpour running off the parched earth when the bush is panting for moisture. Yet good cultivation can mitigate both these extremes. Our object should be to build up a retentive soil in which, under normal conditions, the bushes will flourish and throw off much disease.

As for pests, the methods of attacking them are nearly as numerous as are the pests themselves. We should aim at simple remedies as far as possible, harmless to man and domestic pets.

The theme of this book then will be straightforward: to pass on advice and information about 'growing roses'. Beginning with the nursery, we follow propagation, growing, and feeding the plant; how it is prepared and dispatched; how to get ready for its arrival and what to do when it comes; the plant and its roots, their structures and requirements; what the plant needs, and how to supply its wants; afterwards, having planted it, how to prepare for its awakening and growth. The pruning problem can loom large, as thorny as *Rosa omeiensis*, but once explained, is as satisfying a task as any in the year's round. We shall need a full chapter to discuss this. Having dealt with the basic facts of 'Growing Roses' we shall come to 'Showing Roses'. The great variety of uses probably accounts for the rose's great popularity. Each type opens a new vista of use. Indoor decoration as a cut flower provides an outlet for artistic ability and brings pleasure and distinction into any home. The wide field of exhibition claims a share, and provides a thrill which increases with achievement. Then we may use roses for their perfume's sake, so that those deprived of sight may yet enjoy our roses with us. These are some of the uses of the rose we shall discuss. But having come so far, we shall want to know more about our roses, so the final sections will be on 'Knowing Roses'. The story of the distribution of the rose family, its heredity and its possibilities, is a fascinating study. The gradual evolution through the centuries, the sudden forward surge when artificial hybridizing came into being—well over a hundred years ago—demands a book by itself, but must here be confined to three chapters. Toward the end of the book we shall consider how new roses are tested and proved worthy or wanting, and in summing up we shall draw up a list claiming your special attention.

In concluding this chapter let it be emphasized that our object should be to grow roses for pleasure. While we would not ignore the thorns—and they can be very beautiful as well as useful—we will seek to concentrate on the bloom with its fragrance, charm and beauty.

 CHAPTER II

Propagation

Growing new plants has a thrill of its own. Few can be unmoved as the sturdy seedling thrusts its head through the soil and shoulders its way into a world filled with gifts as well as dangers. There is a special pride of achievement when we see a new plant brought into being, aided by our skill. We may have no more actual participation in its form than the midwife who helps to bring an infant into the world, but who would deny her the pride in what she has done? So as the rose grower's knowledge increases, he longs to produce a new bush which could never have survived without his care and encouragement.

We may grow many plants from seed with the expectation of some degree of uniformity, as pedigree dogs mated together will usually produce similar progeny. But raising roses from seed is like mating a bloodhound with a collie. Who will predict the outline of such a mongrel? The rose has a chequered history, and the present-day rose is a mongrel from mongrels, so that its seedlings are unpredictable, and one can be certain of one thing only: a rose seed raised from its parents will not be like either. Such production by seed is sexual and leads to variety. To obtain uniformity asexual reproduction is essential.

The rose must be propagated vegetatively. In other words enough living tissue containing the plant in miniature must be transferred to make a new bush. This can be done in two ways: by using an established rose plant of another type as host, which has already its own root system and vigour, or by taking a sufficiently large portion of the wood to supply enough nourishment while that piece begins life on its own. First, it must make its own root system and then its upper plant structure. We shall consider both methods in detail. Whatever method is used the wood should be taken from healthy vigorous bushes only. (See 'Virus', page 96.)

The first method of propagation can be by budding or grafting. As grafting needs heat and is an expert's method with no advantages for the amateur, it will be ignored. We shall concentrate on the method of 'budding'. We shall meet the term 'bud' or 'eye' continually and to avoid confusion will always speak of 'bud' or 'eye' as the dormant shoot lying just within a leaf axil and protruding slightly from the bush. The term 'flower bud' will be used for the flower in its early stages of development.

The advantages of budding are the rapid multiplication of full-sized plants, possessing the additional vigour of the host plant and uniformity of growth. One plant can supply up to fifty budding eyes in a season. While this method takes two seasons to reach maturity, it produces uniform plants capable of full flower production in the summer following their autumn transplanting. Only one eye is needed to produce a plant, and this is of great importance where the variety is new or scarce. When one thinks of the millions of the rose 'Peace' which were all produced from the one original plant, one sees how important it is to use an effective method of multiplication.

A special type of knife is essential for the work of budding and must be kept clean and sharp the whole time. Sharpening is best done on a small carborundum stone with the blade held at an angle of twenty-two and a half degrees with the stone, using a circular motion. Each side should be given equal treatment.

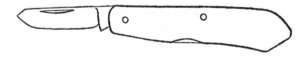

A good budding knife

The 'bud' or 'eye' is removed with sufficient bark surrounding it to ensure its safe transfer. The base of the knife-blade is inserted 0·85 cm ($\frac{1}{3}$ in) below the trimmed leaf stalk to make a shallow cut so that as little depth of wood as possible is removed. The cut continues for another 1·25 cm ($\frac{1}{2}$ in) above the bud, when the bark above this level may be torn away from the shoot by keeping the blade of the knife under the cut eye for support while this is being done. The complete cut is made by drawing the blade across the advancing incision, so that when completed, the knife-blade will be at its point. By this method the cut is made smoothly with one sweeping motion, thus avoiding a see-sawing effect which would leave jagged edges. As the branch surface is convex and the cut through the back of the shoot containing the eye straight, there is a small portion of wood tissue adhering to the cut portion. This wood, unless extremely thin, is better removed, so that the growing tissue beneath the bark and bud can come in direct contact with the growing tissue (the cambium layer) of the host plant. When the shield-shaped 'eye' has been cut out and the wood removed, the 'host' or stock is prepared by making a T-shaped incision on the smooth portion of the upper root just above ground-level, see plate 3. This cut is only possible when the stock is in active growth and the sap beneath makes the lifting of the bark simple. Once the opening has been made, the shield is slipped in beneath the bark, the surplus tissue is trimmed, and the cut is bound with raffia or closed with one of the new budding ties. The union between the growing tissues between 'eye' and 'host' is rapid, often a fortnight is enough, and all the essentials of a new rose plant have been completed. 'Budding' is done during July and August, and although a few buds grow at once, the majority remain dormant until the following spring. To induce growth the stocks are 'headed back', that is, the top growth is removed, leaving a small stump of root above where the budding took place. After this stage, which may be carried out in January or February, the amateur is well advised to remove any weeds and put a 60-cm (2-ft) stake close to the budded stock, ready to tie in the new growth when it is sufficiently tall, otherwise a gale may tear the young bud from its stock, and the labour and plant are lost. This is a risk the nurseryman must take, although he lessens the risk by nipping back the first growth to 10 cm (4 in) in length. During the cleaning, the plants may be fed in readiness for their later need. On the nursery, a crop of sixty good bushes for every hundred stocks planted may be reckoned as average. This would need at least eighty to eighty-five live buds per one hundred stocks to cover small bushes and loss by damage.

The place for the budding of standard roses differs with the stock used. The method employed is the same as for bushes. Standard roses are usually budded on tall stems of *R. canina* or its varieties, or on *R. rugosa*. They are budded at about 1 m (3½ ft) above the ground. Half-standards will be 0·76 m (2 to 2½ ft) high and 'weeping standards' which have ramblers budded on them are usually up to 1·5 m (5 ft) high. If the stems of *R. canina* standards are of over one year's growth they must be encouraged to send out side shoots towards the top of the stem. The three, or possibly four, best are chosen and the others rubbed off. Budding consists of inserting the eye on the top side of the new growth as close to the parent stem as possible. Certain named *R. canina* are especially grown for standards and, after cutting to the ground, send up one shoot of sufficient vigour in one year to be tall enough for transplanting and budding the following year. In such cases the buds are inserted three to a stem at the desired heights.

R. rugosa stems having made their growth the year previous to transplanting are also budded on their main stem.

In all cases, the 'heading back' consists of cutting away all but 15 cm (6 in) of the wood beyond the bud to induce the buds to break into growth; one has to keep a sharp lookout for 'suckers' (see plate 10) and rub these off at once. When growth begins from the buds and has reached the fifth leaf the tip should be pinched out, leaving not more than three or four leaves. It is a wise procedure to nip out flower buds during the first summer to encourage new growth, but full flowering should be allowed during September and October to harden and ripen the wood. The shortening of the young growths prevents their breaking away at the union. To complete the whole process the 'snag', the parent stock wood above the bud, should be carefully taken off before the trees are moved to their final quarters. Painting the cut end with a white lead paint is worth the trouble for the amateur for whom each plant is precious.

One may wonder which type of stock, brier or *rugosa*, is better to use for a standard. *R. canina*, the old dog rose, was the most popular for many years. Undoubtedly, the *best* briers are unbeatable, but very few such standards are available and their use is uneconomic, for out of a hundred stocks grubbed laboriously from the hedgerow, many will die on transplanting and few will attain the height and growth needed for full standards. These arguments are not true of the named seedling brier such as 'Pfander', which has been grown uniformly and rapidly, and can be budded directly on to the stem. Generally speaking brier stocks may be recognized by their smooth bark, often green or light brown, with few but large hooked thorns. Their flowers are single and pale pink. Probably one gets better results on heavy land from standards when grown on brier, provided the root system is young and plentiful.

The most generally used stock is the *R. rugosa*. This stock was especially bred from the wild form and produces a tall 1·5 to 1·8 m (5 to 6 ft) stem in its second year, from a rooted cutting, hard-pruned in the spring. Its vigour, uniformity and compatibility make it ideal for producing a large head in one season. Its roots are very fibrous and it needs shallow planting to give its best. It is particularly good on light, well-drained soils, and well-grown standards of ten years and over are not unusual. So far it is the only satisfactory standard from an economic viewpoint which must decide the average producer. The rugosa stems may be recognized by their dark, almost black stems, covered with numerous bristly thorns. It is used in its dwarf form, being more compatible, for rose 'Mermaid' and certain species. (Plate 1.)

On the nursery the dwarf stocks are usually planted by machine. Rows of stocks are usually planted 0·9 m (1 yd) apart with 20 cm (8 in) between plants. This means about 20,000 stocks to 0·405 hectares (1 acre) if allowance is made for turning of tractors.

Various types of stocks are chosen and preference is given to seedling stocks as these have a deeper rooting system and tend to damage less on transplanting. Also, a most important factor, they do not transmit virus (see page 96). It is possible to grow stocks from cuttings but this is usually an uneconomic process. *R. canina* in its wild mixed form has almost ceased to be grown having been superseded by a number of cultivated forms which give greater uniformity of growth but at present the ideal type has not been found. The stocks are grown by specialists and are usually imported, the complete change of soil seeming to make for a better finished plant. These seedlings after a season's growth are graded by the circumference of the root before it splits into fibre. These sizes are 4–6 mm, 5–8 mm, and 8–12 mm. The 5–8 mm, most usually planted, are about the size of a diary pencil and will be the thickness of an ordinary pencil when budded. The stocks grow rapidly during September and finish their first season with about 1·25 cm ($\frac{1}{2}$ in) diameter. The advantage of *canina* stock and its types is their adaptability to varying types of soil and climate, and the fact that the main roots anchor deeply into the soil, so resisting drought, while they produce enough fibrous surface roots to respond to feeding.

More generally grown than any other is *R. laxa* largely because it sends up few suckers, and although it produces fewer shoots these are stout and strong, making for a high-grade bush although the root system is coarser than some forms. For the best results it must be budded early and ideally with greenhouse wood for it begins growth early.

A further popular stock is the *R. multiflora* (polyantha). This is a rapid grower, with many surface roots, and makes a large tree. Those grown from seed make a good stock for floribunda types, but being more surface rooted suffer more rapidly in dry weather, and because of this may fail to bud well. Another fault is its tendency to early growth which can lead to damage in exposed places or 'frost pockets'. Easy to grow from cuttings, and easy to bud in this form, the plants produced suffer from freezing, and the root system dries out easily, so making transplanting less certain. A further disadvantage is its dislike of alkaline soil.

One other stock is grown, usually especially for standards. This is a commercial form of *R. rugosa* named *rugosa* Spek. Produced by cuttings and treated specially, it produces stems up to 1·8 m (6 ft) in two years. It is surface rooting and resents deep planting.

The stocks are planted with about 2·5 cm (1 in) of the smooth brown root above the ground for easy budding at a later stage. They are earthed up to protect this little bit of protruding root which will receive the bud later. The beds are then sprayed with a weed deterrent or hand hoed and tractor cultivated. The soil has been well prepared before planting, using up to 60,960 kg (60 tons) of farmyard manure to the acre, to which is added artificial manure and ground chalk according to the analysis of the soil. Many soils are lacking in magnesium, and this is added in the form of Kieserite, a crude form of magnesium sulphate. When budding time comes, the wood, after having thorns and leaves removed, is handed to two propagators. With a boy to clip in the buds for them with Fleischure ties, they will bud 2,400 to 3,000 a day. The stocks may be sprayed for weeds once more, and then the bed is left until 'heading back' in the spring of the following year. This 'heading back', the removal of the upper portion of the stock, is done by using compressor operated 'Pruneasy' secateurs. Each bud which has 'taken', i.e. is alive, will show a green shield (the live bark) and a tiny centre, the bud. As the sap rises, this bud swells and begins growth. Usually growth is rapid, and by late June the first shoots are in flower. In the meantime the stocks are watched for 'suckers'. These are growths from dormant 'eyes' on the original stock and these shoots if left would soon smother the young plant. They are therefore removed completely by tearing them out of the bark. This suckering must be done regularly, otherwise the new plant will be strangled by these growths of the original brier. Once the bush has established itself and is able to absorb the full supply of food and moisture from the understock, suckers are less evident, but as we shall see, ceaseless vigilance should be exercised through the plant's life lest a neglected sucker take control of the whole bush.

The object of the nursery should be to produce a plant with a good fibrous root system, and hard, well-ripened shoots. It is better to have a well-ripened bush with two strong shoots and good roots, than a many-branched plant whose root system is inadequate (see plate 2). Grading must vary greatly with the variety, as a bush of the rose 'Topsi' when established will reach less than 0·6 m (2 ft) and 'Queen Elizabeth' 2·4 m (8 ft), but the

B

principle of adequate root system for the branch spread always applies.

The aim of the nurseryman is to obtain a well-ripened bush. For this reason adequate space must be given between plants, and as far as possible late autumn growth is discouraged. The only artificial fertilizer used after an early spring dressing of balanced type is sulphate of potash. This potash helps to promote sturdy growth and so produces a hardier plant more able to withstand freezing. Spraying for weed control, and routine spraying for mildew and black spot, are carried out where these troubles are prevalent.

Most roses continue flowering into late October, and the nurseryman is torn between his wish to send out a mature bush, and the urgent demands of his customers for early delivery. Much may be said for beginning delivery in mid November for the present-day rose continues to grow and flower in October, but economically this is impossible, and the earlier plants have to be prepared by stripping their leaves. This prevents undue shrinkage during transit.

Most roses are loosened in the soil mechanically, and are pulled or eased out as required. The bushes are then graded and 'heeled in' in special sand and sawdust beds to ripen and mature the bushes. It is the object of the nurseryman to dispatch his roses so that they arrive as fresh as when lifted. With unavoidable delays in transit this is not always possible, but should the wood appear dried and shrunken when the bushes arrive, they may soon be brought back to normal condition. Dig a shallow trench about 23 cm (9 in) deep, lay the bushes in so that the roots and tops can be completely covered by soil. Replace the soil within an inch of the surface. If the soil is light or dry, fill the depression with water. When this has drained replace *all* the soil. The slight mound will define the position of the bushes. Leave for a minimum of three days; a week will not be too long, and the bushes will have recovered.

Reputable nurseries are anxious to send out only first-quality bushes, true to name. Labour problems are often acute, and if mistakes occur and inferior bushes are sent out their return will be welcomed, so that such mistakes can be rectified.

Today most roses are shortened before dispatch. This reduces transport costs, but more important, it reduces the loss of moisture, both while the plant is in transit and while the bush is becoming established. What to do with these bushes after their arrival is a subject dealt with in another chapter.

Before going on to this, we should consider the method of propagation by cuttings. For this, sufficient well-ripened wood is needed to support life while major cell structure changes are in progress. The shoot should be about 23 cm (9 in) long and hard enough to withstand weather changes, but not too old for their cells to have ceased growth. What must occur is that the cells of the lower shoot will change their form, and cease to be shoots, taking on the structure of the root. It is possible to encourage more ready rooting by the use of hormones, which are available as powders into which the base of the cutting may be dipped before planting. While these changes are taking place, losses of moisture should be reduced to a minimum. By planting the shoot at least two-thirds of its length below the ground major protection is afforded. Ideal conditions of growth are warmth and air. Cold wet soil should be avoided but may be improved by adding coarse sand or grit, especially at the level of the shoot's base. By choosing a sheltered border, or even using a glass frame, further help can be given. Autumn is the best time. No one should expect full success by this method. The number of rooted cuttings will vary with the variety. Usually the more coarse and strong the growth, the higher percentage of crop. Spacing can be anything from 5 to 15 cm (2 to 6 in) apart, but one must be prepared to transplant at least once before putting into final beds. Also, there will be considerable variation in growth, and an even bed of one variety, produced by this method, is seldom achieved. This is in part due to the root system, which lacks the penetrating roots of the *canina* stock, as the roots produced are surface and fibrous and so transplants with more damage, and has less area to draw up moisture in dry weather. Ramblers and the more vigorous floribundas are the most suitable. Varieties which grow easily from cuttings are the ramblers 'American Pillar', 'Albertine', 'Excelsa', many of the vigorous floribunda roses of the Poulsen type (red and pink), 'Masquerade' and those with firm hard wood. As a rule the more pithy the wood, the less easy it is to root cuttings. One should never attempt to nurse a weakly cutting into a healthy tree. These should be discarded when the best are transplanted. The only hope of producing serviceable trees is to be ruthless at this stage. A weakly rose, like an ailing person, may hang on for many a year but like the chronic invalid will demand that more care be lavished on it, to ensure survival, than a whole bed of healthy trees could expect.

Hybrid trees, especially the more pithy varieties, are the least suitable for rooting as cuttings. It is an interesting method of propagation, but for permanent improvement of the garden falls far short of propagation by budding. The gift of a rooted rose cutting can be an embarrassment to a keen amateur. He has to choose between offending the giver by planting it in an inconspicuous corner, or spoiling the look of a prominent border by admitting an apparent starveling among its opulent fellows.

 CHAPTER III

Preparation, Planning, Planting

The soil is an amazing medium, built up by ages of erosion. Rocks have crumbled through the ceaseless wear of weather; frost and water have played their part; glaciers have transported foreign matter to its present home; rivers, long since diverted or flowing into seas now unknown, have left deposits strange to the neighbourhood. All these materials have contributed to the present soil as we know it. Sand, clay, limestone, these are the inert materials which form our soil, together with many less common minerals. But the living, vital soil, on which we depend for fertility, has been built up by the continuous action of plant and animal growth. Fertility depends upon humus, the vegetable and animal matter introduced by growth and followed by decay, which is encouraged by a host of bacteria without which the foods we have placed in the soil, or which are naturally present, would be unavailable to our plants.

Soil is not a dead material, not just so much filling by the cubic metre. It is a living, fertile medium, to be treated with respect and knowledge. How many promising gardens are ruined by the careless introduction of a bulldozer, which in a few hours can bury or destroy the patient accumulation of centuries! 'Top soil', the dark matter above the subsoil, must be conserved and improved at all costs.

Few people are able to choose the site for their garden. The house and the area are usually overriding factors. However, a keen rosarian may well, on retirement, consider whether roses will thrive where he intends to settle. The best way is to look over the hedge of one's neighbours to be! If there are no neighbours, the hedges will tell the story if vigorous dog roses can be seen. It is worth consulting the local Horticulture Officer whose knowledge of the district will make him a better guide than the local handyman, who having lived there all his life may have an outlook as limited as his experience.

If the soil grows good roses, the next question should be 'Is it easy to work?' A tenacious clay may yield to the muscle and skill of a young man who can spend years on improving its texture, but a man near retirement needs land easy to work. This means medium to light loam without too many stones. Given the land, the ideal site would be a slight slope to the south-west open to the sun on the south and west but protected at a distance on north and east. Above all, the site should be open, and big trees should be far off. A general plan for the whole garden and a detailed plan for the rose garden should be prepared. Do not fill the whole site with roses unless you have easy access to other soil. When purchasing a site or preparing plans for the house, leave room for wheeled access from back to front. Carting ripe farmyard manure through the kitchen, a pail-full at a time, may be a labour of love, but will never be loved labour! Three metres (10 ft) more of frontage purchased in desperation as an afterthought, can be as expensive as exasperating.

Levelling of the site should be avoided whenever possible. Gentle slopes should be encouraged, as they add variety to the scene, and promote natural drainage. If the position must be levelled, then the top soil should be removed, heaped and replaced after the subsoil has been shifted to the required levels. This is a costly, time-consuming task and should be undertaken only after careful thought.

What is the best soil? One which has been cultivated regularly, where the top soil is at least 30 cm (12 in) thick, where the more yellow subsoil is retentive of moisture but permits ready drainage. Above all else, if choice is possible, always prefer a light, workable soil. The ancient fallacy that 'roses like clay' is a lie which should long ago have been nailed down in its coffin. Roses like a well-drained friable soil, but more important, their owners do. The soil should be manageable at all times. Heavy soil can be a disaster both in very wet and very dry weather.

Both light and heavy soils can be improved. A light soil contains at least 50 per cent sand. These coarse gritty particles have no food value but they are an excellent workable medium for a beginning. The addition of humus is the first consideration; this acts as a sponge, absorbing water and foods; it encourages the growth of useful bacteria; it darkens the soil, which thus becomes warmer as it absorbs heat more readily. The ideal form of humus is found in animal manures of the farmyard type, where there is sufficient food to feed the bacteria, which in their turn break down these foods into suitable material for plant absorption. This 'breaking down' is the first step and demands nitrogen. Digging in a green crop can actually deprive a plant of nitrogen, as the bacteria get first choice, and if this food is in short supply the plant may starve while its meal is being prepared! For this reason, compost, unless well made, should be used with care. Both composts and peat demand the addition of a balanced fertilizer if the best effect is to be obtained. Where obtainable pulverized bark makes an excellent substitute for peat.

Unfortunately, good farmyard manure is scarce in the country and unobtainable in the town, so we must resort to compost or peat.

Compost as a name covers many strange and some unwholesome concoctions, but if properly made it can supply most of the plant's needs and also encourage good health. It is not a haphazard mass of putrefying rubbish, but the result of a carefully controlled decomposition of vegetable matter, in which bacterial and other activity, such as that of worms, is encouraged, so that the ready-to-use materials are free from disease and full of readily absorbed food.

The average garden will provide only a small but useful amount of material for composting, but all waste from the house, of vegetable or animal origin, should be used as well. One of the essentials for good composting is uniform heating, and this means that the sides and top of the heap must be protected. A simple box with the soil for its base and its top small enough to fit inside so that it can move up and down as the contents increase or diminish, is all that is needed. The sides of the box should permit some air to pass into the compost, for air is essential if the useful bacteria are to get busy. The site should be well drained. There are many useful detailed books on the subject but the principle is simple. Ingredients are: a 12-cm (5-in) layer of vegetable matter allowing air to pass through, such as prunings, sticks, etc.; a sprinkling of dried blood or poultry manure; a layer of closer material such as lawn mowings, fallen leaves, vegetable waste; a sprinkling of lime. This should be continued layer by layer, until the top of the box, probably 1 m (3¼ ft) high, is reached. The lid should be weighted enough to compress the material. Some ventilation is essential, for while heating is to be encouraged, this should be as uniform and regular as possible. This is helped by having layers of open material at intervals and also by making small ventilation shafts from top to bottom by piercing the heap with a suitable pointed post. At times it may be necessary to dampen the materials, but soaking should be avoided as this will drive out the air and prevent bacterial activity.

Two such boxes kept in use throughout the year can produce up to four tons of excellent compost. When the compost in the first box has become well decomposed and heating is less evident, it should be transferred to the second box, putting the materials on the top and edges into the centre and packing the sides with the warmer, more decomposed, compost from the middle. The second box will not need ventilation shafts and the compost will mature. Usually the addition of extra sulphate of potash at some stage is advisable if a balanced food is to be produced.

The fact that this matter is of vegetable origin and that it has been changed by active bacteria is as vital to plant health as vitamins are to the human body. Good compost not only feeds the plant but promotes health. Additional materials such as straw and sawdust may be composted to add bulk to the existing material, but some weathering in both cases is needed before these are put in the compost heap.

With the scarcity of farmyard manure a greater need for humus manures has been felt. Many local authorities are now composting their dustbin refuse and sewage sludge to an excellent product, free from smell or disease risk, and first-rate for roses. Among them are Leatherhead, Rawcliffe (Lancs.), Dumfries, East Lothian, and

Edinburgh, all of which will sell small quantities sent by rail or road, but the demand is so great that they have waiting-lists at times. So far as rose growers are concerned this Municipal Compost is weed-seed-free, it carries no pests or diseases, and contains all essential plant foods, though it is low in potash, so that some sulphate of potash should always be used with it. Still more important are the trace elements it contains, essential to healthy plant growth but absent from the 'straight' fertilizers in general use as artificials. Where the city dweller is able to purchase such material he need have no hesitation in using it freely. It has many advantages and will benefit all types of soil and promises to afford the country a new source of soil fertility. Remember it is not a 'concentrate' but a bulk food which needs using freely.

A further source to which you might be referred is mushroom manure. This should be used with great caution on rose trees as the heavy lime content may well produce chlorosis. My personal experience has been such that I would hesitate to use it for rose trees under any conditions.

Peat is readily available but a few words as to choice may not be out of place. Firstly, there is texture. The coarse, sedge peats are ideal for heavier soils and these should be used very freely. Up to 10 cm (4 in) thick may be spread on the bed in course of preparation, adding at the same time 227 g (8 oz) of bone meal and 56 g (2 oz) of hoof-and-horn meal or nitro-chalk. This should be worked into the top 37 cm (15 in) of soil. The same method should be used for light soils, but a finer moss peat is more suitable. These peats should be of horticultural types chosen for their suitability. Half-decayed leaf soil, peat taken at random from a moor or bog, may be totally unsuitable and may lead to complete failure. The reason for this is most important. As we know, 'pH' is a term expressing the acidity of the soil and this 'pH' can make or mar the suitability of soil for rose cultivation. Ideally the 'pH' should be 6·5, just verging on the slightly acid. Fortunately this is quite a normal type of soil. The addition of peat has a tendency to lower the 'pH' and the use of lime can quickly raise the 'pH' until the soil is useless for rose growing. Never add lime to a rose bed unless it has been found to be very acid. There are certain indications in the way the roses thrive which will help you, and indicate whether it is worth getting the opinion of your County Horticultural Adviser. Briefly, if red and pink roses thrive but yellow and white roses fail, the land is too alkaline. The colours of the foliage will vary with their mineral content and the availability of plant food. This latter indication will be dealt with under 'Feeding'.

Drainage may be essential. If so, this should be done expertly, as a whole. To attempt to drain one bed by altering the subsoil with coarse drainage may encourage moisture to flow in from outside the area and so create a bog, even worse than the surrounding soil. The only way to drain a heavy site is by taking levels and piping the surplus water to the lowest point, where some provision must be made for its disposal. Slight improvement may be made where the soil has slow drainage by raising the level of the bed, but this method has many disadvantages beside the ugly effect of these 'plum-puddings' dotted over the site.

Plan your rose beds carefully. Where can you site these? Usually we have little choice, but normally we can choose back or front of the house; and if the site runs east to west we may manage to use both. A north site which is largely sunless is to be avoided. If it is used, the roses will probably make more leaf than flower and will give far less than their best. The site should be as open as possible, and if shrubs and trees are to be planted much thought should be given to their effect in maturity. A small plant can become a very large bush when it is full grown. Above all, we should avoid shutting off light and excluding air. Plan your garden as a whole. On taking possession of a new house the first wish is to get something to grow as soon as possible, and roses can flower within four months of planting. Remember, however, that rose planting is an investment which will pay liberal dividends for at least fifteen years. Do not jeopardize your final satisfaction by clearing a small patch immediately, and planting 'just a few roses as a beginning'. Look ahead. If you can use a simple design with a few beds, and further, if you can leave as much room between the roses as the beds occupy, you may save much work later on. When the time comes to change the bushes, instead of renewing the soil in the rose beds, one grasses down the beds and turns the existing lawn into

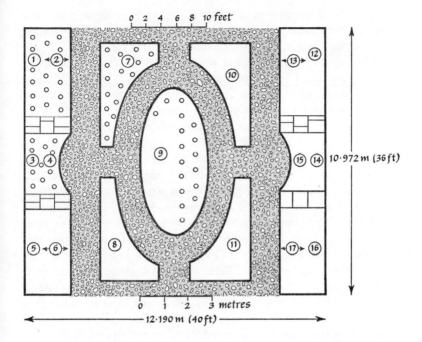

The above scheme, based on an oval 6·096 m × 2·438 m (20 ft × 8 ft), may be adapted to the shape and area of the site by omitting the side beds or altering the dimensions of the oval.

KEY

FLORIBUNDA	H.T.	FLORIBUNDA
(1) 6 'Matangi'	(7) 14 'Just Joey'	(12) 6 'Orange Sensation'
(2) 11 'Red Sprite'	(8) 14 'Alec's Red'	(13) 11 'Allgold'
(3) 4 'Vesper'	(9) 30 'My Choice'	(14) 4 'Arthur Bell'
(4) 7 'Snowline'	(10) 14 'Piccadilly'	(15) 7 'News'
(5) 6 'Rob Roy'	(11) 14 'Grandpa Dickson'	(16) 6 'Evelyn Fison'
(6) 11 'Chanelle'		(17) 11 'Plentiful'

rose beds. A narrow garden often demands straight lines, but break those lines if possible. An oval bed can relieve this monotony and can be made simply by the following method.

First, one has to use a right angle and this is easily checked by making a triangle in the following proportions. The two sides are 3 units and 4 units with the hypotenuse at 5 units. A very useful gadget is such a triangle 3 × 4 × 5 units *in these proportions* kept hanging in a shed for those occasions, occurring more frequently than we expect, when a right angle will be required.

The first decision we have to take with the oval is where the axis is to run. We will call this AB. It is best marked by a garden line. The next item is to decide where the centre point of the oval is to be. This, of course, will be half-way on AB, the centre line. We will call it C. Suppose the oval is to be 3·048 m long and 1·219 m wide (10 ft × 4 ft). From point C at right angles mark a point half the total width of the bed; DC will be half 1·219 m, i.e. 0·610 m (2 ft). Insert a pointed stake here. From D a string is run which is half the total length of the bed, i.e. 1·524 m (5 ft). Where this bisects the garden line AB at points E and F, stakes are inserted. This gives three stakes, at D, E and F. A string is run round the triangle formed by these stakes and joined. Now comes the result. Removing the pointed stake at D, which is now loosened from the soil, and using its point to trace the design imposed by the limits of the loop which is kept taut all the time, you will find that the extreme limits of this string will form a perfect oval as stake D slides round the boundaries imposed by the loop. Points E and F remain fixed, but point D will follow the course these prescribed limits dictate.

Test your bed by making a trial shape elsewhere first. Proportions which look good on paper may not appear so attractive after translation into fact.

It is always easy to plant your garden a little at a time, if you have a plan to which you can work. Before you plan the garden, try to live in the house for a little while, and look out at your garden. A rose bed planted just far enough from the kitchen window to be seen from the sink may lighten toil, and be seen far more frequently than the front bed—the pride of your neighbours.

Another argument for waiting a season before planting is that it gives time for germination and destruction of the weeds which have usually had free quarters during, and often before, building operations. Unplanted land can be cleaned repeatedly at far less cost in labour than odd-shaped beds and borders partly planted. Further, the soil can be rendered more fertile, and the hard compacted soil reduced to a good tilth. It is not wise to apply farmyard manure to all the land. Apart from the expense, neither the weed seeds nor the nitrogen brought in with it are helpful in a lawn. Reserve the manure for your rose trees. Well-broken soaked peat is a great asset and should be freely used. Keep the soil cultivated. A small rotary cultivator hired, borrowed, or purchased is invaluable at this time.

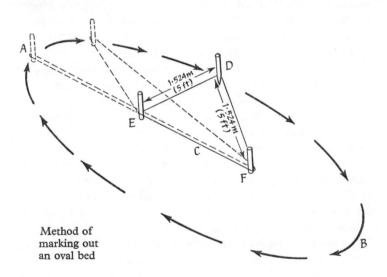

Method of
marking out
an oval bed

The whole idea should be to build up the fertility of the soil: far better to encourage good root growth the first year. Heavy feeding should be discouraged in the early stages.

If we think for a moment of the plant and its needs, we find that each part of its structure has basic requirements. The roots are of

two types, those which go down deeply, and those which are just
beneath the surface. The deep roots provide anchorage for the
plant, and draw on reserve supplies of moisture in the lower soils
beyond the reach of the shallow fibrous roots, which, growing near
the surface, are always pushing forward and branching out. All the
foods from the soil must come through the ends of these minute
root hairs on the tips of the fibre. They can easily be damaged by
too deep cultivation, by drought, or by competition with coarser
foreign roots from trees and hedges. The ends of these root hairs
are protected by a 'root cap', loose dead cells which come between
the frail absorbent tissues and the hard earth. Further protection
for the fibrous roots from drought or too much sun may be afforded
by a mulch—a covering on the soil of peat, manure, or if possible
pulverized bark, for lawn mowings will sow annual grass which is
always costly and difficult to eliminate. This forms a protective
layer, smothering most weeds and protecting the roots from loss
of moisture and sudden changes of temperature.

The food to be taken in is partly prepared by an excretion from
the roots sufficiently acid to help to dissolve some foods for the
plant's use. The entry of the food from the soil through the root
into the plant depends upon 'osmosis', which is made possible by
the solution in the plant being stronger than that in the soil around.
For this reason, too heavy feeding, especially in dry weather, may
actually cause a plant to collapse, by drawing out the moisture in the
plant to balance the strength of soil and plant solutions. 'Little and
often' is a far better rule for feeding than one heavy dressing. If
plants are to be fed during dry weather then before this is attempted
the soil should be well soaked.

The work of the root has been dealt with at length, because,
being out of sight, it may well be forgotten. The medium in which
it works, its form and function, its ceaseless activity, should be
remembered and catered for. It is in this sphere that the rose
bloom receives the extra something which leads to perfection.

The stem is of equal importance, for by it the plant supports its
starch-forming leaves and finally its flowers. The stem has a
different series of cells to perform its varied functions, such as
protection, growth, conduction of water and food, and finally food

storage. To produce strong healthy shoots able to perform these functions fully should be the aim of the rosarian. This is where correct pruning can make or mar the plant. Mature shoots carry the winter supply of the plant's starch without which it will die back during the winter.

The major activity of the leaf is to breathe. It controls the loss of moisture from the plant. It is essential for this loss to take place, for as moisture is given off, suction is caused which brings up more liquid containing the plant foods brought in through the root hairs. By the energy obtained from the light the leaf takes the water from its cells, the carbon dioxide from the air and builds up starch. In its turn the insoluble starch is changed into sugar and either used or transferred to storage cells where, as starch, it waits for the plant to need it. This highly complicated process is known as 'photosynthesis'. In similar ways simple elements brought in by the roots are built up into complex foods to be used or stored as the plant requires. It has been shown that the plant readily absorbs most suitable elements of the right type through its leaves. Just as a human being in a crisis may benefit from an intravenous drip or a 'shot in the arm', so the plant under abnormal conditions, when suffering from a mineral deficiency, may be fed through its leaves. This should be considered an abnormal method for unusual circumstances. At such times foliar feeding may be a real asset. This may be necessary after a long cold spell in early spring or on soils which are too alkaline. It is possible to grow roses on chalky soils by using iron sequestrine. This is an expensive but effective method but should be done in consultation with an expert.

We lavish all our care upon the rose to produce its flowers. To build up a good flower we must have a healthy plant, and as far as possible, slow, steady growth all the time should be our aim. Stimulants at the last moment may mean soft growth, and petals without stamina or lasting qualities. We must decide when pruning if our aim is to be quality or quantity.

The natural function of the rose is not to produce fine flowers, but plentiful seed, and we must be on the alert to prevent this. Once the seed has been formed, the rose has done its work, and all its energy and food will go into producing viable seed. Out comes the reserve food from the storage cells, up to the seed pods, and away goes our hope of a succession of flowers. Do not wait until the seed pods form. Remove the flowers as soon as they begin to die. Where there is a cluster, the removal of each dead flower is the ideal. Failing this, remove the whole head immediately flowering has finished. On examining a flower head one finds that usually the first leaf below that head has less than the full number of leaflets, and that the leaf bud in the axil is small and pointed, or even non-existent. This leaflet should be ignored and the flower head should be removed to the first full-sized leaf with a plump rounded leaf bud in its axil.

Having seen what our plant needs, and suggested methods by which this may be given, we come back to the actual making of the beds and planting. Planning beforehand is the first essential. A rose bed should be well prepared long before the plants are due to arrive. First plan what you want. Is it to be one bed of roses only? If so, where, and what shape? Is it to contain one variety or many? There are many factors which will help to make the decisive choice, including the shape of the garden. A curving sweep to the garage may provide a clue. Here is a hard kerb, for instance. If we put the lawn up to the edge, who will cut it? Why not make a rose border here? The position of the sun, the distance from the house, the size of the frontage should all be considered. If the border is long, try for at least three rows of bushes, with the centre row broken in height by standards at intervals. Far better to have one sweeping border up to 1·8 m (6 ft) wide, than a series of small narrow beds, costly to keep up and insignificant in effect. Try to avoid little beds. A 'rose garden' of tiny beds with roses planted three in a bed gives a messy, untidy effect, but the same site planted with one bold mass will be a joy and will need far less labour in upkeep. Shall we mix the bed or have one variety of one colour? Make your individual choice. Never mind what Smith says, or the landscape gardener: he may have a surplus of one variety! It is your garden and should be for your pleasure. If you want a bed of mixed varieties, then mix them thoroughly. Never mind about blending colours in such a case but find out which are the tall bushes, so that the smaller grower is not hidden by the strong variety. If you wish for a bed of one colour keep to one variety. Few varieties of a similar colour grow alike, flower at the same time, or have similar foliage. There can be more variation in an assorted bed of one colour than in a mixed bed of many different sorts and the former is less pleasing.

If you decide to have a number of beds, each in its own colour, more care is needed. Height, colour, contrast or blending, growth, all need consideration. A visit to a nursery or a letter to an expert may give you great help or at least a basis for decision.

How wide apart should the bushes be planted? A bush planted on good soil in ideal conditions will grow three times as freely as one in adverse circumstances. As a general rule 60 cm (2 ft) apart may be accepted as a happy medium.

To prepare the bed for the roses is not an archaeological excavation! A good rule is never go deeper than you must, but never fail to go as deep as you should. The first test is to find how the land drains. Dig a hole 0·9 m × 0·6 m (3 ft × 2 ft) wide and 0·6 m (2 ft) deep. Fill it with water, but if you find the water going as fast as you put it in, stop. Drainage is no problem there. If the water fails to disappear within the hour of filling, some drainage will be needed. If the water disappears at once, your problem will be to retain, not dissipate the moisture.

Now, mark out your bed or beds. Never prepare one bed in a whole series until each bed has been pegged out and your circle or square has been completed. If you fail to do so you may find at the end that you have room to spare or that the last square is a rhomboid! The next part is just hard work and there must be no remission. Happy the wife who has a muscular husband or a conscientious workman! It is always easier to work where there is elbow-room. If the beds are small, not more than 1·8 m × 3 m (6 ft × 10 ft), throw out the first 30 cm (1 ft) of top soil, half on one side and half on the other. This will give you a bed of the same size 30 cm (1 ft) lower than the normal level. If the soil is light or medium, spread a 10 cm (4 in) thickness of broken, soaked, medium-grade neutral peat. On this sprinkle 227 g (8 oz) of bone meal and the same of hoof-and-horn meal to 0·836 sq. m (1 sq. yd). Fork this material as deeply as you can into the subsoil.

It will probably be about 15 to 20 cm (6 to 8 in), making a prepared
bed 46 cm (18 in) deep in all. Replace the earth which has been
excavated, and mix in half the quantity of peat and plant food you
put in the lower layer. Your bed will now be about 15 cm (6 in)
above the level of the surrounding surface. However, the earth will
settle down rapidly, especially if a few heavy autumnal rains soak
it. If this work can be done during September, the beds will be
ready for planting in late October. If your soil is heavy but well
drained, choose the same method but use dry, broken, coarse sedge
peat, adding a further 113 g (4 oz) of basic slag to the lower level.
If you are making these beds where lawn grass has been for some
time, it will be easier to skim off the first 5 cm (2 in) and cast away
than to chop up and mix in the lower spit, although this may be
done with advantage if wished. Further, much clearing up will be
avoided if a few sacks or covers are laid down before the earth is
dug out so that the soil does not lie on the grass itself.

When the bed is made, mark out the position of the plants,
putting in a stake for each. If the bed is 1·8 m (6 ft) wide three rows
should be needed and the centre row should be 'staggered' so that
its plants are between the two outer rows of bushes. This will give
the appearance of greater depth to the bed, and will seem less
formal. At least 30 cm (1 ft) is needed between the edge and the
first row, to give room for the lawn to be mown.

Before planting, the bush should be prepared, unless it has been
received as ready. Bushes, if sent as lifted in the nursery, will need
trimming, although many firms now prepare them. This is not
'pruning' but shortening the tall growths to prevent wind rock in
the autumn and winter gales. If the bush is rocked by the wind, it
will have no chance to root, and a small hole will be made in the
soil at the base of the plant. This will let in rain and frost, and the
vital part—the junction of plant and root—may become damaged,
leading to death. Not only should tall shoots be shortened but any
damaged or unhealthy growth should be cut back to sound wood.
Similar preparation of the root is advisable. Sometimes the roots
may be very long: do not attempt to plant these to their full length,
and on no account twist them round in the hole. Shorten the roots
to 25 cm (10 in) and remove damaged portions, cutting to a healthy

piece. This main structure will give anchorage, but new fibre must be formed before the plant can grow.

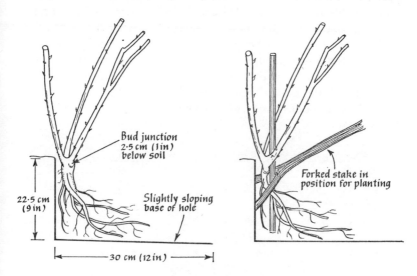

Planting and staking roses

To plant, the same plan must be used all through. Dig the first hole 30 × 30 × 22·5 cm (12 × 12 × 9 in) deep (see diagram) with the stake in one corner, then plant the bush with its junction of root and plant an inch below the soil, spreading the roots fan-wise across the hole. The hole should slope slightly away from the stake, so the roots farthest from the plant are a little lower. Now dig a similar hole at the next stake, using the soil to fill in round the plant just positioned. The last hole made will receive the soil from the first hole which was dug. This method is suitable under all normal conditions. The object should be to get fine earth close to the roots, so that air pockets may be avoided. If the roots are gently shaken as the earth falls upon them they should settle in without trouble. To do this, a helper is required. Failing such help the rose tree may be held in position by a forked stick until the soil holds it.

When the hole is filled to within 5 cm (2 in) of the top, the soil should be consolidated by gently but firmly treading the earth, pressing it against the roots. Level up the soil in the hole, leaving the top 2·5 cm (1 in) loose. Care should be taken, if the earth is very wet, not to compact the soil to exclude air. A better plan when the soil is wet, as so often happens at that time of year, is to have a barrow-load of prepared dry earth kept under cover until planting is done. A portion of this dry earth may be sprinkled about the roots, and being dry and fine it will fall between the smaller roots, so making a better contact when firmed.

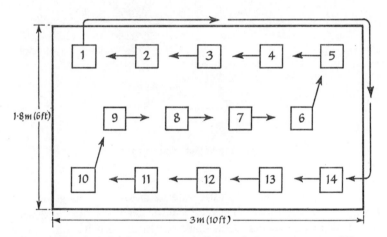

Preparation for planting: remove soil from hole 1 to near 14. When planting rose at 1, cover with soil from 2 and continue in numerical order, when soil for 14 will be the surplus from hole 1

All the above directions are for the winter months. Should the weather be dry at the time of planting, which is quite possible in the spring, the hole should be filled with water after planting but before the final 2·5 cm (1 in) of loose earth is levelled in. Where the soil is very thin and poor it may be necessary to remove the subsoil or chalk for at least 46 cm (18 in), replacing with imported good earth. John Innes No. 3 would be the correct type (see note on iron sequestrine, page 47). In such cases it is essential to mulch and feed freely so that the fibrous roots are given every encouragement to keep within the limits of the prepared beds. After planting in dry areas, especially in the spring, it may be advisable to draw up soil from the surroundings, about the bush itself, leaving the tops of the shoots just peering through until the trees have become established. This method will conserve the natural moisture in the wood until new roots have formed to replenish the supply. When growth begins, the soil should be carefully removed, remembering that new shoots may be forming from the base below the present soil level.

If planting has to be done in the late spring, then the bush should be pruned at the time of planting, and at such a time 'hilling up' will be even more advantageous.

An additional paragraph is now called for on the treatment of container-grown rose bushes. Plants in containers vary greatly in quality and size both of the bush and container. The plants so obtained should be growing quite freely and appear completely healthy. Given these conditions they may be planted at any time, although if planting is done in hot, sunny weather the plants should receive some shading until established. The soil into which the plant is going should have as good preparation as advocated above. When the container-grown plant is collected it should be examined and if dry, watered thoroughly and allowed to drain before removing the container, for the polythene or other container should be finally peeled from the plant to keep the ball of earth or soil-medium intact. Never break the soil from the roots nor attempt to spread them out. If this is done while the roses are in growth they will probably collapse. Dig out a hole where the soil has been prepared beforehand slightly below the depth of the soil in the container. After removing the covering very carefully the ball of earth should be lowered gently into the hole. This will leave the container-soil surface well below the surrounding earth. Fill in the surrounding gap with some of the removed soil and firm gently, making sure both container-soil and surrounding earth are contacting. This should leave a slight saucer-shaped depression. Fill this with water once or twice, allow to drain off and then level back the

soil. Container roses may be grown in soil-less compost which
depends upon artificial feeding to maintain health. In this case
additional fertilizer may have to be used to maintain health until
the roots have entered their new soil. Where the compost used
contains a fair proportion of earth this should not be necessary.
The main advantages of container plants are that quick results are
possible and gaps caused by accident can be filled immediately, but
the best results will still be obtained where first-quality bare root
bushes are planted in the dormant season under good conditions.
If the soil of your new garden is weedy and rough it is wiser to
spend the three or four months cleaning and preparing the earth
than planting for immediate results. Given the right conditions
excellent results can be obtained.

You may well think that too much care has been demanded for
the preparation and planting of the rose trees. It cannot be over-
emphasized that rose trees will amply repay for the extra care and
attention lavished on them. More, they will go on paying extra
dividends during a long life of abundant and healthy flowering. If
you should inherit a batch of unhealthy plants it will be revealing
to dig them up and contrast those puny twisted roots with the
healthy root spread of a well-grown plant. The pleasure a good
cook sees as a well-prepared meal disappears before the onslaught
of a hungry man is as nothing compared to the joy of a proud
gardener watching the results of his care flourishing before him.

 CHAPTER IV

Pruning

A great deal that is wise, and at least as much that is foolish, has been written and talked about pruning. Like the hieroglyphics on a doctor's prescription, there is much mystery and unnecessary complication surrounding a practice which in principle is simple, but in use needs adaptation, observation and common sense.

One of the most controversial questions is when to prune. I am at a loss to know why. There is one time only which is always safe and that is when the sap begins to rise. This condition will vary with the position of the plant in the garden and with the area in which the garden is to be found. The time may well vary from mid February in the south of England to late April in the exposed hills of northern Scotland.

A little reflection will show why. When the shoot is pruned, the pith in the cut is exposed to the weather and to the introduction of disease spores. For safety's sake, this period should be as short as possible. No healing can take place while growth is dormant. If this cut is made in winter the pith may become saturated with rain which then freezes, bursts the cells, and encourages the die-back spores by providing the ideal conditions for their hibernation and, later, their increase. This has happened and will always happen where the site is exposed and spring growth delayed.

The fallacy of early pruning has attracted adherents because in some places the trees are sheltered and in some years never cease growth. In such places, any period would be suitable. If, however, one lives on the exposed East Coast or at a high altitude, pruning during the winter can lead to the devastation of the beds.

55

It is necessary to stress that one should try to prune when the bushes begin to awaken from their winter's rest. If a large number have to be pruned, it is better on balance to prune a little early than a little late. Even so, a little top growth need never cause any worry although it is very unwise to wait until the sap is flowing fast enough to cause the shoots to 'bleed', i.e. to be able to see the sap running down the shoot after it has been cut.

Books which speak about removing dead wood and old shoots early, never explain how such shoots are there in the first place. Such wood should never be allowed to develop if correct pruning is practised.

There is little evidence, if any, to show that earlier pruning brings better and earlier flowers. Possibly, again because the garden is sheltered, this may appear so. Delayed flowering may be induced by very late pruning but only at the cost of good blooms.

Shrub roses may have their exhausted wood taken out whenever one has the time, as may climbers and ramblers.

Nature's time-table is controlled by weather conditions, and when the sap rises and the small eyes redden and gleam, the time for pruning is at hand. Get busy!

Once the main idea has been clearly grasped, all that is needed is practice. Why should one prune? The answer may be found in the hedgerow or in the neglected garden. At first the brier throws up a strong shoot from its base. This grows vigorously the first year and flowers freely in the second. As the years go by the shoot loses its vigour until another growth springs from the base and the primary shoot slowly dies of starvation and disease. What nature has accomplished over the years may be brought about by the intelligent practice of pruning immediately the shoot shows loss of vigour. Pruning should have certain definite objectives: encouraging growth, shaping the bush, discouraging disease, removing old and worn wood, and fitting the plant for its position. It is this adaptation to its environment which is so important, and for this observation is essential. A long, vigorous shoot may warrant light pruning, but its position—one among a bed of many—may demand its being cut harder. On the other hand, in a specimen bush every piece of healthy wood may have to be left almost its full length.

To encourage growth it may be necessary to balance root and top, and this is an essential part of pruning, especially in the first year. Observation shows that normally not more than three 'eyes' (see Chapter II, page 28) (growth buds) break into growth at one time. However long the shoot may be, this is a general fact. This means that if a shoot is left 0·6 m (2 ft) long, only the top 12·7 cm (5 in) will carry new growth. The remainder of the shoot will present 45 cm (18 in) or more of hard stem which will become harder and thicker as the years pass. This has many disadvantages. It is unsightly; a bush presenting 45 cm (18 in) of bare thick branches at the base spoils the look of the bed. It is uneconomic for the plant; all the food needed for the top wood has to pass through an unnecessary length of hardening tissue. As this wood ages it may become more prone to damage and disease, thus threatening the health of the growth above it. It is dangerous; heavy top growth puts a great strain on the root system, not only in the gales of winter but even more in a wet and windy summer, when the top growth, heavy with leaf, flower, and water, pulls at the anchorage roots, and as the bush moves tears off the fibre and root hairs which should feed the plant.

If, on the other hand, the shoot is shortened to produce the maximum number of growths on the minimum of wood, a well-shaped bush, close to its food supply, with wood all of equal age, will develop satisfactorily. What the best length is will be determined by observation, but certain general rules will have to be applied. A useful rule is that where soil and growth conditions are good, the weaker the shoot the harder one prunes, the stronger the growth the lighter the pruning. When the bush is established, the golden rule is to prune at least one shoot each year almost to ground-level, thus inducing growth as low as possible, so ensuring wood for renewal when older stems are failing. Once the wood has been produced, the rules of hygiene must be observed. Light, air, and space for free development need to be given and this begins with pruning. If two shoots are likely to compete against each other, one should be removed. Normally the branch nearer the base of the plant and away from its centre would be left: the exception would be if this plant might then overshadow its neighbour.

In such a case the intruding shoot would have to be shortened and pruned to an inward, not outward, eye. The centre of the bush should as far as possible be kept clear. The normal practice would be to prune with the top eye facing in an outward direction, so encouraging a cup-shaped growth. In a few cases where branches grow parallel to the ground the pruning would be reversed, cutting to an inward eye to produce the desired cup-shaped bush.

One of the main objects in pruning should be health. Cut out all weakly and diseased wood. 'Weakly' should include all over-grown, soft, late wood, so often damaged by frost. This frost damage may be determined by the colour of the pith. Healthy pith is white, frost damage causes it to go brown. After a sharp winter, the pith may be injured far below the apparent damage to the outer cells. It is a temptation to prune to an apparently healthy eye which may be promising to break into growth, even if the centre of the shoot is brown. In such conditions growth may begin, but the dead pith will continue to die back further, until the shoot collapses and the damage is beyond remedy. Once this 'die-back' has reached the junction of bud and stock the whole plant will die even if it lingers on for a year or two. 'Cut back to white pith' is a rule which should never be broken if cuts are to heal and the bush is to recover.

Good pruning is a first essential in the health of the tree. Much disease may be directly carried over on the later growths of the season. It has been proved that mildew is over-wintered in the leaf buds of the shoots, especially those near the top of the growths. The removal of such unsound wood, and its later burning, ensures the destruction of much latent disease. Light and air produce healthy conditions. Free-moving air and sunlight give the plant ripened wood, and discourage diseases and pests which propagate in stagnant air and on soft weak shoots.

The difference between good and bad pruning lies in the way the cut is made. This must be clean so that the cut can heal quickly. A correct cut should throw the water so that the growing tissue at the edge of the wound can make new cells to exclude weather and disease spores from the cut. This thickened growth, the callus, may be seen completely covering a pruned shoot within the year. The cut should be sloping, beginning on the side farthest from the eye and slanting towards it, finishing just above it (see plate 4). If you are wondering which tool to get, my personal opinion is, use a good knife every time. The secateurs are the nurseryman's best friend, killing more bushes than frost, disease, or old age! So often secateurs crush the wood rather than cutting it cleanly. A pruning knife should be slightly hooked and the blade need not be more than 7·6 cm (3 in) long. A smooth wooden handle is lighter and easier to hold, and pruning with a knife is much easier and less tiring. Hold the shoot to be cut at the tip; with the left hand bend

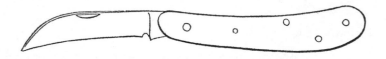

A good pruning knife

it very slightly towards you and cut the shoot by drawing, not pulling, the knife. The cut should begin at the base of the knife and as it is drawn across the shoot, this will be severed before the knife has been drawn to its full length. A knife must be kept sharp, and should even be sharpened when needed during the pruning, using a carborundum stone. It may seem difficult, but a little practice will soon make the user perfect. Only dead wood should need secateurs, and a pruning saw should be used rarely, although some large specimen bushes and old climbers may need such an instrument at times.

If secateurs must be used—and I consider them unnecessary except where old, extra hard or dead growths have to be removed—then make sure they are kept clean and sharp. When the cut is made, slightly more wood, about an eighth of an inch, should be left above the eye but the cut should slope in the same way. When using secateurs, cut cleanly, and on no account wring. Equally important when pruning is a pair of serviceable but flexible gloves. The ideal type are made from horse hide which, after wetting, will dry back to the normal, supple texture, but any strong leather gloves may be used.

It is wise to have a 10 per cent solution of tri-sodium ortho-phosphate into which the cutting blade may be dipped if sickly bushes are being pruned. This may save spreading canker and other diseases which attack the rose wood. Before pruning proper begins, much heavy preliminary work may be done as time and circumstances permit. Old and unhealthy wood needs treatment as soon as it is seen to be there.

Some repetition may occur in the following instructions but better to overlap than to cause disaster by being too summary. Definitions of the types of roses will be found in a later chapter.

Hybrid Teas

In the first season after planting, prune down to three or four eyes, choosing an outward eye for the top. Heights above ground will vary with the variety, but will usually be 10 to 12 cm (4 to 5 in). If the shoot is weakly, shorten to one eye; if very weak, remove. Sometimes the new bush appears as a single shoot with secondary growths higher up the stem. Ignore these branching growths and still cut to three or four buds from the ground. A single thick shoot so treated will make an excellent bush. The following year treat the bushes similarly, pruning the new growths to three or four eyes above where the new growths started. This should mean a gradual increase in height of the bushes by 10 to 15 cm (4 to 6 in) a year. Always remember to cut one shoot hard to ground-level, leaving one eye only, each year, thus ensuring abundant basal growth. Succeeding years should see a repetition of this pruning. However old the bushes, the wood will never be of great age because of the continual renewal of wood as advocated. It will become necessary at times to check on the general shape and health of the bush, and extra wood may need removal after a wet season of abundant growth. Better to leave too little wood than too much. A great deal has been said about pruning for exhibition and pruning for abundant flowering but with this type of pruning, judicious thinning of new growths to throw more energy into fewer flowers will accomplish the purpose where exhibition flowers are required. More details of this treatment will be given in Chapter VIII, 'Exhibiting Roses'.

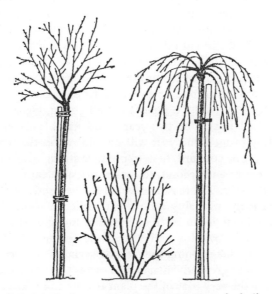

(*left*) Standard rose; (*centre*) bush-rose type, including H.Ts., floribunda specimens; (*right*) weeping standard

The pruning of floribunda and polyantha roses is a slightly different matter. Here quantity and succession of flowers are all-important. The first season the pruning is the same as for hybrid teas, i.e. to three or four eyes, the outer eye being at the top. As growth occurs especially freely in the autumn, thick shoots will spring from the base bearing large clusters of flowers. The object of pruning for this type is to produce an annual crop of these strong basal growths. Two forms of pruning will be carried out on each bush every year after the first year. The thick new basal shoots will be pruned lightly, removing the flower head down to the first strong eye. Sometimes, where a strong basal growth has grown early in the season, it may flower and then grow again, just below the first flower head producing a second shoot, which flowers in its turn. In this case, light pruning will consist of removing the second flower heads down to the first healthy eyes (the first flower head should have been removed after it had flowered in June or July). Here common sense comes in and says: 'If there is one only of these extra-tall shoots among a collection of roses, it is better ignored and cut off to the level of its neighbours.' Given other growths of similar nature the bed may well be left 0·6 m (2 ft) high. This is half only of the pruning. All older and weaker growth should be pruned to one or two eyes to ensure a crop of basal growths the next year. To repeat: cut all young, vigorous growth lightly and all weakly or two-year wood hard. This means that wood lightly pruned one year will be 'old' wood the next. In its turn this must be cut hard, first, to produce strong basal growth for the current year and second, to make sure of plentiful flower for the following year. The reason is twofold. The lightly pruned wood will flower early, probably a fortnight earlier at least. The hard-pruned wood will produce strong autumn-flowering shoots, which in their second flowering will extend the season a fortnight the other end, thus lengthening the total flowering season by at least a month. This is a great advantage. The second reason is that by this method only the very base of the plant is ever more than two years old, and the plants remain at an even height all their flowering life, which can well be up to thirty years. When pruning floribunda roses for hedges, the foregoing method should be employed for the first two years, but after that the height you wish your hedge to become should be the deciding factor. Normally, if the light pruning is extended for a further year, sufficient height should be obtained without sacrificing rigidity or density of the hedge. This extension consists in leaving the lightly pruned shoots for a further year and again lightly pruning the extra growth made the second year. This will add 30 cm (12 in) to the height of the pruned bushes and should mean about 0·75 m (2 to 2½ ft) extra at the end of the season. Even where hedges are required, the same principle should be applied as with all floribundas. All old wood should be cut out at a fixed age, making sure there is just enough short growth left to produce new basal growth each year for renewal. There is one problem which should be faced, and which may demand considerable courage from the novice. Supposing the two- or three-year growth which is due for removal produces a really vigorous shoot 15 cm (6 in) up the stem? Cannot this be left? The answer is No! This method stands or falls by its regular use. Once deviate, and the bush soon ceases to throw up basal shoots. Floribunda roses have a remarkable power of rejuvenation and with encouragement will produce these basal shoots all their lives, but some growths must be pruned each year to ensure this desirable result.

POLYANTHA

Polyantha roses should be pruned as for floribundas but, as they have less vigour, they should not be grown as hedges.

MINIATURES

The pruning of miniature roses has received little or no attention. Although these plants are very hardy (*R. rouletii* was named after a Swiss doctor who rediscovered it) it will be found that most of the upper growth dies back each winter. This is due to the fact that almost all this upper growth is flowering growth only, so that there are no leaf buds on it. The simple way is to cut the bush down to 2·5 cm (1 in). It is preferable to cut away all dead wood completely but this is not essential. The dead twigs can be broken off cleanly at the base if care is used. The principle is exactly the same but as the strong 'eyes' are at the base, cutting cleanly to an inch is enough. They may be cut to an 'eye' if vision is keen and back supple, but the easier method works satisfactorily.

SPECIMEN ROSES

There are certain varieties which naturally make excellent bushes planted on their own. Their vigour ensures plenty of long stems and healthy growth. The roses 'Peace', 'Queen Elizabeth', 'Dainty Maid' and 'First Choice' are roses of this type. In all cases the pruning should ensure sufficient hard cutting to encourage at least one new growth from the base each year, sufficient clearing of the centre and sides to allow light and air, drastic removal of every weak, damaged, or spent piece of wood, and enough shortening of the tall growths to avoid top-heavy bushes. Given these factors, allow the bush to grow naturally to the limits of its capacity. Remember 'the bigger the bush the bigger its appetite' when it is being fed.

SHRUBS

There is another group which we will call shrubs. These go by various names such as 'hybrid musks' but have a common factor in that they are perpetual-flowering and usually have large flower heads. They naturally grow tall, and unlike specimen bushes cannot be kept low without destroying their natural growth. After the first year, when weakly growth should be cut out and strong growths shortened to 30 to 37 cm (12 to 15 in), they should be left to grow naturally. They should have their flowering tops removed, and any overcrowded shoot should be cleared away. Where the flower heads are very heavy, their supporting growths may be shortened to strengthen them enough to carry the blossom without damage. Height may vary considerably in this group and the pruning will be governed by the natural height of the variety.

SPECIES

There are certain very charming natural varieties which may vary in height from the dwarf *R. nitida* to *R. moyesii* at 3·6 m (12 ft). These may be left to grow as nature made them. Some will become a thicket of densely growing pendulous shoots, for that is their natural habit. Do not destroy it, but keep an eye open for dead shoots or weak branches, and here your saw may be used as you cut out a whole branch. Cut it down at the base first, even if you have to cut up the branch piecemeal to get it out of the bush. Certain hybrids such as the lovely 'Frühlingsgold' group should be considered as species. Most of these are once-flowering so that the old branches may be removed any time after blooming as circum-stances permit. The so-called 'old garden' roses contain many sorts which flower on their two-year wood. Here, observation is essential, for an annual pruning of the wrong sort may remove the flowering wood. Some types, such as the moss roses, may be treated as raspberry canes, cutting out wood which has flowered directly flowering is finished, and shortening the tips of the shoots. Normally these only flower at the top of the shoot, so that by cut-ting the shoots at differing heights one may give the flowers more light and air and also produce a better-looking bush.

While much has been said by others, and well said, in detailed instructions on the pruning of 'old garden' roses, everything has been covered under different headings in these notes. The diffi-culty will be in identifying the groups and their needs. Even these groups vary greatly in their individual requirements. The moss roses for instance may vary from the dwarf 'Little Gem' to the tall 'William Lobb'. Bearing this in mind, one asks: 'Is this rose a small bush making relatively little wood like a hybrid tea, or is it a shrub or even a vigorous specimen bush?' Once this has been decided, and one can see many varieties with their habit of growth in the Royal National Rose Society's *Select List of Roses*, it is possible to prune: (a) for specimen blooms, where wood will be well pruned as for hybrid teas; (b) for quantity of flower—in shorter types prune as for floribunda roses; (c) for specimens—treat as for shrub roses. Common sense reminds one that a heavy new growth high on the specimen bush will damage itself and its neighbours in a high wind by whipping itself and other shoots to shreds, so shorten it enough to produce a rigid shoot unaffected by the wintry gales. Observa-tion will show also that certain types like the *R. alba* group flower freely on their old twiggy growth. These may be left until worn out, when they should be completely removed as low as the first vigorous new shoot. Much of this thinning of old wood can be done as soon after flowering as possible, but the more drastic pruning should be left until the plants are dormant. As for other roses, if the soil is very poor, light pruning—just removing very weak growth and unripened tips—is enough until the plant is estab-lished.

C

RAMBLERS AND CLIMBERS

There is great confusion concerning the pruning of ramblers and climbers. These have been so hybridized and mixed in growth and behaviour, that only observation of their habits will give the key to the best form of pruning for each. Far more important than the pruning is the training of the shoots, and as this must be done at the time of pruning we will deal with it here. We have all seen the climber on the house with its bare branches for the first 2·4 m (8 ft) and the few flowers well out of reach, where the shoot has been bent to keep it out of a window. Here is the key to the training it needs. Ramblers and climbers should be trained horizontally if flowers are desired. Never let the shoot go upright if this can be avoided. A vigorous climber, if well trained, will give up to three hundred flowers in a year. Light, air, and room to spread, are essential (see plate 6 for illustration). This is easy where there is a wall or trellis, but not so easy on a post or pergola or in limited space. On a post or pergola the shoot should be zigzagged or twisted rather than allowed to go straight up. Anything discouraging the flow of sap will encourage the freedom of flowering. Now comes what may be a counsel of perfection, but if followed it will save much trouble in the future. Where trellis or netting is used, always tie the shoot to the support. Never, never tuck the shoot in 'just for the time being'. Keep a few ties or a little fillis handy so that, in passing, the shoot can be tied in at once. Pruning is a simple matter where the shoots have been tied on the support. Once the ties are loosened the shoots can lie out on the ground and be observed clearly. Old growths can be cut out and removed and those left can be retied in a few moments. The chaotic mess an uncared-for climber can get into will never repay its rehabilitation and is better removed.

When you require climbers, have a clear idea of what you need. How much room can be spared? What is the maximum height? Can you reach that height easily or will the tree have to take care of itself without pruning as it straggles and struggles over an inaccessible roof? If you are uncertain as to choice, get the information from an expert: there is such a wide variety of uses for these climbers, as well as a great assortment from which one may choose.

Climbers are blessed above ramblers in that they will continue to give good flowers in most cases on older canes. Enough wood should be left to space shoots 45 cm (18 in) apart. Again one should strive to encourage basal growth. This is not always easy, for even hard pruning may not always succeed. A method which seldom fails, but will mean extra work, is to detach the tree and spread its shoots on the ground just as vigorous growth begins, usually in late April. The sudden check to the sap flow often induces dormant buds to break from the base. When this has occurred the climber may be retied after a few days. Having determined how many shoots may be required, cut out the oldest no longer needed, but keep a few shoots in reserve. Climbers can be very brittle, and have a habit of snapping, just as they have been fixed in position. It may not be necessary to cut down each shoot every time for retying, but on balance this is wise. A permanent tie used one year may well cut into a shoot which has had an additional year's growth of girth. One-year growths tied in, need no pruning beyond tipping, i.e. cutting away the soft and thin top. Two- or three-year shoots may be pruned like bushes. Their laterals (side growths) or sub-laterals (growths from the side growths) should be pruned hard to one or two eyes from the main branch. From these side shoots flowers in quantity, but not of such high quality as from one-year growth, will be freely produced. It is because the one-year-old growths give better flowers that they should be left where possible. If there is a superabundance of one-year growth and some of this has to be removed, select the medium, well-ripened shoots for tying in, the thickness of one's little finger, rather than the very coarse shoots of double that thickness which sometimes appear. If a variety is not flowering freely, give as much room as possible and leave as many shoots as long as possible, always provided that they have a minimum of 45 cm (18 in) between each shoot. This extra distance apart prevents overcrowding. In such a case, it pays to leave long secondary growths even if they are far from the root. Certain varieties are too coarse for free flowering, as their wood fails to ripen enough. Avoid planting such a variety as 'Climbing Peace' which gives wood in abundance but seldom flowers in our climate.

The treatment of newly planted climbers consists of pulling the growth as nearly horizontal to the ground as possible and shortening the growths as soon as planted. Many newly planted climbers and ramblers with large tops die from losing moisture before the roots can make new fibre to replace such losses. (It is a wise procedure for a polythene bag from which the bottom has been cut to be slipped over the rose during the winter and early spring to conserve the moisture in the wood, thus protecting it from drying winds.) In all cases, balance the top by cutting back. A few of the less vigorous climbing 'sports' may resent this and refuse to climb again, but this shortening is the lesser of the two evils. One of the causes of loss in newly planted climbers and ramblers is their inability to get moisture to their wood before rooting is established. This is aggravated when the full length of wood is left. It is seldom realized how extremely dry the average location for a climber is. Most of the scant rain we get during a dry March and April and indeed right into the early summer comes from the north-east, so that rose trees planted near a wall or protecting post may be sheltered from all rainfall, while in the open, the ground may be saturated. It is wise when planting in such positions to insert a 12·7 cm (5 in) flower pot level with the soil and about 37 cm (15 in) from the rose stem. The flower pot should be left unfilled and regular and copious waterings made through this will give a definite supply directly to the root which needs it. So often a cursory watering ends by the moisture running off the hardened surface and either evaporating or entering the soil well beyond the range of the newly planted climber with its shortened root. Once established the tree will look after itself.

The less vigorous, perpetual-flowering types usually flower on a short shoot, then throw another shoot of similar height, just below where they have flowered, so slowly growing taller as they flower. For this reason, older wood must be kept in longer to give greater coverage, but horizontal training is just as important. Immature growth and unripe tips should be cut off. It may take some years for climbers to come to perfection. Even vigorous climbers need at least three years to give their maximum flower.

The ramblers are mostly hybrids with *R. wichuraiana*, a delightful, glossy-leaved, sweetly scented white rose with many thin pendulous shoots. These have many traits in common with this parent, but more vigour has been produced by hybridizing, and the majority are useful for coverage. Some, like 'American Pillar', are not only very vigorous but are also extraordinarily hardy. They are ideal for covering the top of an old shed or the roof of a summer-house, or the end of a building. In this last case they will need a support. Little pruning in such situations will be possible or desirable. A weakening shoot, damaged by frost, may be removed. Should such ramblers get completely out of control and be filled with too much rough wood, the simple and only remedy will be to cut the whole plant back to within 46 cm (18 in) of the ground, and then allow only the youngest (green rather than brown) wood to remain. This will mean the loss of one year's flowers but the resulting growth from the cutting back will be extremely vigorous and should give considerable coverage the first year, with abundant flower of good quality the second year.

In theory all ramblers flower on the previous year's growth, and after that wood has flowered it should be cut away and new growth of the current year be tied into place. *Wichuraiana* hybrids, with their extra vigour, often throw very strong growths well up the older shoots. Provided that one or two shoots are cut to the base each year to ensure future new growth, some of these strong secondary shoots may be kept and tied in, so giving a much longer range of coverage. For this pruning use secateurs.

STANDARDS

The pruning of standard roses of whatever type follows the principles of the same dwarf type, but one has to remember that a bush at the end of a long terminal stem is a long way from much of its food supply. Bearing this in mind, one cannot expect quite the same vigour, nor the same rate of recovery after damage by frost or wind. Pruning must be used to encourage new wood, but undue severity may lead to a permanent weakening of the bush.

HYBRID TEA TYPE STANDARDS

The first year, prune to two or three 'eyes'. Make sure that the cuts are clean and it is well worth applying a waterproofing substance over the cuts to prevent water penetrating the open pith. The following year, shorten the new growths to three or four eyes. Keep the centres open. As a rule wood will not be made so easily, and older wood may have to be left. In such cases keep only healthy wood thick enough to produce flowers. Where this is on three-year wood or older, cut back to one eye. It is far more important to get suitable varieties for standards. Good varieties for this purpose are limited and while it is possible to bud every variety on a standard stem, this is a very unsatisfactory policy. A rose needs to be vigorous and free branching to make a success in this form.

FLORIBUNDA STANDARDS

Similar methods apply to the pruning of floribunda roses, bearing in mind that single blossoms on a stem are not desirable. It is better to hard-prune a main growth shoot than to prune to sub-laterals which, you will remember, are side growths from a side growth. When vigorous breaks occur from where the plant was budded, or even near it, these shoots should not be pruned as lightly as with their bush form, but be cut back to four or five eyes.

WEEPING STANDARDS

When one comes to weeping standard roses, the need for courage and discretion is most obvious. We have already said that the old-type rambler flowers on the wood made the previous year and that pruning consists of removing the wood which has flowered as soon as possible. This is done to allow maximum light and air to the growing shoots which in their turn, i.e. the following year, will give their crop of flowers. Good weeping standards are those (1) which flower on their twelve-month-old wood; (2) which make flexible and therefore pendulous growths when budded on the tall standard stems. There are only a few varieties which comply with these demands. It is possible in order to increase the range of colours to bud some *wichuraiana* hybrids, but their stiffer growth and habit of making vigorous growth some way down the current flowering growths, need adapting, by tying in the shoots carefully and early. At the same time one may leave some of the older wood if vigorous new shoots are a little way down the stem. In all cases the weeping standard when transplanted should be cut back to 15 or 20 cm (6 or 8 in) from the bud. This will mean sacrificing the flower of the first year but it is essential to promote maximum growth to ensure plenty of blossom each succeeding year. An adequate support is needed, and although these wire umbrella-shaped trainers are expensive, they are very necessary if full satisfaction is to be obtained.

Old Bushes

One of the problems facing a novice in an old garden, is what to do when pruning old bushes. So often, through inadequate pruning in the past, these bushes have one or two immense trunk-like shoots supporting a bush 60 cm (2 ft) above the ground. The tendency in such cases is to treat such trees as half-standards. The correct way, and a very rewarding one, is to cut down half the shoots the first year and the other half the following year. Should there be one of these shoots only, then it should be cut down, and the risk taken of its growing from the dormant eyes, set deeply in its bark. However old the shoot the eye can be seen, if only as a scar with a tiny eye, hardly discernible, set deeply in the ageing bark. The cut must be made in the same way but with more care, and the weight of the top growth must be supported lest its heavy head, in falling over, tear the bark, not yet completely severed. The fresh wound should be protected. An old bush or old bed of roses may be completely rejuvenated by this method. Better to carry it through in two years, as the shock to the plant is considerable. After pruning, a heavy dressing of good fertilizer, preferably farmyard manure, should be given. Only healthy trees will respond to such treatment. Old and unhealthy bushes are heavy liability which should be disposed of on the first good bonfire.

Perhaps this chapter, read at one sitting, will produce mental indigestion, but the principles are simple, and many armchair problems arising from this perusal on a winter's evening will resolve themselves when, with knife in hand, we begin to prune our trees. Begin the right way. Try pruning some top wood cleanly before pruning lower down on wood which will remain permanently. Once you have obtained the knack of cutting with a clean upward slope you will proceed apace. You may have to count the buds on a few shoots at first, to find where 'four eyes' lands you, but after that you will be able to estimate where the cut should be made.

Few achievements are so rewarding or give such a pleasing awareness of a job well done as a properly pruned bed of roses.

Although spraying should be left to another chapter, the dormant period immediately after pruning is finished gives a unique opportunity for beginning the new season with a clean bill of health. Because there are no leaves to scorch, a much stronger spray may be used which would be fatal if employed later. For this reason one may use sulphate of copper at 28 g to 4·5 l (1 oz to the gallon) of water. Such spraying should materially decrease the carry-over of black spot spores wintering on wood or in the soil. When you are spraying, both wood and soil may be given a copious covering. If any tender leaves of other plants are in the area of spray drift these should be covered, otherwise they will be blackened, and if not killed outright their crop of flowers will be ruined for the season.

 CHAPTER V

Aftercare

The aftercare of the rose garden or border can be thought of as a task which cannot be avoided, or a pleasure which brings relaxation and delight. It can be either, and depends partly upon our outlook, but more upon the planning and thought we have put into its preparation.

Simplicity should be the keynote to planning, and in aftercare we reap the benefit of every golden thoughtful moment well spent before we even began the original laying out.

Let us consider a few straightforward but important rules in aftercare. First of all and most important, the garden should please the eye, not only in its proportions, and these really matter, but in other ways we will consider later. Think what 'proportion' entails: the beds should be wide enough to cultivate easily from both sides if possible; they should contain a minimum of three rows to give depth, but for ease of cultivation they should be a maximum of four rows wide if tasks are to be manageable at all times. To be able to carry out hoeing, mulching, feeding and spraying without tearing one's clothes or soaking one's feet is a great advantage. A bed of 1·8 m (6 ft) in width presents no difficulties for the owner who, working away from the surroundings, can approach his roses at any odd time without having to change his clothes, so that he can pick up his task again where he left off, for those few minutes before the meal is ready. Not only does such a bed make work easier, it also means that each individual rose can become a personal friend. A fine flower or a sick shoot, a leaf attacked by a pest, each can be passed under rapid review, and the appropriate measures taken. The same is as true for watering or spraying as for cultivation. For ease of movement the bed should not be too long. The actual length must be determined by the position and area of the whole garden, but it is better to break up a very long border with stepping-stones across it at intervals. It is so much easier and quicker to get to the other side, and how often the end roses in a long border are damaged by the hosepipe as it is run out, or brought round to the other side. Little things? Granted, but worth consideration. We have already emphasized the use of wide paths, wide enough to become rose beds later. Bear this in mind when planning, and these proportions will enable you either to make lawn into rose bed and return the spent bed back to grass, or peel turf off the lawn, change over soils and replace the grass, if the area prevents a complete changeover of soil from elsewhere. It is true such a change should not be necessary more than once in ten to fifteen years, but how much time and temper will be saved when that time comes!

The reason for the necessity for changing the soil is not readily understood. The one fact which experience drives home is that new roses will not, I repeat 'not' flourish in old rose soil. Despite the evidence, many rosarians try to ignore this truth. Look at the actual results of planting new roses in old soil: the rose trees will probably live but they will languish; instead of the old wood remaining green and virile it tends to die back. Weakly growths will begin from nearer the tree's base, for which failure the nursery-man is blamed. If at this stage we lift the trees, there will be little or no rooting from low down. Any growth will be just below the soil surface and will consist of young fibrous roots springing from near the top of the main root. If the anchor roots are tested, they are found to be rotting from the tips inward and upward. Evidently the trouble, whatever it may be, discourages re-rooting. Two theories may be put forward. The first is that the soil's food depends on its conversion by bacteria and other agencies into suitable plant food. Roots give out a toxic material which upsets the soil's bacterial balance and so the conversion rate of the plant food is too slow for the plant's need. If this is so, why does the old rose continue to grow? The only answer one might give would be that the fibre of such a rose is far from its stock environment, and so on a better source of food. A second suggestion concerns a plague which we in England are mercifully spared to a large degree, namely eelworm infection (nematodes). These minute creatures play havoc with some crops, such as chrysanthemums, narcissi and potatoes, and it is highly probable that their presence may be the cause of the debilitation seen in old rose soils. The only known cure is soil sterilization by steam. This is practised to a large extent in rose forcing houses abroad, but is not possible out in the open. It is possible to use Dazomet as a soil sterilizer if this can be obtained. With care it is most effective. Formalin may also be used under warm soil temperatures and adequate coverage using a 2 per cent solution watering in (4 to 6 gallons) 18 to 27 litres per 0·836 sq m (1 sq yd). The answer is to be found in changing the soil completely to a depth of 37 cm (15 in). Any good garden soil in which roses have not been grown recently will do. If it is a physical impossibility to exchange the earth, then the beds must be rested for at least two years and other crops such as annuals and bulbs may be bedded out in the meantime. A green crop may be grown and dug in for a period of two years. One of the most successful deterrents to eelworm appears to be the marigold and if a vigorous type is used, one planting cleans the soil. It is not necessary to dig this in as a green crop. The old plants may be removed when they have died down. The beds may be sown down to grass, but if so, at least three years should elapse before the beds are remade and the soil is used again for roses. Cultivation and aeration are vital factors in renewing the health of the soil. One need have no hesitation in using the soil for other crops, and the old rose soil may be used at once in other places for growing vegetables or flowers other than roses.

As well as in proportion in lay-out the eye should find the garden pleasing and restful at all times even if we are hard at work. Cleanliness is a must, not only as a maxim of health but also from an aesthetic point of view. Weeds, jagged path edges, unruly suckers, ill-kept grass, broken shoots, dead flower heads, and decaying leaves are all undesirable, and indicate both unnecessary work to come and bad planning in the past.

Probably the right knowledge of good tools and their use will make all the difference when time is short and demands upon it severe. Cleanliness is more than a matter of good looks, it is the keynote to health. It is debris lying about that encourages pests and diseases. All healthy waste should be sent to the compost heap, all diseased matter and unhealthy wood should be burned.

A third point, again an aesthetic one, is concerned with the health of the foliage. Good foliage may prove a delight long before and long after the wealth of flowers is gone. The very wide variety and texture of the leaves, together with their great range of colour, presents an added delight which may be doubled by their perfect health. Here is the hallmark of the good rose grower. Here is the source of joyous anticipation for the keen rosarian. Here too is proof that the garden is in the hands of one who knows and loves his job.

We have spent quite a lot of time on the general statement of facts, but here is a basic one: dealing with pests and diseases should always be a secondary activity. Growing good plants should be our main objective.

Let us deal first with cultivation. It cannot be said too often that rose roots are fibrous and grow very near the surface. Forget the deep anchorage roots. These have had their foundation prepared when the bed was made, and nothing can improve them now. But the ever-growing, ever-hungry fibres are searching every inch of top soil for food and moisture. Feed them freely, encourage their spread, protect them from deep cultivation and from change of temperature. Two types of feeding will be necessary. One is a long-term, slow-acting one, the other a quick-acting, temporary form of feeding. The slow-acting food may be hoed in, in the autumn, the other may be added in the spring, and again after the first flush of bloom, when the second crop of flowers is being prepared by the plant. To conserve both food and moisture a good mulch is the ideal. A mulch is a layer of material laid on the bed between the plants, covering the earth. It may be farmyard manure, peat, pulverized bark, or even dark paper. While it helps to conserve moisture and protect the surface fibrous roots from extremes of temperature, it also builds up the general fertility of the soil and checks weed germination if itself sterile, as peat is, or well-decayed heated manure can be. The mulch will vary in thickness but usually 2 in (5 cm) is the maximum.

Farmyard manure probably makes the best mulch if of high quality, but unless it has been well made and rotted, my preference would be for a good medium near-neutral peat. Peat retains much moisture, but as it usually arrives in a compact and pressed block, completely dry, it needs to be well soaked before it is applied. Otherwise it will shed the rain and in its dry and light form blow away in the first strong wind. Once in position it forms a cool insulating layer. Any food to be given should be applied before the peat mulch. A great advantage with peat is its freedom from weeds and the odd perennial weed pushing through the peat layer from the soil below can easily be removed. The best time to apply these mulches is after pruning, when the bed has been cleared up. A mulch of this nature will slowly disintegrate during the years and will build up the fertility of the soil. It has a further advantage in that disease spores washed from the fallen leaves do not splash back and reinfect young growths. At the end of the season, in late autumn, any remaining loose mulch should be removed with the fallen leaves and dug in, in the kitchen garden, where rose disease spores will perish for lack of hosts on which to breed.

After mulching, feeding is probably the next most important contributor to good health. Briefly, three important elements necessary to growth must be added: these are nitrogen, phosphorus and potash. Nitrogen is an essential for growth. Plants work in the opposite way to the animal kingdom where food is concerned. They begin with simple substances and build them up into complicated materials, from simple nitrates to complicated proteins. This means that if we feed with proteins (fish and meat meal for instance) these must be broken down before the plant can use them. This takes time, and so our feeding programme must be suited to the time when the rose needs its meal. Nitrogen encourages growth. It shows its effects in the deep green colour of the foliage, in its vigour and lushness, and is an essential part of the programme. One should bear in mind, however, that too rank and soft a growth can cause weakly, sappy stem and foliage, prone to disease and the production of poor-quality flowers. Our object at all times must be balanced feeding to produce firm, strong, mature growth. This ideal will build up resistance to disease as well as helping to produce ripe wood and flowers of healthy quality with intensity of colour.

The nitrogen which is so essential to plants is usually available to it in the form of nitrates which are very soluble. Nitrogen is quickly expendable and can be washed from the soil very rapidly. A shortage shows in the yellowing of the leaves and in feeble spring growth. Readily available nitrogen in the form of nitrates and ammonium compounds should be used in the spring and early summer, when the winter rains will have reduced its level.

Forms in which these are most readily available cheaply are ammonium sulphate (21 per cent nitrogen (N)) which takes a fortnight in warm weather to become available; nitro-shell (20·5 per cent N), or nitro-chalk (15·5 per cent N). These last two are excellent for quick action, and the nitro-chalk does help to prevent additional acidity; and as it is granular in form, it can be spread without sticking to the foliage, which might otherwise be scorched. Generally speaking it is wise to use a balanced fertilizer. Of this we will speak later. Ammonium compounds, especially ammonium sulphate, have to be changed to nitrates for the plant's use, and this is done by the ammonia combining with the calcium in the soil to produce calcium sulphate and calcium nitrate, and as a by-product two equivalents of 'acid soil'. In practice it has been found that slightly more calcium carbonate by weight needs adding than ammonium sulphate used, if the loss of calcium is to be made good. A further disadvantage with sulphate of ammonia is that because soil acidity is increased, biological activity is reduced to a low level. Indeed this is a recognized practice where ammonium sulphate is used on lawns to discourage worms and the stronger grasses. Generally speaking there is much to be said for using nitro-chalk in preference. There are now a number of slow-acting dispensers such as urea or the complete slow-acting food such as Osmacote; but, if obtainable, these are very expensive.

After nitrogen, phosphorus is of great importance. Much of its action is indirect, and its functions are now known to lie in the activity of the cell nucleus and in cell division. It has the reprehensible habit of getting 'locked up' by consorting with other compounds, and becoming useless in its insoluble state. The results of application are less spectacular than with nitrogen, but it helps to promote general well-being, earlier growth (exhibitors please note), hardier plants, better root systems, and ripening which aids winter hardiness. An important item with the rose grower appears to be its encouragement to the plant to produce starch, and cells well filled with starch stand up to cold and 'die-back'. Generally speaking phosphates are even more necessary in areas of high rainfall and late development. The form used is superphosphate (18 per cent water-soluble phosphoric acid (P_2O_5)), triple superphosphate (47 per cent P_2O_5), the latter in a granular form. Basic slag is a slow-acting phosphatic manure and has a variable content. It is useful for preparing heavy soils, but the more soluble forms should be used normally. Heavy and regular dressings would add too much lime to the soil. A very popular form of phosphatic manure which also has a small proportion of nitrogen, are preparations of bones. Steamed bone flour is more readily available for the plant and contains 27·5 per cent P_2O_5 with just a hint of nitrogen. Bone meal has 20 to 24 per cent P_2O_5 and 3 to 4 per cent N. Two things should be said of it. While not a complete food it does have a stimulating action on the root system, and by increasing the area of the plant roots' absorption, adds to the plant's food supply. Like other organic compounds (derivations of animal matter) it is expensive, as there is a strong demand for it for animal feeding compounds and other manufacturing processes. To be on the safe side handle with gloves on; small broken bones cut and anthrax is possible.

The third important item is potash. This aids ripening and counteracts the soft growth. It also increases starch formation. Although not so essential on heavier soils, where it is naturally in better supply, it is vital to health. There is a common saying that nitrogen increases the area of the leaf, while potassium increases its efficiency. A compound manure for roses should always be high in potash content. A word of warning should be given. Never use muriate (chloride) of potash. Admirable for some farm crops it is a killer on rose trees. Only sulphate of potash (48 per cent K_2O)

should be used. The lighter and more chalky the soil, the more
vital is sulphate of potash.

These three elements nitrogen, phosphates and potash are the
most important correctors of plant food deficiencies. The carbon
and oxygen are obtained from the air by the plant leaves, and con-
verted into sugars which in their turn are changed into starch for
storage. This remarkable process, known as photosynthesis, depends not only on the above elements, but upon minute quantities
of trace elements, although most of these have an indirect effect,
only carbon and hydrogen, with small quantities of nitrogen and
oxygen and minute traces of magnesium, contributing to the process. It is because farmyard manure contains the complete wastage
from animals that these trace elements may be found in this source
of plant food, and account for its greater value when compared
with pure sources of plant food, such as peat for humus with the
addition of artificial manures.

One other most important element is lime. While not in itself a
food it is essential for healthy growth. It makes food available and
neutralizes acidity. The average soil is more likely to have enough
lime than too little for the rose crop, and soil should always be
tested for deficiency, and this lack should be proved before lime is
added. Roses prefer a slightly acid soil and the careless addition of
lime in any form can ruin good rose soils almost beyond recovery.
Experience proves, unfortunately, that because lime is cheap it
may be grossly over-used. Where it has to be added, ground chalk,
being slower in dispersal, is to be recommended.

The following elements play a necessary but restricted part in
plant growth besides those previously mentioned. The hydrogen
and oxygen comes from water and the carbon as carbon dioxide
from the air. Three others are necessary in appreciable amounts—
iron, as iron sequestrine, magnesium as Kieserite or Epsom Salts,
and sulphur. Essential in tiny amounts, certain trace elements,
boron, manganese, copper, zinc, molybdenum and chlorine, must
be available, but in any concentration they can be actively harmful.
It is because organic manures contain such trace elements that they
are invaluable, and undoubtedly the ideal organic food is good
farmyard manure. This mixture of straw, dung, and urine is not

only rich in the main necessary plant foods nitrogen, phosphates and potash, but also contains many trace elements essential to the life cycle of the plant. The emphasis here is on 'good'. The slightly stained straw and sawdust which are hawked round by avaricious dealers should be avoided at all times. It is far better, if good farm-yard manure is not obtainable, to look for suitable substitutes. Here peat or spent hops can provide the humus which may be supple-mented by bone meal for phosphates and a little nitrogen; dried blood for nitrogen and some phosphates and potash; shoddy, old cloth, a slow source of nitrogen; or hoof-and-horn meal, a more balanced food with small, slow supplies of nitrogen, phosphates and potash. It should be remembered that plant foods bought in the organic form are far more expensive than their equivalent in arti-ficial counterparts. This has a twofold cause. These products are needed in other markets and so competition raises the price; also, being more bulky, transport and packing costs are higher. They are, however, an insurance against waste, for they cannot be washed from the soil as quickly as soluble artificials, and therefore are especially useful in light open soils. Their texture helps to build up fertility, and again their impurities mean replacement of suitable trace elements in the necessary tiny quantities. An added advantage is their beneficial effect on living organisms in the soil. It is a reasonable supposition, therefore, that if a manure compound contains organic material, it will be more expensive for the same feeding value as an artificial compound. On the other hand, organic manures will offer qualities difficult to evaluate. Broadly speaking the light soils will benefit more than the heavy soils if organics are used although both types will show the difference. Much of the value of an organic manure lies in its bulk and in its property of improving the mechanical nature of the soil. This means that a generous proportion may be used, and used with safety, but much greater care must be used with artificial manure. I would strongly advocate that in all artificial compound manures the correct strengths be used. That little bit extra, that generous handful, may do much harm. Haphazardly applied artificials may not only ruin the plants but also destroy the texture of the soil. Unless you are expert, it is wise advice to buy a balanced fertilizer, which not only has a guaranteed analysis, but has those materials in a usable form. Analysis showing insoluble proportions should be ignored. They are of no immediate use and may never become available to the plant. The soluble portion should be considered the valuable part. As a rule the less soluble the manure, the earlier in the season it should be used. When the mulch is removed in the autumn, manures such as bone meal may be distributed and hoed in. On the other hand, most manures of inorganic nature usually in use should be applied just as the plant begins to grow. If pruning is carried out in late February or early March, then the first feeding should be done as the beds are cleaned up. Never leave these feeds lying on the surface. Put them into the soil, but only just beneath.

If the total application is at the rate of 113 g to 0·8 m (4 oz to the square yard)—a heavy dressing amounting to 558 kg to 0·4 hectare (11 cwt to the acre)—split the dose into two lots, giving one early, and the other just after the first flush of flowers is over. A heavy dressing at one time may upset the balance of the soil or prevent the plants from obtaining the maximum advantage. It is essential to add artificial manures to damp soils. If feeding is carried out in dry weather, the ground should be soaked first, then fed, and next the food must be watered in.

Some indication of mineral deficiency may be gathered from the discoloration of the foliage. The commonest nitrogen deficiency signs are the pale yellowish green of the leaves, which later become more varied (orange, red and sometimes purple) first in the older leaves, and the fact that growth is weakly and poor. The application of a nitrogen fertilizer shows spectacular results in such cases. Phosphorus deficiency is revealed by many similar symptoms. The main difference is that the leaves turn a dull blue-green and later tints are purple rather than red and yellow. Calcium shortage usually shows in the young leaves and growing tips, which are distorted and die back. Lack of magnesium may often be confused with other ills, and indeed these symptoms need expert diagnosis, but shortage of potassium can lead to apparent scorching of the leaves either at the tips or edges. There has been so much discoloration of foliage, especially in the early part of the year, that caution is necessary. One fact is emphasized over and over again. Moderation in feeding is essential. Read instructions, and never exceed doses.

As already seen, spraying instructions must be just as scrupulously observed. In fact, in many instances the rainbow-hued specimens I have seen may be accounted for by active scorching from an overdose of spray. If such an unfortunate effect should occur, the simplest and easiest method is to feed with a foliar feed. This is a very weak solution of plant foods which are immediately soluble, and of essential trace elements, all in available form. This quick restorative can give the plant the energy needed to recover from the shock it has received from misplaced kindness.

Better by far to obtain a well-balanced fertilizer, organic for preference, which has been carefully adjusted, than to make up one's own mixture. The percentage difference cost per tree is negligible, and the risks are out of all proportion to the small monetary saving. For the amateur their greater expense is offset by their value as insurance for health. There are rose fertilizers made to the formula of the Royal National Rose Society now readily available under proprietary names.

In 'aftercare' one item should be touched on. It may be called 'summer pruning', which is rather a drastic description for what is really the removal of worn or unproductive foliage and shoots. The objective may be twofold: quantity or quality of flower. If quantity of flower is needed, every shoot capable of producing flower without expense to its neighbour should be left. Even here, the removal of the flower head, when this has died, is essential. A little more wood beyond the flower head may have to come off. Observation shows that usually the leaf bud immediately below the flower of a hybrid tea is undeveloped. Examine the leaf buds on such a shoot. The majority will appear full and globular, but the top leaf bud will seem thin and pointed in comparison, while the rose leaf will have less than its full complement of leaflets. It is safe to cut to a plump bud which will produce a normal growth giving maximum flower. Where cluster flowers in floribundas or hybrid teas are present, then the first cut should be under the whole flower head at the first plump bud. One seldom has to make the decision with the floribunda, as growth will be well under way before the head above has finished flowering. A more drastic pruning is necessary for exhibition purposes, but this will be dealt with in Chapter VIII, 'Exhibiting Roses'.

The slaughtering of a plant for bloom is indefensible. Foliage is the factory for food making and storage, and to remove this essential to health is mortgaging the future. This does not mean that one should not cut flowers, but a sense of proportion should be maintained, and one or two long-stemmed shoots per plant should be the limit, at least until a mature, full-size bush is established. During the first summer the flower heads alone should be removed. Should there be top-heavy growths, these should be removed before winter to help the plant to keep a firm root hold. Wind rock can do much damage both by tearing the fibrous roots and by forming a hollow between plant and soil which, filling with water and then freezing, can do untold harm.

If one examines the eye in the axil of the leaf, it will be seen that there are really three growth points: the large, plump, central one, and far back in the wood, at each side, two tiny scars which are little dormant eyes. These are known as 'guard' eyes and in many cases will never develop. They are there to ensure continuity of growth should the central eye be damaged. There are some varieties where these 'guard eyes' break freely. Such a case is 'Violinista Costa'. Usually, if three shoots develop from one leaf axil, it is better to rub off the two smaller side shoots while still very young, and let all the energy be concentrated in the main growth. These guards are nevertheless present as insurance in emergency. Should the centre shoot be damaged the side shoots will grow to replace the lost growth.

Remembering this, we are faced with the common problem of 'suckering'. Not only do shoots have these 'guard buds', but hidden away in the roots are 'adventitious buds' which in emergency can produce growth shoots, if the wood above ground is hurt in any way (see plate 10 for illustration). These growth shoots are called 'suckers' and, as they will be produced on the root stock, they will be foreign to the 'bud' of the cultivated rose which was inserted above. Once started, they have a great advantage. Being below bud level, they have first call on the plant food and can soon reduce a healthy plant to a weakly specimen. The first problem is to remove this 'sucker'. It is worse than useless to cut it off, because a whole nest of new growths will begin at the cut, and also those two dormant guard buds will spring into life, producing vigorous shoots straight from the root. As soon as these suckers are seen protruding from the soil, one must play the detective. Follow this 'sucker' back to the plant from which it came. It may not be anywhere near the bush you imagine to be the culprit. When you have traced it to its source, remove the covering soil from that part of the stock, and then with a sharp inward and upward jerk tear the sucker from the root. It may be advisable to place one's foot on the root of the plant, so steadying it and preventing tearing the other roots from their hold in the soil. This tearing will not only remove the sucker but also tear out the guard eyes, and ensure the complete removal of the trouble.

Often suckering is a sign of ill-health, and may be started by damage to the root caused by too deep cultivation. A severe frost, killing back the wood of the bush itself, anything indeed which breaks the even routine of growth may give rise to the trouble. If one is unfortunate enough to inherit a bed of suckering roses it is wise to dig up the bushes carefully, and then remove the growths. It is interesting to see how many suckers can arise from one cutback shoot.

It is always a problem for the beginner to decide which is a 'sucker' and which is new growth sent up from the bush itself. There is one golden rule when in doubt. Remove the soil round the plant, and see whether the growth comes from the root or from the bud, which will appear as a gnarled knot compared to the almost smooth root. If from the root, pull off. Usually it is not hard to distinguish the stock sucker from the genuine rose. Normally the sucker is a paler green and has smaller and more numerous leaflets which are also narrower. This applies to polyantha and brier stocks. Rugosa suckers, more often seen on standards, have larger leaflets, but these again are more numerous and are a dull green. Do not confuse the vigorous red shoots thrust up from the base of the plant springing from the 'bud'. These must be preserved at all costs, for on them will depend the rejuvenation of the whole plant.

Confusion can arise from certain species, and in this case it is better to leave the sucker to flower during its second year when the small blooms in June will reveal its true character and it may be removed in the usual way.

Staking is an important item in the satisfactory growing of roses. If one has planned the purchase of standard roses it is a wise precaution to obtain the stakes in good time. These should be 2·5 × 2·5 × 152·5 cm (1 in × 1 in × 5 ft) and should be thoroughly saturated with Cuprinol to preserve them. When the hole is due for the reception of the plant, the stake should be driven well into the lower firm earth and the tree itself put in and tied fairly loosely for the first month. This will allow for settlement of soil and plant. The stem may be fastened permanently after a few weeks.

Stakes should be examined in the autumn and again in the spring. There is much to be said for an iron stake for weeping standards as the strain is considerable, especially in the summer, when the head is heavy with flower and growth. It is a common tragedy for a well-grown weeping standard, just attaining maturity, to be snapped off in a summer gale.

When you furnish posts for ramblers and climbers, avoid 'arty' lichen-covered larch poles which deteriorate almost as rapidly as silver birch. Only two woods should be used, unless one is prepared to spend a fortune on teak. These are sweet chestnut or riven oak, both of which are extremely durable. If less enduring woods are used, they should be treated with preservative under pressure, and an added precaution is to cement these into hollow drain-pipes which should be sunk to within 30 cm (12 in) of their top. This will give a post with a very long life.

Trellis can be a bane, and it is wise to have these made with bold 12·7-cm (5-in) squares and have them fastened to blocks of wood fixed on the wall. This will allow air to circulate between the climbers and wall and the trees will keep more free from mildew.

Under 'cultivation' one should mention the use of sprays to control weeds. Simazine is the general ingredient largely used. As a rule this is at 50 per cent strength, but quantities should be used as prescribed by the suppliers. This spray does not kill weeds, but prevents the germination of the seeds. It works while the coverage is unbroken, so that raking, hoeing, or other cultivation must cease. Quantities used on such small areas are minute, for only 0·9 kg (2 lb) of Simazine are used to the 0·4 hectare (acre) and would have to be sprayed on with great care. Rose bushes are unaffected by the spray. Arguments against this anti-weed treatment, are the hardening of the soil and the fact that weeds such as thistle and annual nettle are untouched by it. Before using the spray, every weed must be removed, and efficiency will depend upon abundant moisture at the time of application. If this treatment is to be given, choose the time after pruning and feeding. For the amateur a peat mulch is preferable.

No calendar for treatment is given. Do the job when it needs to be done and this will vary with the year's weather.

With practice will come skill and speed, and routine tasks will take less time and seem far less formidable.

 CHAPTER VI

Maintaining Health

It has been said that rose growing should be a pleasure, and if one is able to keep plants in good health, pests and disease should cause little real worry. A wary eye directed frequently on the bushes can keep pests under control. The finger and thumb are still a very effective deterrent for the lesser pests. Probably a drenching from a forceful hose will keep aphis at bay: it is as good as a heavy storm for dashing this pest to the ground.

There are times when pests must be treated by spraying. When this is necessary it is essential to use a sprayer which will produce a fine mist giving complete coverage, and this demands considerable force. One would suggest a pneumatic sprayer which can be pumped up beforehand, so giving the hands freedom while actually spraying. The choice will depend upon the quantity of material to be used at one time and the strength of the user. There are a number of small, light and very efficient sprayers on the market which can be pressurized before spraying by using a hand pump or other device. Where a large number of roses have to be sprayed I would strongly advocate a small motorized knapsack unit which cuts out all hard work while maintaining a constant pressure and leaves the hands free.

Here a word of warning is needed. An increasing amount of damage is occurring each year from the careless use of sprays. Never mix up the spray until the directions have been read and re-read. Quantities should be exact. You are dealing with complicated chemicals, finely balanced to produce maximum results. Undue dilution may make the spray ineffective, but extra concentration can scorch foliage and ruin a promising batch of roses.

Never carry over last year's supplies of spray material. Age diminishes their effectiveness. Never mix together sprays for different purposes, unless the firm concerned states that this may be done safely. It may save a little time, but the application of unnecessary sprays may not only waste money but also cause damage. The exception is a pesticide against greenfly which may be mixed with a spray for disease, but even so, the second spraying for greenfly should be carried out long before the next disease spray is necessary.

Never spray in bright sunlight or a cold drying wind or your foliage may be damaged. The ideal time is in the evening, as often in the early morning the leaves will be wet with dew. A dust, properly applied, can be as effective as a wet spray when the weather is dry, and may penetrate better for some leaf-rolling insects.

Above all, one needs a sense of proportion, and the rose hypochondriac who imagines his trees have all the pests and diseases and all the mineral deficiencies, will soon reduce a healthy rose garden to an experimental station for disease. Let well alone whenever possible. One should bear in mind that the city-dweller, or those living in or near an industrial area, are blessed by immunity from black spot and rust, so that preventative spraying for these diseases need never trouble them. With the coming of the Clean Air Act fewer areas are becoming immune to these troubles but a little care at the right time will keep diseases controlled.

A warning note is necessary on the extremely poisonous nature of many of the insecticides offered today. A single splash in the eye from one concentrated greenfly killer, and the unfortunate operator might be blinded for life. Scrupulous care is the rule, and rubber gloves should always be worn when mixing up such compounds. Systemics, poisons absorbed by the plant to re-poison sucking insects in their turn, can be highly dangerous. So many poisons nowadays can be absorbed through the skin, and their effect is cumulative and highly dangerous. A great advance has been made with systemics although it appears there is a limit to their movement in the plant but one may expect further advances in this type of spray.

It is far safer to leave such lethal materials in the hands of commercial growers who are not only insured, but who wear protective clothing and even masks when using them. The following five materials are recommended as combining the most effective destructive power with the greatest safety to the user:

B.H.C. (Known as Lindane, Gammalin 20 or Strykol B.H.C.) An excellent spray against sucking insects such as aphis. It is dangerous for bees and harmful to fish and livestock for about two weeks after application.

Derris is available as a spray or dust. An excellent insecticide, it is highly dangerous to fish although harmless to warm-blooded animals.

Dipterex 80 (contains trichlorophon). An organophosphorous insecticide which should be used with caution. It is harmful to fish but an excellent spray against caterpillars and other leaf-eaters.

Malathion 60. An organophosphorous compound giving excellent control for a series of sap-sucking and leaf-eating predators including scale.

Pirimor (contains Pirimicarb). An excellent partial systemic against sucking insects. Used as a wettable spray or as dispersable grains. It is harmful to livestock but of little persistence needing about a week to clear.

One may divide the pests into two types: sucking insects which live by obtaining the sap from the plant, and insects which eat the plant itself.

Of the sucking insects the rose aphis is the worst enemy (see plate 11 for illustration). This can be encouraged by over-feeding with nitrogen and so producing soft growths. The main problem is the rapidity of its reproduction and its periodic migration. It mates once a year, in the spring, then propagation goes on unhindered by every fly during the summer and the rate of increase can be fantastic. This type of insect breathes through holes in its body, mostly in the abdomen, and besides poison, any material which seals the breathing apparatus ensures rapid death. One snag, however, should be borne in mind. Even while the fly is being killed, the tiny progeny can be reproduced, and unless immediate steps are taken, the build-up can be rapid. This being so, it is wise to spray twice, with a three-day interval between, so ensuring complete destruction. Remembering these warnings on poisons, use either Malathion 60, Derris, or B.H.C. where these are effective. These substances are harmless to human beings, but efficacy depends upon complete coverage, and the use of a reliable spreader such as saponin or soft soap. It should be remembered that Derris is deadly for fish, and any drift or rinsings should be kept away from ornamental ponds or running water. Aphides migrate at times, so that rapid infestation can take place at any growing period.

The rose leaf hopper can cause much damage. In the larval stage it eats the underside of the leaf, giving a mottled appearance. The larva remains on the underside of the leaf, causing it to drop early. The larger adults continue the damage, but are active and hop and fly. Malathion 60 should be used.

The cuckoo-spit insect is easily traced by the frothy sap covering it. Within this froth is the small yellow body. The frothy mass must be penetrated by a forceful spray for good results. Any of the materials named may be used. Normally, hand picking is enough.

Rose caterpillars and maggots of various sorts can be an unsightly nuisance, but may be treated by crushing between finger and thumb or dusting where the leaves are rolled. The larger caterpillars may be destroyed with Dipterex 80. The ideal time to catch these predators is in the evening when they come out to feed.

Two sawflies are particularly troublesome. The first is the slug-worm which reduces the leaf to a skeleton. The yellowish, almost transparent, slug-like larvae feed mainly on the underside of the leaf. Prevention is effected by spraying with Derris or Dipterex 80, the lower surface of the leaf, at the end of May or in June when the larvae themselves are easily killed. It is an unsightly pest, but its inroads seldom reach harmful proportions.

On the other hand, the leaf-rolling rose sawfly is a menace which increases year by year if unchecked. The attack is more general in sheltered corners, and under warm hedgerows where stagnant air encourages the flies to hover. It is particularly common in rose gardens over-sheltered by surrounding trees. Once the leaves have curled, no spraying is of use. The damage is done when the irritation from the laying of the egg in the mid rib of the leaf causes the leaflets to curl up. Hand picking and burning at once are the only remedy. A preventive spray with Malathion 60 in May and June will catch the thin-bodied adults which, on the wing, look like flying ants. Neglected, the plants may become completely defoliated, for the leaves turn yellow and drop off once they have fed the larvae to maturity. The yellowing of the leaf before fall may be confused with chlorosis, which is due to iron deficiency.

Only three diseases need concern us. Others are of minor importance. Undoubtedly, outside the industrial areas (as already noted) black spot is the biggest threat to the growing of roses. It is not a killing disease but it is very unsightly, and repeated attacks weaken the plants which lose their resistance to cold, as insufficient starch is produced to keep the wood cells hardy.

Prevention is the only line of attack. The black spotting of the leaf is an indication of the disease already within, and it is then too late to save the leaf. The 'black spots' are purplish-brown to black and have ragged edges (see plate 12 for illustration).

Cleanliness is the first requisite. This consists of removing and burning old leaves, only possible where a removal mulch is spread beneath the plants, and peat so used presents the double advantage of helping to keep the plant growing during the summer, and then acting as a trap for any falling spores in the autumn. This also should be collected and dug in, in the kitchen garden, where it can do no harm.

The second stage is the treatment of dormant wood. Spores over-winter on the younger wood. By spraying plant and soil thoroughly with copper sulphate (28 g to 4·5 l water (1 oz to 1 gallon)) immediately after pruning in late February or early March one begins the season with a clean bill of health. So common is the disease, and so easily spread, that regular routine spraying is the only safeguard for perfect health. Two sprays may be recommended. Probably the best known at the moment is Maneb. This is effective if regularly applied, but it does encourage the retention of leaf with late growth—not always an advantage. Such growth in October can become badly mildewed in the cold nights then experienced. If Maneb is used, precautions against mildew must be taken. What is certain is that healthy plants retaining their leaves until the frost, do not die back in winter. Maneb may be mixed with a mildew preventative A.M. 62. This acts as a mildew preventative while Maneb itself has been found to give a strong measure of prevention against rust which has become more prevalent of late.

Maneb's great advantage is that as well as giving excellent and dependable results against black spot it also gives considerable coverage against rust, so providing an insurance against the two most damaging diseases which afflict roses.

In all cases, adequate coverage, especially of the lower leaves and their undersides, is essential. Full directions for spraying are given and they must be strictly adhered to. The time to spray is when the leaves are dry. If dry weather continues, one spray will last a long while. Don't put off spraying until the rain, promised on the weather news, is over. It is essential to have a layer of spray on the leaf before rain falls, so that spores may neither fall nor be splashed upon the bare surface of the leaf.

In a normal garden, if the autumn and spring treatment is given, and the garden is not badly affected, one may get away with spraying in mid July for the first time, but mid June is a wiser starting date. If an early spraying is done before the leaves are mature, half strength should be used. Infection can be very rapid when encouraged by warm, wet weather. Usually, if black spot begins in August complete defoliation can take place by late September. Where this disease is really bad, regular spraying from early leafing onward is essential.

If the bushes are kept healthy and have a balanced food, low in nitrogen, high in phosphates and potash, black spot should not be an insoluble problem. It is often confused with purple spot, caused by a mineral deficiency. Experts who have kept careful records go so far as to say that black spot itself is not so widely prevalent as was once supposed. It is common enough to be available for every rose if conditions are favourable, and as this is so, we must rely on prevention, for there is no cure. The only chance is to build up resistance by growing healthy plants and to give them adequate protection before the disease appears.

Mildew, the outdoor variety (see plate 13 for illustration), is very common at times, and may be extremely disfiguring. Correct pruning will help, see page 58. It appears in very wet weather when much lush soft growth is produced and the cool temperatures encourage the trouble. On the other hand, extremely dry weather can produce mildew on what little growth appears. Two conditions aggravate the tendency to mildew, draughty positions and borders where temperature extremes are encouraged by corrugated iron or similar screening. Again, a mulch, by encouraging equable growing conditions, is very helpful. A new spray which has given very promising results is Milfaron (contains chloraniformenthan). This is harmful to fish. Karathane has been much used but this is highly soluble. Both sprays are most effective unmixed. If the number of roses is small, or only one or two susceptible varieties are affected, a dusting with green sulphur powder is enough. Small canisters, with blowers incorporated, will provide sufficient dust for the purpose.

Rust is easily recognized by the bright rusty-red spores on the underside of the leaf which ripen to black, and the dying leaf crumples and soon falls. This is a killing disease which has been less common since the war, but is prevalent in the West of England where the wetter weather conditions, together with higher temperatures, help it to spread. Regular spraying with Maneb gives control while helping against black spot.

I regret to suggest that the safest and best method is to destroy the bushes by burning at once. If one hesitates to sacrifice the bushes and is willing to take a 'kill or cure' risk, one may defoliate by spraying with copper sulphate (28 g to 4·5 litres (1 oz to a gallon of water). This has been done successfully with a large bed of 'Chrysler Imperial'. Attacked in August, the bed was treated, all foliage was collected and burned as it fell, and the bushes recovered and flowered well the following year. But this is a great risk. Not only may the roses themselves be killed, but infection may spread.

Again, at the risk of wearying the reader, it is wise to repeat that the hygiene of good cultivation with good feeding, is cheaper, better, and more effective than all the sprays. Use sprays by all means when necessary, but only as a second emergency line of attack.

Such advice can be given generally. There are certain bad areas as there are also good positions. If one is unfortunately in the midst of such an infected spot, then full precautions of all kinds must be taken. This means fortnightly spraying through the season, beginning at half strength when the leaf has opened but is not fully mature. After this first spray use full strength. Continue fortnightly until October. It is sometimes forgotten that this regular spraying is needed not only to continue protecting the old foliage but also to cover the many new leaves which are constantly forming.

One can achieve much by ruthlessly removing susceptible varieties. It should be remembered that a forgotten climber, infected by disease, can spread trouble over a wide area. Don't miss the odd climber or specimen bush when spraying: it must be all or nothing.

A trouble which has been confused with black spot is due to the larva of the capsid bug. This is more frequently found near grass banks or long grass, such as uncut borders where bulbs have been grown. If it becomes really troublesome the banks and hedgerows will have to be sprayed with B.H.C. It is unlikely to reach epidemic proportions, but the nervous beginner may well think these black spots are the first assault of his major enemy. If the leaf is examined it will be found that the damage is on the underside of the leaf only, and a search through a magnifying glass will reveal the enemy, quietly and methodically eating its way round the edge of the darkened area.

A very disfiguring trouble, difficult to eradicate, is the leaf-cutting bee. This industrious lady cuts out circular pieces of leaf to build her nest for the egg she intends to lay. These cuts are made with mathematical precision and can cause much speculation as to their reason. Spraying the foliage with Derris will act as a deterrent.

One should remember that 'aftercare' of the rose is demanded at all times, and regular pruning, carefully performed, will remove much disease and many pests. 'Canker' causing the formation of diseased portions of wood, and 'scale'—an insect pest protected by a very tiny shell-like covering, attacking older bushes—may be kept at bay by the skilful use of the knife.

To complete this chapter it may be advisable to pass on information supplied through the courtesy of Dr. R. H. Cammack of the Plant Pathology Laboratory of the Ministry of Agriculture at Hatching Green. Considerable confusion can arise through certain unusual symptoms appearing in the leaves of a few roses. These are caused by virus diseases. In the U.S.A., rose streak and rose mosaic are common, and in Australia rose wilt is a serious disease which kills the plant. Fortunately no virulent type is known in Britain. Virus is distributed in the rose trees sent out, but a few varieties are totally infected. Of these 'Masquerade' and 'Queen Elizabeth' are badly affected. I have also seen 'Circus' and many others affected at times. In New Zealand a trouble known as 'petal break' is a very common occurrence although there is some doubt as to whether it is the result of a virus. The colour of the bloom is uneven and at its worst the petals appear distorted.

Virus symptoms are best seen in mature leaves. Young foliage does not show them. Symptoms vary with the rose and the type of virus. Common forms are shown in plate 14. These are 'vein banding' (Fig. *a*), or 'vein mosaic' (Fig. *b*), and often the affected areas along the veins spread out in patches between the veins. A symptom noticed frequently on some varieties is 'line pattern' (Fig. *c*) and occasionally on some floribundas a 'ringspot' is present (Fig. *d*). Effects vary considerably, and show up as areas of pale green or bright yellow against the normal green of the remainder of the leaf. This may be partial, not necessarily a general infection, so that some shoots may appear quite healthy even if on an infected bush.

The severity of symptoms and the effect of the disease on the plant vary with the susceptibility of the variety. In general the yellow forms of mosaic have little effect, but the green forms can cause puckering and distortion of the foliage. Virus infection weakens the plant and so reduces vigour, lowering the quality and quantity of flowers.

The virus is not known to spread by natural means. It is, however, multiplied by budding and grafting both by using infected bud wood and infected stocks. Make sure that only mature healthy budding wood is used. Do not use cutting stocks which may be infected and will pass on the trouble to the budded plant. As virus is not seed borne, use seedling stocks only, where these are compatible with the variety to be budded. There is no evidence that the virus can be carried on pruning or budding knives, but it would be wise to sterilize both knives and secateurs regularly, ideally after each successive operation. A convenient way of doing this is to dip the blade into a 10 per cent solution of tri-sodium orthophosphate. This chemical is safe to use and readily available.

Some stocks used for standard roses appear to be infected. These are rugosa stems which appear normal when budded but the growths from the buds appear unhealthy and make little growth. Such trees should be destroyed rather than wasting time in trying to resuscitate them. This virus is known as strawberry 'ringspot'.

There are other soil-borne viruses transmitted by root eelworms. The symptoms are broken yellow rings on the leaves and leaf distortion. These types are very rare at the moment, but one should make sure in all cases that only the mature and healthiest wood is used for propagation.

With care it should be possible to maintain healthy stocks of roses by normal methods, but experiments are being made in the use of immature, quickly forced wood to produce virus-free stock from infected bushes.

As with all disease, the object should be to recognize the enemy early, and so ensure its swift destruction before it has secured a firm foothold. Spend care and energy on producing healthy trees, and pests and diseases will give little trouble. Never bud from any but the healthiest stock.

The rose family is a large one and nature has decreed that it should play its part in providing for the voracious needs of many organisms; but nature always makes sure that one pest has another to feed on it. The ladybird and its larva is only one predator and there are many others which will help to keep order in this unruly kingdom. If the cheeky sparrow as well as other feathered friends throw the peat mulch on the lawn when taking a dust bath, they will also destroy a host of aphides and other insects. Encourage nature to fulfil her function of keeping a fair balance, and use artificial measures as a second line of defence only.

D

PART II

SHOWING ROSES

 CHAPTER VII

Garden Usage

The increased popularity of the rose in recent years owes much to the adaptability of its types for many purposes in the garden. From coverage of grass banks and unsightly borders to the lofty branches of a dead tree, from the formality of a paved court to the informality of a woodland dell, there are varieties and types suitable for all these and many other purposes.

A major difficulty which must be clearly faced is of giving an indisputable definition to the modern terms used in seeking to describe the varieties of roses. The reason for this will be dealt with in Chapter XIII, 'The Genetics of Hybridizing and Cross-Breeding'. In the meantime it must be realized that the antecedents of the present rose trees, as catalogued, are so varied, and yet have so much common blood, that borderline cases may be found in all groups. The definitions must be in general terms only. There will be no botanic significance except for the few.

THE HYBRID TEA

Why the name? Some varieties arise from the mating of pure strains showing little change from generation to generation; others, from the mating of two differing strains give rise to progeny having qualities obtained in varying proportion from either side. These latter are known as 'hybrids'. In the last century, a forward move was made, when purposeful crossing took the place of chance sowing of seeds produced from natural hybridizing carried out by wind and insects. At this time, the hardy perpetual-flowering qualities of roses known and grown in Europe were combined with the new shades, types and growths of the Asiatic roses. This process took many years. The final grouping evolved a long pointed bud, bushy growth, and perpetual-flowering combined with increasing hardiness. Thus 'hybrid' is certainly true but 'tea' is a relic of a small part of the blood in the veins of the present hybrid tea rose. Whether 'tea' scent applied to the freshly picked tips of the tea plant, the aroma of the China tea, or the tea-chest itself is anybody's guess and anyone's choice! It is a name hallowed by time, and probably with some small foundation in fact, as is usual in tradition. People will still ask for 'tea' shaded roses, probably meaning the subtle shades of pink and pale yellow such as are found in mother-of-pearl which were often present in the earlier roses of the tea type. The tea roses, bred from *R. indica*, were lovely flowers, but were so delicate in the British climate that most were grown as pot plants, bedded out for the summer and over-wintered in a frost-proof frame or greenhouse. To dismiss this name in a few sentences should not blind us to the fact that centuries, more, thousands of years of patient selection by keen Chinese gardeners went into the selection and production of the varieties which became available for hybridizing, or for using as seed parents before any deliberate cross-pollination began. Briefly, we owe the repeat flowering and cluster qualities to the Chinese varieties, together with the softer yellows and pinks, also the clear reds. The fact that our dwarf varieties 'sport' to climbers shows a reversion to the original climbing form of all the Chinese progeny. Many of these varieties were scented, but not with the perfume still supposed to be 'old rose' perfume. This damask perfume comes from what one might term the European ancestors of the present hybrid tea. 'European' should really be 'Near East' for these roses became known in the Mediterranean region, although their origin is probably still farther East. This European section contributed to the deep red colour, the strong damask type perfume, the bushy factor, and also, through one type, helped to strengthen the repeat flowering factor. To follow the development of the rose is a fascinating study, but sufficient has been said to show that the hybrid tea type is of very mixed ancestry, and we can think of the group as having medium to large specimen blooms, usually coming singly, although in the autumn a shoot may have a veritable candelabra of flowers. The illustration on page 61 will show the types which are more easily recognized than described. The other distinguishing mark is that flowering is usually inter-mittent. The blooms come in big bursts with a waiting period between. To this class belong the specimen blooms exhibited in box classes at the leading shows.

THE FLORIBUNDA TYPE

It is this hybrid tea class which has maintained the ascendancy for some seventy years, but it is now being outmoded by the floribunda type. The word 'floribunda' has no botanical significance in this setting. It is used to describe the perpetual-cluster-flowering roses. Some sub-divide this section into 'floribunda roses, hybrid tea type' containing the large, more double group, and 'floribunda' which have the same habit and are either smaller in size of flower or with fewer petals. Whatever is said and done is purely arbitrary, and it is possible to show a disbudded floribunda hybrid tea type in the exhibition class in the early summer and as a floribunda in the autumn. There are too many borderline cases to allow us to be dogmatic. There should be one unfailing criterion for judging a floribunda. It should be continuous-flowering, not intermittent. One should always expect to see a secondary flower shoot well developed, just below the first flower head of a true floribunda, before this first flower head has finished blooming. There should be flower in the mass, for it is this freedom which has lifted this type into its present position of the best bedding plant in the world.

THE MINIATURE TYPE

A class known as 'miniatures' are quite distinct. They began as descendants from *R. chinensis minima*, a form of which is *R. rouletii*, named after a Dr. Roulet as already pointed out. Their origin is obscure, but hybridists know that the dwarfing quality is always hidden in any rose, and in *R. roulettii* the dwarfing quality or factor is so strong that it dominates its progeny. They are in all

ways like tiny replicas of the ordinary rose, usually growing 15 to
20 cm (6 to 8 in) high if grown from cuttings. If budded or grafted
they are apt to be over-tall for their purpose.

Specimen Rose

Other types are the specimen roses. These may be species, hybrids
of species, or just over-vigorous hybrid teas and floribundas. One
expects the bushes grown on their own to rise to 1·5 to 3 m (5 to
10 ft), and they may be continuous- or once-flowering.

Climbers and Ramblers

The same confusion exists with climbers and ramblers. There is
no clear division. The only distinguishing feature is in their
developing rods. The climbers usually flower on their second-year
wood but in some cases they will flower on one-year wood. The
breeding of both is even more varied than for hybrid teas and
floribundas, for they have added climbing species blood to the
other types. Because of this very mixed ancestry one has a combination of a great variety of characters.

When one considers the list of names given (see page 328) one
finds that a very great advance has been made in the increase of
flowering time of modern roses. Today no climbing rose would be
considered unless it gave a second crop of bloom at least, and
usually the flowering is intermittent throughout the growing
season at least from June to October. There are a few climbers
which may be forerunners of others which are used primarily for
ground cover. Two types, one 'Temple Bells' with tiny almost
evergreen leaves on long trailing shoots giving much coverage and
another, 'Nazomi' with less vigorous growth and small pointed
leaves and leaflets which are smooth and mat, both flower once
only but may offer a new type of plant coverage.

Species

Sufficient has been said to open a wide vista on the abundant
choice possible. Beginning with roses in the shrubbery, one may

choose any height from 0·9 to 3·6 m (3 to 12 ft). The choice may range over foliage and hips as well as flower. If so, specimens of the *R. moyesii* group are ideal. Of tall, almost ungainly growth, their single flowers, coming in May, vary from a strange coppery orange to pink. The very large urn-shaped orange-red fruit are very ornamental. The variety 'Sealing Wax', with its bright red hips, is a little shorter and more compact. There is a group with creamy yellow to golden yellow flowers. In this case their ferny foliage is an added attraction. More compact in growth they make large rounded bushes. Probably the best is 'Canary Bird' (*R. xanthina spontanea*) with its golden yellow, 2·5 cm-wide flowers. Unlike many of this class, it throws odd flowers throughout the season and is a joy from early May until late autumn. *R. primula*, with glossy brown wood and small fern-like leaf, not only gives a crop of lovely yellow single flowers, but in the evening perfumes the air with its incense-laden wood and foliage. A shorter shrubby rose with similar qualities is *R. ecae*. The Frühlings group, 'Frühlingsgold', single, 7·6 to 10-cm (3 to 4-in) flowers, growth 2·4 m (8 ft) high, with pale primrose flowers massed on pendulous shoots; 'Frühlingsmorgen', similar in flower but shaded pink, are the two best known in this lovely group raised by Herr Wilhelm Kordes. The above varieties are once-flowering, but the so-called hybrid musks, originally made popular by the hybrids from the Revd. J. Pemberton, contain a series of perpetual-flowering shrub roses with a wealth of large clusters, some single, some very double. Many are of pastel shades, but the most charming of all, 'Buff Beauty', is an unusual shade of biscuit with a strong perfume and large clusters of double flowers. More recent additions to them are the reds, again from Kordes, such as 'Prestige', 'Kassel', 'Bonn' and 'Berlin'. Before we leave this section I must mention 'Lavender Lassie' which carries huge corymbs of heavily perfumed lavender-pink flowers. Last, but not least, comes the brilliant bi-colour 'First Choice'. This is a single flower, scarlet with golden reverse, scented and when in full bloom is unforgettable. Yet one has hardly touched the fringe of these fascinating, adaptable beauties. Few of the choicest of shrubs can match such roses for long-term effect and sheer loveliness.

Of course, one may always train a vigorous hybrid tea or floribunda, as a specimen, and a 1·8 m (6 ft) high bush of 'Peace' or a
2·4 m (8 ft) tree of 'Queen Elizabeth' can take their place with
any shrub. Not only may these be grown in the shrubbery but even
better, grown in separate beds in grass or on the edge of a copse.
They may well be used as a transition from the formal garden to
the informal woodland.

The defining of climbers and ramblers is as difficult as any
definition of the branches of the cultivated rose. Climbing was a
natural characteristic of the Chinese roses. The dwarfing factor
which is now so widely represented was a recessive (hidden)
character which only came to the surface by careful selection.
When a dwarf hybrid tea or floribunda throws a 'sport' (chimera)
it is really a throwback to one or more of its ancestral natural
qualities, which show in their alteration in growth, colour or form.
Even so, there are two types of these climbing sports. There is a
sport where the change has been complete and progeny from such
roses will breed climbers and usually give one hundred per cent
true climbers, i.e. 'Climbing Lady Sylvia', when budded. There is
a partial 'sport' where only the rind, the cuticle (skin) and cambium
(growing tissues) have changed. These latter usually flower in the
autumn as well as the summer but are less vigorous and give quite
a high proportion of dwarfs when climbing wood is propagated by
budding. Such a variety is 'Climbing Ellinor Le Grice'. This is
important as a deciding factor, for generally speaking the vigorous
climbers are complete sports and flower only once. The partial
sports grow less vigorously and often give a second crop of flowers.
It is useless to try to get a perpetual-flowering vigorous climbing
sport. One cannot have the best in both these worlds. Generally
speaking, the more continuous the flowering, the less tall the plant
grows. These climbing sports have the same type and quality of
flower as their dwarf variety, although their additional growth and
vigour often mean better and bigger flowers. It is possible to obtain
prize-winning blooms for the show bench from these climbers. An
example of this additional vigour is to be found in 'Climbing Mrs.
Sam McGredy', which is far superior to its very beautiful but
rather weak dwarf form.

In addition to these climbing sports are a few true climbers, hybridized for that purpose. Of these, 'Guinée', an exceptionally dark red, and 'Danse du Feu', a vivid orange-red, are particularly good. There are others also of less vigour which are a little more perpetual. One of the basic problems with the tall varieties of climbers is their satisfactory fastening to the wall of a house. A wide-meshed trellis is advised, but this is usually better kept on the lower level of the house, up to the first floor. Beyond this, vine eyes, pointed galvanized metal strips with an eye in their top, are best put into the wall when the house is being built. An alternative method is to have strong holders fastened into the projecting eaves from which wires may be run to the trellis below. Put in at 45 cm (18 in) apart these will provide support for the complete coverage of the wall by the roses. Under 'pruning' it has been stressed that rose shoots should not climb up the wires but across, to promote free-flowering.

Perpetual climbers are not necessarily always in flower but they do carry a much heavier crop of blossom over a more extended period. Of these the old-fashioned 'Zéphirine Drouhin', the thornless, deep pink, scented variety, and 'New Dawn', silvery pink, scented, with glossy foliage, are two good examples. Others are more like elongated bushes and one should always choose with care, and if in doubt get expert advice. Of the perpetual type, some of the most useful are single or semi-single and flower much of the growing season. Of these 'Soldier Boy' has single bright scarlet-red flowers over a very extended period and is sufficiently vigorous to grace the second storey of a house. Less vigorous but of great beauty is 'Altissimo' which revels in sunshine and is at its best facing south, although it is hardy enough for any position.

A modern book on roses would be incomplete without treatment of the section known as *kordesii*. These possess the qualities of both the massed profusion of the ramblers and those of the climbers and some, indeed most, give extended flower over a wide period. Their colours vary widely, and when over thirty different varieties were planted at the Royal National Rose Trial Grounds at Oaklands Institute they created the sensation they deserved. These are still being distributed, and although some of their names

are not easy to remember or pronounce this is the only drawback.

We owe this wonderful break to the patience and skill of Herr
Wilhelm Kordes, who was granted the distinction of having a new
race of roses given his name. This is one of the classic examples of
skill combining with patience to produce a desired result, after
long and repeated effort. Three of these varieties are characteristic:
'Hamburger Phoenix' (*kordesii* × seedling), deep red, fragrant
clusters of bloom which is repeated, very vigorous; 'Leverkusen'
(*kordesii* × 'Golden Glow'), full light yellow in long sprays, a pillar
rose up to 2·4 m (8 ft), with recurrent bloom and 'Dortmund'
(seedling × *kordesii*), very large, single, open, fragrant flowers
which are red with a white eye and carried in large clusters. This
last is a very vigorous climber with profuse recurrent bloom.

Enough has been said to show what a wide variety of material
can be found in the useful climbers and ramblers.

The fact that the rose may be used as ground cover is sometimes
lost sight of because of its adaptability for so many locations, but
the hardy short rugosas, in white and red form, make excellent
coverage even on the sea-coast, while the common form with its
large red, rounded hips, gives very popular pheasant feed. With
their thorny wood they should be kept well away from frequented
paths. A charming creeper with characteristic perfume is the small-
flowered, almost evergreen foliaged *R. wichuraiana*, a parent of
the vigorous 'American Pillar'. Many of the pendulous shooted
ramblers may be pegged down and used as coverage for banks and
ground cover. For further discussion on this matter see the pre-
previous pages.

'Coverage' however, may embrace a much wider field than
ground or bank hides. Few, if any, other climbing plants can be
more effective in quickly hiding unsightly objects which obtrude
on the garden scene. Wide-meshed trellis has already been suggested, but where a larger area has to be covered and the necessary
support given, a cheap but excellent material is wire-meshed pig-
netting or the newer plastic-covered netting painted black. To use
this to advantage, supports should be strong and well prepared,
treated with rot-proofed material and fixed firmly in position.

Where an almost evergreen form is desired, 'Alberic Barbier' is as good as any. For mass effect at one time, 'Albertine' is a joy, and the foliage will be a pleasing cover for many months. Where extreme vigour is essential 'American Pillar', 'Minnehaha' or *R. filipes Kifsgate* may be used.

With supports, ramblers and climbers can make excellent hedges, but one must remember that they have to be kept in hand by adequate training and pruning, no easy task. Keeping the ground weed-free below them can call for 'blood and sweat' if not tears.

Preferably hedges can be made of floribunda roses, a few hybrid teas, and the taller specimen or park roses. These last are the 'awkward squad', too short for pillars, too tall for bedding. Here again, if one wishes for the best results, the varieties must be carefully selected. I would hesitate to use such hedges for boundaries between properties unless these are also well defined in some other way and privacy is not important, nor the inclusion or exclusion of animals a necessity. They are ideal for hedges of demarcation in the garden, as a cover for the kitchen garden, as a break to relieve monotony in a flat area, as a directional guide to the eye leading it to a focal point. A brilliant hedge of floribunda roses can improve and dignify an approach to a factory, boosting everyone's morale. Well grown, a single row should be sufficient, for when fully grown such a hedge would reach at least 0·9 m (3 ft) in width. Planting should be 0·6 to 0·9 m (2 to 3 ft) apart, according to variety. It is in such a position that profusion of flower is of absolute importance, and the single flowers of cluster roses can excel in such positions. There is much to be said for a hedge of one variety only. To mix sorts, or to have part of the hedge of one variety followed by another sort, leads to a ragged effect and does not have the appeal of one mass of colour. Good red-flowered hedges are 'Scarlet Queen Elizabeth', tall; 'Fervid', less tall and 'Evelyn Fison', the shortest of the three. 'Dainty Maid' is most effective grown in this way. Its clear pink colour and resistance to wet make it attractive at all times. 'Queen Elizabeth' may be very effective if its addiction to legginess, with all the flowers at the top, is checked by judicious shortening of a few outside shoots. A few rules are useful guides. Avoid roses which do not lose their old flowers cleanly. Many sorts are perfection at best, but look as bedraggled as a lady clad in a summer dress who has been caught in a thunderstorm, when after a period of heavy rain their blooms hang sodden and pitiful, clogging the remaining buds and ruining the hedge's beauty longer than they adorned it. If one cannot remove the spent flower heads, then one should limit the varieties even further to the few sorts which do not have seed pods.

For a really tall effect, the hybrid musks may be used, but here I would prefer to think of these as a break rather than a hedge, for there must be space between the lower part of one bush and another. A few species make very lovely hedges. Probably the most beautiful of all is 'Canary Bird'. Its naturally pendulous shoots link up plant with plant in a very charming manner.

The most important way of using roses is for bedding. It is here that the majority of hybrid teas and floribundas excel. When one considers that a bed of roses may look delightful from the time they are in full leaf (May) until the winter gales (October) they compete with any bedding plant on this point alone. Add to this hardiness and long life, freedom of flower, variety of colour, and often abundance of fragrance, and what more can one ask?

Bedding may be formal or informal, and both have their uses and advantages. For formal work we recommend one bed of one variety, chosen by height and colour, to grow with another of similar height and contrasting colour. Far be it from me, an outsider, to dictate what owners should grow in their own gardens, but even so, an effective scheme can be ruined by planting a bed of 'Topsi', 45 cm (18 in) high next to 'Peace', 0·9 to 1·2 m (3 to 4 ft) high, or 'Allgold', at 0·6 m (2 ft) against 'Shepherd's Delight' 0·9 to 1·2 m (3 to 4 ft). There is sufficient choice for such disparity to be avoided. Possibly three colours are difficult to blend with others: 'hot' shades of orange-scarlet, white, and mauve. Of these orange-scarlet should be used with discretion in a formal setting, and there is much to be said for keeping such roses by themselves where they can be boldly massed to awaken a dull patch into ebullient life. White is useful for contrast, and if possible this should be used as a centre bed surrounded by other coloured beds. Treated in this manner, each colour is enhanced and the eye, resting for a moment on the white, passes refreshed to a new feast of colour. Lavender and lilac shades in no way clash with other colours, being neutral. Always keep an eye on the all-over effect. Probably lavender-lilac sorts like 'Blue Moon' and deep brown like 'Jocelyn' may appear drab from a distance if left on their own, but plants of 'Lilac Charm' backed by 'Dairy Maid' or the purple 'News' with 'Moonsprite' produce most charming effects.

To propose beds of one colour only, may deprive the rose lover of the assortment he needs and craves. There is no reason why roses should not be mixed if one is limited to a few beds or even one bed. In that case, however, one is better to mix all colours thoroughly rather than attempt a blending of 'sorts'. Few, if any, varieties will clash under such conditions. The living green of the foliage acts as a foil for all colours and is often itself adapted to the colour of the flower. It is a pity to choose too similar varieties. 'Sarabande' and 'Paprika' are both excellent roses and are quite distinct apart, but bedded together their similar characteristics outweigh their differences and they tend to detract from one another.

One should be warned that any indication of heights is factual purely for one particular area, but they can be comparative. Two varieties listed as 60 cm (2 ft) may grow to 0·9 m (3 ft) on good soil and only 38 cm (15 in) on poor soil, but they should both be shorter in all localities than one listed as 0·9 m (3 ft).

It is not the usual lot of most rose lovers to plant up massed schemes, but one who has seen the bold areas in parks and the sides of the roads abroad, must realize that many of our public authorities need guidance and encouragement to plant roses more generally than they do. Some enlightened councils are doing so, and many park superintendents would be delighted to have the opportunity of improving sites and encouraging the visitor to emulation. How beautiful and effective a roundabout can be made when planted up with masses of dwarf floribundas. Nothing gives so much for so little, and what a transformation may be effected when a ragged mound of spent earth is changed into such an attraction. The whole status of the town or city is raised, and the roses leave a pleasing memory to linger in the mind of the passing traveller, while the town-dweller returns home determined to improve his own small patch.

Here, then, are some ways of using roses. Roses for decoration and exhibition will be dealt with separately. Others may be a challenge to ingenuity, but at all times he who grows roses not only has roses in his heart but gives a wealth of pleasure to the passer-by.

 CHAPTER VIII

Exhibiting Roses

A professional rose grower nowadays hesitates to venture an opinion on the Exhibition rose as it is still produced. For him this is a dying and unprofitable art, a relic of bygone leisurely times, glimpsed occasionally through the eye of an old-timer who remembered those 'great days' of the Crystal Palace Exhibition. I have been told by such a one that he reckoned on getting a good new suit of clothes out of the price of the blooms he sold at the end of the show. As much as fifty pence would be paid for a winning bloom from a championship class. Today the few professional stalwarts who continue to exhibit would hesitate to say what they lost in cash on the venture, but they still gain immeasurably by their delight in producing a flower which sets the standard for others.

The real specimen, or exhibition bloom in the box, is produced by a comparatively few amateurs, whose skill and patience are rewarded by this offspring of their love of the rose. We should be ignoring the general trend of rose shows if we gave a disproportionate amount of time to this one type. I am compelled, perhaps reluctantly, to admit that a Championship in the Exhibition Boxes is the acme of accomplishment for rosarians. To put the matter in perspective, let us examine the schedule for the Royal National Rose Society's Autumn Show in 1975.

In the Nurserymen's Section there are four classes. Of these two classes are for Specimen Blooms in Boxes, one for twelve blooms, one for twenty-four. In the Amateur Section there are seventeen classes for Decorative Roses, seven shown in bowls and ten in vases. There are eleven classes for Floribunda Roses, six in bowls and five in vases. There are, however, still sixteen classes for Specimen (Exhibition) Blooms, eight for boxes and eight for vases. In addition, there are nine classes for Floral Arrangements and for the first year two classes for Miniature Roses. Out of fifty-nine classes, sixteen are for specimen blooms, and undoubtedly these specimen blooms set a standard by which other roses tend to be judged, or, some may feel, misjudged.

Bearing these observations in mind, we go back to preparing for Specimen Roses. Everything starts from the making ready of the soil, and every item of cultivation which follows. The exhibition hall or tent is the culmination of months of care and years of experience. To counterbalance the great experience of the regular exhibitor and to encourage the beginner, there are usually special classes for the novice.

Good cultivation is the first consideration. Second should come attention to detail and third experience. Exhibitors are, as a whole, a kindly, friendly fellowship, and will go to great lengths to set a novice at his ease and give him many tips. Naturally, one should not intrude at the last moment, when the exhibitor is trying to decide whether to change a large and slightly tired 'Grandpa Dickson' for a smaller but fresher 'Princess', whose rough outer petals have not yet reflexed enough to hide their coarse exterior. Wait until the deed is accomplished and until the prize is won. Then comes the time for relaxation, reflection and reminiscing.

The late Dr. W. E. Moore, a past president of the Royal National Rose Society and a great exhibitor, used to tell how, returning from the Summer Rose Show, he saw a fat red shoot, full of promise, thrusting up from the base of a 'George Dickson' (and that dates the tale). 'That', he declared to his wife, 'is the championship bloom of the Autumn Show', and so it became! But of the care and attention bestowed upon that shoot, nothing was said. The vision became fact, because expectation was backed by knowledge and experience.

Good cultivation must be routine for the exhibitor. A good bloom does not come by heavy feeding at the last minute. That way leads to fast weak growth, thin petals and poor colour. The foundation lies in well-ripened wood of the previous year, laying the foundation for the healthy new wood which, without haste, can come to maturity at the right time. Included in this term are clean foliage, efficient pest control, freedom from disease and balanced fertilizer. Spare the nitrogen and harden the flower.

A few items to remember for the specimen bloom are that the whole plant is the 'larder' for the bloom. At an early stage eliminate competition for the same space. Two shoots may be growing into or against one another. Rub out the weaker of the two. If two or three growths come from one eye, keep one only. Light and air are essential, besides which two shoots in proximity may scratch each other to shreds in a gale. Also remove any 'blind' growth shoots. They are unwanted and obstructive. Stake the shoot if you decide to cover the flower with a bloom protector. These are made of waterproof cloth or similar material, fixed to a rigid cane by a clip which permits raising or lowering to give the rose bloom a measure of protection from sun but more especially from wet. Their use is a matter of experiment, but such types of rose as 'Red Devil' and 'Memoriam' seldom come to perfection without such aids. This again requires care, for carelessly placed the 'protector' may do more harm than good.

As the shoot grows, the terminal flower bud will develop, and probably other smaller buds will appear on the sides just below. As soon as these other flower buds are big enough, they should be carefully removed. To do this at a later stage wastes the plant's energy, and may leave ugly wounds on the stem where they have been pinched out. The exception is where a terminal bud may 'split'. If a variety is prone to this trouble, by taking the first side bud instead of the terminal, a slightly smaller but more shapely flower will result. 'Rose Gaujard' is a variety which does this. The same treatment delays the flowering which may be useful if a bloom is needed at a later date.

Before one attempts to exhibit, the schedule should be read very carefully. Choose the class or classes you should excel in. Better to err by entering for the few rather than the many until you are well established. Number of blooms, forms of presentation (bowls, vases, or boxes), space to be occupied, cards for naming varieties, all these should be checked in good time. Salient points may be underlined in the schedule. If decorative vases are to be used, some material to hold the rose stems in position is advisable. Stems of *Lonicera nitida* or coarse rush, thrust loosely into the vase, give the right type of support. These should be cut and bundled in readiness whenever time permits.

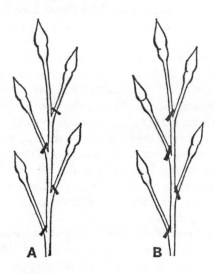

(*a*) Disbudding a normal rose
(*b*) Disbudding for a rose which splits leaving the second bud terminal and removing the other side buds

It is probably much wiser to begin showing locally first. Time and transport will be on your side. The ideal time to cut is just after the morning sun has begun to dry the petals. There is a time when buds develop into flowers with amazing rapidity. After that period they will remain in a fixed position for quite a time. A memory still haunts me of a hundred flowers brought two hundred and fifty miles. In tight perfection at 5.30 a.m., only a dozen remained fit to show at 8.30 a.m. and the hoped-for award for a new rose vanished with the rising sun. If you are wise, go through the stages of cutting, preparing and exhibiting for the class you intend to show in, as soon as your first flowers bloom. Only by 'try, try, and trying again', will you succeed. It is practical experience which holds the balance. The real triumph is not when you obtain a 'first', but when, despite disaster in weather or transport, you can turn up smiling, and fill the place you have booked with the best exhibit possible at that time. The person who scraps his exhibit because winning is impossible is not only a poor sportsman but is losing invaluable practice.

There are available excellent diagrams and photographs by keen rosarians who have made their own flower containers to take their blooms to the shows. These should be light enough to carry easily, and the containers should stand firmly and be deep enough to give a good drink to the flowers on their way to the show. Whether they be painted sweet tins or aluminium pails will not matter, if sharp edges are avoided. Probably the best way is to decide your means of transport with the area available, and build to that. More harm is done by transporting blooms in too much space, when they chafe and shake about, than by tight, firm packing, when each bloom supports another.

For exhibition blooms, special boxes are obtainable with individual flower holders. These are, front to back, 45 cm (18 in) × 30 cm (12 in) for six blooms, 45 cm (18 in) × 60 cm (24 in) for twelve blooms. These boxes contain detachable lids which are placed in position for transport and removed during exhibition. There are also removable holders which fit in tubes for retaining water. If a box of spare blooms is kept, and this is advisable, the blooms can be exchanged rapidly if necessary.

Today more and more specimen blooms are shown in specified vases and bowls often supplied at the show. Not only do the blooms look more natural with the longer stems required in these classes, but the cumbersome exhibition boxes can be left at home.

Whatever classes are entered, there are certain facts which should be borne in mind. Freshness wins every time. Erect flowers, clear colour, glistening foliage, undamaged leaves and petals, these effect a permanent impression of well-being. Good presentation is a most important factor. The exhibition box should have the boards covered, colours of blooms should be chosen to contrast, the best blooms, if possible, in the top left-hand corner, and so working down. Uneven blooms look worse when the largest and finest rest cheek by jowl with the smallest and scruffiest. With adequate buffers between, the contrast is not so glaring and the overall effect is better. Added foliage is not allowed, and to remove the foliage is as depressing as looking at a moulting bird.

When showing in vases, one is asked to show the blooms to the best advantage. This means adequate length of stem. However good a flower, it cannot compete if it has a 10-cm (4-in) stem when its competitor boasts a length of 38 cm (15 in), well covered with healthy foliage. I dislike wiring intensely, but where the head of the variety is too heavy for its stem to support, the judicious use of a wire is the lesser evil. These wires should be inserted in the base of the swollen green ovary just below the flower and carried straight down as far as the first leaf, when the remaining wire is wound round the stem as inconspicuously as possible. Any florist's shop carries a stock of these wires in various thicknesses and lengths, but make sure that such wiring is permitted in the schedule!

The exhibition of miniature roses is new to the Royal National Rose Society. Whether the rulings of the American Rose Society are adopted remains to be decided in the light of experience. The A.R.S. use the ruling that if specimen blooms are shown they must be judged as for H.Ts., if in clusters they will be judged as for floribundas. Such rulings lead to problems, as indeed any rules will, but if adopted another ruling must be remembered that each bloom must be judged as a true specimen of that variety. The bloom shape of a miniature varies greatly, some being pointed, others being flat but circular in outline. This will be another case of reading the schedule carefully and if necessary of buying cultivars having the qualities we need.

When the blooms are cut the first consideration should be, at all times, as long a drink in clean water as can be arranged. If a flower has to travel to a show out of water, for however short or long a time, it must have a long drink, being immersed up to the flower head on arrival. This applies to local shows also and if this is to be the case, it is advisable to cut the evening before, in order to ensure the long drink. Rose blooms, to travel well, should be packed firmly but must not touch each other if wet. Blooms packed wet can rot very quickly. If the roses have to travel out of water, line the cases with polythene sheets. This will ensure that the foliage is perfectly fresh on arrival, but be careful the boxes are not placed where they may heat while being transported and that the flowers themselves are dry when packed even though the foliage and stems are damp. It may be necessary, if a petal is badly damaged, to remove it, but this will tell heavily against the exhibitor. It is his wits against the judge's, and if he can remove it undetected good luck to him! I have known the championship for the best bloom of the show to be lost by one removed petal!

This brings us to 'dressing' the blooms. Correctly interpreted this means opening a bloom in a way natural to its character but before its normal time. To do this requires much practice, and it is probably wiser to depress the outer petals with a broad soft artist's paint-brush at first, rather than to attempt this by using the thumb and finger to press the petal down. It must be a natural effect. If this is done, as it can be, then the colour appears more brilliant, and the natural shape is preserved. To 'overdress' a bloom, making it unnatural, will mean that the flower will be treated as a spoiled bloom and it will receive no points.

Contrast of colour will at all times enliven the effect, and one should beware of showing too many 'washy' colours. Those who have much experience of dressing roses evolve different ways of getting the best from their blooms. A few thin-petalled double red roses are best prepared after the blooms have been allowed to flag. As soon as the petal is flaccid it is drawn back and positioned. After this the base of the stem is cut and the stem is plunged into water, and the revived flower stands erect in perfection! Where there is a rose, there is a way!

Quite enough has been written to show how fascinating this branch of showing can be. One should seek to accomplish it by growing good roses really well.

I remember the shock I received many years ago on visiting a well-known exhibitor who gained many prizes. The first shows were over, and he had gained his usual batch of high awards. All I saw were rows of maiden rose stumps. There was no beauty in the garden, and once the one bloom had been taken from the plant it was discarded, and another batch was budded for the following year. A garden debased for this purpose should be hidden away as a shameful thing. On an allotment this might be forgiven, but surely such 'pot hunting' is not in the best interests of the rose.

It is because this type of exhibiting is dying out that the specimen roses shown more naturally in vases are becoming more popular. In this case the stems are cut from flourishing bushes which have been encouraged to do their very best. Here can be beauty, shared and sweetened by the knowledge that later on there will be more, and possibly better, roses.

When one considers floribunda roses it is necessary to have a clear idea of what is wanted. Study the flower heads and you will see that often the centre bud will open well before any others; after this, another set of good even flowers, to be followed at a later date by yet more, but smaller, flowers which will be the final burst from a single flower head. The late Mr. A. Norman, a past president of the Royal National Rose Society, who will long be remembered as a rosarian most knowledgeable in all branches, maintained that buds which would flower before and after the main burst of flower on the stem should be carefully removed with vine-thinning scissors in an early stage, so that the buds left would have full room to grow to capacity. Results justify such measures but the need for experience is again very evident.

One should remember that exhibiting is the golden key which unlocks the door leading to another delightful experience in rose growing. Not only may there come a sense of achievement, but there is that wonderful heart-warming period after the staging, when, having cleared up the pieces and tidied oneself up, there is time to share experiences with others, and find the pleasure inherent in company with a common purpose and a shared delight.

So far in this chapter we have looked at rose showing from the amateur side. It might be of interest to go behind the scenes and obtain a glimpse of the work entailed in those massive trade exhibits where roses have to be matched by the hundred, and where the scheme has evolved over many years, while plans prepared in the winter months are carried to perfection in high summer.

Preparations for such exhibits begin with the budding list made and carried out during the previous summer. Two distinct types of groups may be seen: the old, massed effect in a narrow high bank where sheer weight of specimen bloom in perfection carries the day, and the newer island site where lightness and artistry display varieties to their best advantage. This transition began with the advent of the floribunda rose. Trade groups in which these were first shown stood no chance of an award. A particularly lovely group of the then new 'Karen Poulsen' surrounded by some very fine blooms of 'McGredy's Ivory' caught the eye of a well-known judge in passing. 'Hybrid polyanthas!' The withering scorn in that voice is remembered today. The group got no award, a fitting punishment for such a recreant, but the well-filled order-book brought its comfort! Now, how things have changed! Probably half the roses grown belong to the floribunda class, of which the Poulsen group were the heralds, and without that mass colouring, the groups or 'islands' would look flat and dead.

These island groups demand thousands of blooms, and unless a grower can boast a minimum of two hundred and fifty thousand bushes he must be prepared to put up a smaller group. This method of showing is extremely costly in money, labour, and above all in plants.

The plans are made. The van is driven to the field. The cutters, with a prepared list, set to work to cut their required number of blooms. As these are cut, boys hasten with them to the van, where they are trimmed of lower thorns and leaves, and plunged into pails of water. A small island site will require a labour force of six for three hours' cutting and preparing the flowers. Once the cutting is done, the van is driven back to the nursery, the blooms, show stands, catalogues, cloth, labels and all items likely to be wanted, are packed ready for the journey. In the meantime those who will be responsible for the show will return to their homes, change, and after a meal, begin their journey which may be of anything up to two hundred or more miles. When they reach the hall or tent, the site has to be found, and the flowers and materials carted to the stand. When the flowers are carried to the show in water, arrangement begins at once. Probably forty stems are used for a bowl, and the man in charge, with the help of a boy, lays out the stand, arranging the tall supports or whatever has been chosen to display the bowls to the best advantage. Arranging the flowers will take many hours, until the final bowl is in place, the last label fixed. Then the stand may be left for judging in the morning. This is the easy way. Those nearer, or much farther off, may decide to work during the night, and 'stands' left blank at 10.30 will be filled twelve hours later, when the fortunate ones return after a night's rest. Even so, no group will be left unvisited at an earlier hour, and one member at least will return to check over the previous night's work.

The weary workers on some championship stand will, cup of tea in hand, wander from stand to stand, assessing their rivals' chances before they pack up the sorry mass of discarded blooms which were cut 'just in case', and return these to the nursery, some to be budded, others for the waste heap.

Older hands could tell of hard days before the war, when the quality of flowers was not so lasting, and one had to cut as late as possible, travel and stage all night, finishing just as the clearance bell went in the morning; of pulling down, journeying back and beginning once more, losing up to three nights' rest in a heavy week. Competition was keen, prices were low, hours were long, but the rose was as lovely in their eyes then as now. Memory lingers on nightmare cross-country journeys with tight rail schedules: of changing trains caught at the last moment, with flower boxes tipped in the haste, and blooms damaged beyond repair and replacement. Of pouring rain, leaking tents, flooded gangways. Of halcyon days when the sun shone, when business was good, and when life and rest were very sweet.

Showing is in the blood of many old-timers, both amateur and trade, and in their common cause they have forged a strong bond of fellow-feeling and mutual respect, expressed in their joint loyalty to the greatest specialist flower society in the world, the Royal National Rose Society.

 CHAPTER IX

Roses for Decoration

It is not intended in this book to consider roses in art, although ancient art shows that at a very early stage the beauty and decorative value of the rose had already made an impact upon the mind of the artist. He adorned the dwellings of the rich with representations of the flower which for many of us has become the emblem of home and homeland.

Nor do we wish to recapitulate, however briefly, the wealth of tradition and story which hover over the speculative beginning of the rose in literature and poetry. Sufficient to say that from earliest times the rose caught the imagination of all creative artists, and from the rose have blossomed some of our best-loved quotations and most honoured customs.

The intention is to consider the living plant and flower, its decorative possibilities in and around the home, and the many ways of using it to the general enjoyment.

The massed effect of the planted rose has been considered, but one method of using roses which should be mentioned under 'decoration' is the method of so arranging our planting that some particular feature, by blending or contrasting, makes a living picture of itself. Great pleasure may be derived from such devices. For instance, a small bed, planted with a weeping standard in the centre, around which other roses bloom to enhance its beauty while in flower, and continue as effective decorations after the main centre-piece has lost its first glow. Contrasting colours in the same border or bed can be very effective. 'Orange Sensation', tall, fiery orange-scarlet and erect, is made more vivid by having the clear yellow 'Allgold', itself short and sturdy, nestling at its feet.

Or again, 'Lilac Charm', short and bushy in growth, may be contrasted with the taller, lovely, single-flowered, creamy white of 'Dairy Maid'. A charming picture springs to my mind, of a small bed of the salmon-pink 'Tip Top' with a group of *Caryopteris clandonensis* in full flower for background.

Granted that the rose stands peerless in its own right, there are times and places where other useful plants may with advantage accompany it. Increasingly one is called upon to plant up a week-end garden, which by very force of circumstance must fend for itself over a long period. What better border than 'Fervid', scarlet-red and tall, or 'Pink Parfait', shell-pink with deeper shadings, combined with the violet-mauve of catmint (*Nepeta*), either in its tall form ('Six Hills' variety) or the more compact form (*mussini*). The colour contrast, both of flower and foliage, is very pleasing, while the border looks well from the Whitsun break until the late autumn. There are other plantings which may be very effective such as of early- and late-flowering honeysuckles planted with climbing roses, of *Clematis montana* where height is needed, or the *jackmanii* group for shorter growers, intermingled with roses to their mutual benefit.

The decorative value of the climbing rose is much appreciated at the doorway, where it blunts the hardness of modern lines and caresses with its fragrance the exit or entrance to one's home. Such wise planting can be a source of lasting delight.

Under 'decorative roses' one would hope to include the less formal types, and nothing can excel the single five-petalled or semi-single varieties. It has become unfashionable to admire these types at the moment, but there is much to commend them in the climate from which we suffer while we grumble and nevertheless excel. What a refreshing contrast to find roses such as the single-flowered 'Dainty Maid', holding up its head in heavy rain, unspotted and unspoiled, unlike the fuller roses which, so often, hang their heavy bedraggled heads in shame, shapeless, pulpy, discoloured and dishevelled.

The story of the single rose goes back to the beginning, for all species depending upon pollen for fertilization could not afford to waste their pollen-bearing anthers by turning them into petals.

When the double flower became popular there were still some single varieties which compelled our attention by sheer merit. In the early part of this century 'Irish Elegance', 'Fireflame' and 'Isobel' were all single hybrid teas of great beauty. Probably the culmination was in 'Dainty Bess', its clear pink with its deep brown anthers—a real brunette of entrancing beauty. These lacked one asset, freedom of flower, and W. E. B. Archer, the raiser of 'Dainty Bess', might well have added to the choice number of beauties which he raised, such as 'Ellen Willmott', had his long and honoured life been increased even beyond its ninety years. He and his daughter excelled in showing the decorative qualities of this type of rose, and we will discuss the importance of preparation for blooms of this character a little later. The single cerise 'Kirsten Poulsen', followed by the brilliant scarlet 'Karen Poulsen', led the way in what later became, the floribunda class, and 'Betty Prior', bicolour pink, achieved deserved popularity. Few roses have had such a long success as 'Dainty Maid'. Here is the clarity of the unfolding wild brier, its fresh pink deepening on the outer side of the petal, but wedded to this dainty elegance is a thick petal withstanding all weathers, capturing and linking the freshness of the morning dew with the splendour of mature noon. Here were roses with large trusses of flower presenting a bouquet in themselves, with little effort required in arrangement. The only foil they needed was the abundant foliage which they carried so effectively. It has been said that single roses are not difficult to obtain by hybridizing. This is true, but it is equally true that good single roses are more difficult to produce than good full hybrid teas. They need to be outstanding in quality, symmetrical in outline, with thick unfading petals which weather well. They must be free flowering and perfumed. Given these qualities, and they have been achieved more than once, few flowers can surpass them in decorative excellence.

It is a fallacy to suggest that decorative qualities can be limited to one type or confined to one standard. A rose bloom is beautiful in many stages, and the art of decoration lies in expressing this fact, so that the picture presented is one of anticipation as well as realization. The bud, with its long embracing calyx, has a grace and beauty of its own, and may be used to enhance the glorious fullness of the mature flower. Neither should we expect to consider flowers only in the opening stage. The exhibitor of prize blooms may think it essential that no centre should be shown, but it would be hard to say whether the swelling blossom, or the wide open flower of 'Peace', were the more lovely.

Each rose is a decoration in itself, but a combined effort is like the great conception of a famous artist who embraces in one canvas many items to create one moving scene.

The fact that one single flower placed with its own foliage in a separate vase is a complete decoration, is recommendation enough of the perfection of its qualities. The combination of many blooms into one fascinating picture is the acme of floral art.

While many volumes will be, and have been, written on the art of floral decoration, no instruction is adequate. One's own home should be the natural outlet for the expression of one's skill and the sphere for experiment. Whatever is learned and used there may be employed in a wider field.

Floral decoration as a means of expression is a grand exercise, and brings relaxation and pleasure in its train. One thing is certain, practice and more practice is essential. Trial and error will lead to the happy moment when your effects really satisfy you—or almost!

General rules for floral decoration apply equally to our work in the house or exhibition hall but there will be additional refinements and greater latitude and variety in competition. At home, the atmosphere and the decoration of the rooms will limit one's scope, both in size of design and in use of colours. More important probably will be the restricting condition that one is planning for a long-lasting arrangement. The average housewife cannot afford material and time for a short-term effect. The exhibitor has a different set of circumstances, and provided that her work lasts for the term of the show the objective has been achieved. One need not do all this experimental work oneself. The best experience is often gained by watching and studying the work of another. There are certain rules which may surely guide. The first is to aim at simplicity and strength of outline. The object in mind should be projected so clearly that the design will impress itself at once upon the spectator. The silhouette should leave one in no doubt as to the shape intended. To this end, foliage, flower and colour should be controlled to give a balanced unity to the finished product. If this balance is to be achieved, the fuller, heavier part of the decoration must be placed at what is the fulcrum of the design. All the airy lightness should spring from a firm foundation produced either by weight or colour of material.

A creation worth constructing should be worth keeping alive, and so the stems should have sufficient water to keep their cells turgid at all times. We may deplore the swift passing of such beauty, but this is surely one of the most satisfying of qualities, for this is a 'living' design, alive with change and interesting to the last.

In such decoration, colour should be as important as outline, and again experiment is the only worth-while teacher. The winner on the show bench excels because of the many earlier attempts made in her home, and each of these has been a striving for perfection. Even if the majority of those who practise this art never enter a competition, they will give pleasure to themselves and many others, and all will delight in the fact that it is one more way of turning a house into a home.

One of the most spectacular changes in showing and all floral decoration has been the great upsurge of floral arrangement societies, and these range from local to national level. One has only to see the long, patient queues outside the floral art tent at Chelsea to realize how their popular arrangements are and deservedly so, for they have added a new dimension to showing and have increased and widened greatly the interest both of the amateur and professional. Joining a local society may be recommended not only as a means of exchanging ideas but also of improving the already high standard.

It is certain that any attempt at indoor decoration will demonstrate the need for suitable containers and vases. One should set one's mind against buying any shallow receptacle or narrow-based vase. Containers should stand firmly and hold enough water to fulfil their main function, that of supporting the life of the flower. As a rule a shallow container should never be used for roses in the house. 'Floating flowers' are as barbarous as the display of a dismembered body. One may obtain a special dispensation as an exhibitor faced by the exigencies of a special class. There may be opportunity and occasion to adapt a novel container, but usually the vase or holder should be of definite, simple, functional design, satisfying the eye and carrying through the intended picture. It should never obtrude, but should have sufficient character to contribute to the total effect.

Clear glass may detract somewhat from the neat overall effect. The wire support used in the vase and the medley of stems thrust into it will be seen too clearly. The same charge cannot be laid against cut-glass. I find this neutral setting unobtrusive and satisfactory indoors. Opaque black is excellent, with silver a good third. However, there are so many opportunities for change, and so many colours and designs to be employed, that once launched the floral decorator will demand more shelf room than the average house can provide. Yet each vase will treasure a memory of some particular triumph or disaster met with in the quest for flawless perfection. A simple rule, but one often neglected, is that all supports should be completely hidden. A neat finish completes the whole, and gives the impression of competence so essential to good work.

Before we look at the mechanics of decoration I would ask you to glance briefly at some of the materials at your disposal. For this we might consider two types. First there is the rose itself, its flowers, foliage and fruits: next there are those other many and lovely blossoms and plants in a wider field which may well be used with roses. The rose is peerless, we agree, but it is not exclusive, and may enhance the overall beauty of a floral composition, which, without it, would lose its crowning glory. It is well to face the fact that with outdoor roses the stems must be comparatively short, and even the tallest forcing rose would not compare with the long stems of such flowers as delphiniums. There are times when the size of the building or the position of the vase demand height and width. Even so, the bold use of well-advanced blooms or the large heads of floribunda clusters may be used with great advantage in such cases.

While this is true, the average rose lover will prefer a composition with roses only, as far as possible. There are times, such as autumn, when the wealth of berried shrubs in conjunction with grey foliage can make the perfect foil for a brilliant mass of orange-scarlet floribundas, which, like the glowing flames of an open fire in a dusk-filled room, bring comfort and inspiration as one enters it.

Fundamental to all such decoration is the cutting and preparation of the flowers themselves. At what stage should roses be cut? Nothing but experience will show. The rate at which the flower has grown is an important deciding factor. A flower that has taken fourteen weeks to develop will open slowly and last for a long while. 'Baccara' has become famous not only for its length of stem but also for its 'lasting' qualities, and the latter trait has made 'Garnette' and its progeny very welcome additions to the florists' lists. A bloom matured in heat and grown under damp conditions will have but a short life. One needs to be particularly careful about single roses. As a rule these need to be cut in the bud and opened in water. This will take up to forty-eight hours and if timing is necessary, and it usually is, a stem should be tested well in advance. Despite every care, a sudden thunderstorm can ruin carefully laid plans, for often under such conditions the blooms open with surprising swiftness. For this reason one should never be without spares if one is not working at home.

The secret of keeping flowers fresh is to keep their cells turgid. A turgid cell is one filled with its maximum content. One may have seen leaves in the early morning exuding moisture in tiny droplets from their edges. Such leaves are more than turgid, they are full to overflowing. They demonstrate very strikingly the outflow of water which is taking place at all periods of active growth. This moisture must be replaced if the foliage and flowers are to remain upright, for erect carriage depends upon full cells. We all know how plants in the open, on an intensely hot day in dry weather, protect themselves by 'flagging'. The wilting of the leaves closes their stomata (breathing pores) and so saves loss of moisture. A cut flower behaves in a similar fashion. The trouble is, that once severed from its parent stem, each cell carrying moisture must have an adequate filling for the water to rise. Once an empty cell forms an airlock, the upward journey cannot be resumed. If, therefore, a decoration of flowers begins to flag, the stems should be lifted

E

out, recut by removing the old discoloured end, and the bunch plunged, foliage and stems, into water, where it will recover.

Bearing these factors in mind, one will find the ideal time for cutting roses is in the dusk of the evening before dew falls, or in the early morning. If the latter, the blooms must be given time to dry before they are pressed together. Whenever they are cut they should be placed in a receptacle deep enough to permit foliage and stem to be immersed up to the flower bud. An amazing amount of moisture and food can be assimilated through stems and leaves by this means—and the soaking should continue for at least five hours —then the blooms will travel well, even if removed from water. If this is done, the flowers upon reaching their destination should be immersed once more for as long as possible. If one can cut in the evening and leave in water all night the flowers will remain fresh for a surprisingly long spell. Crushing or bruising the stems of roses is not necessary and does not appear to lengthen their life in any way.

Prepare your blooms and foliage indoors where it is cool before going out. Strip those leaves and thorns you know will have to come off, as soon as possible, removing a few stems at a time from the container and returning as quickly as possible. It is much easier to take out the right stem from the bunch once this has been done, without pulling out more unwanted victims at the same time.

Premature drooping of flower heads is caused by anything which deprives the stem of water. This can be because the cells are blocked. While an airlock is possible, it is equally likely to be due to bacterial activity, by the early decay of tissue induced by impurities in the water or container, or by the method of collection. For this reason tap water is safer than soft water.

There are proprietary materials on the market which can prove effective on certain occasions, and may, by stopping decay, slow down the death of the flower. Such materials contain dextrose to feed the plant, alum, potassium and sodium chloride. The quantities are minute and experience suggests that there is little advantage over blooms which are placed in sterile water as soon as cut, and if possible with the foliage immersed.

Far more difficult to control is the position in which the decoration is to be placed. A hot, dry tent is bad enough, but when the steward, more intent on the visitors' comfort than the exhibits' well-being, partly pulls down the canvas sides, so creating a draught, then trouble comes surely and swiftly. A plant will endure humid heat but not moving air. So, to place a vase of flowers between window and door, or in the autumn, near a radiator, is to shorten the life of the flower very considerably. This is equally true of the sun's rays which draw the moisture from the leaves quicker than it can be supplied.

Clean water, no draughts, shade, cool temperatures, these will help to keep the flowers much longer. If one's exhibits have to remain in the tent overnight, soak the surrounding area, which will reduce the immediate temperature and moisten the atmosphere. Many knowledgeable exhibitors use a scent spray filled with clean water to freshen up the flowers before judging begins. Care should be taken if this is done after the show has been open for some time lest the dust, sometimes an almost invisible film, runs together on the waxy petals and so leaves a dark stain, like the tear-streaked face of a dirty urchin. Then truly, the last stage is worse than the first!

At the moment he would be a bold man to say the ideal flower holder had been evolved. To position the stem just where it is needed and keep it there is most difficult. One thing is certain, some form of holder should be made and tested as soon as the vessels are chosen. Some will swear by wire-netting; others, with good cause, will swear at it, but whatever method is used it should be chosen and fixed beforehand. The best mesh is 5-cm (2-in) with the netting pressed together carefully into the vase's shape. This should be done at leisure. If the want of a nail for a horse's shoe lost a battle, the careless choice or omission of adequate arrangements for support has ruined many an exhibit and wasted hours of care and preparation in other ways.

One of the most revolutionary materials as an aid to showing has been the introduction of 'Oasis'. This is a rigid yet spongy green material in blocks which absorb much water. It can be cut to shape as required, but because it is light must be fixed in or on a heavy base to prevent the arrangement overturning. It is most versatile in its uses and their adaptation. It is essential to soak the material until no more water can be held. The ideal is probably for the block to be shaped so it can fit inside a container. If this is not possible the block itself will hold sufficient moisture to keep the flowers fresh for up to a day without 'topping' if some receptacle can catch the drops. I have slipped the soaked blocks into polythene bags which when tied have been suspended by their tops. Stems have been pushed through the polythene and the blooms will remain fresh for three days but one should be careful not to pierce the bag near the base, or the water draining from the Oasis will escape. This material has much to commend it. It is expendable in so far as the holes made by the rose stems remain unclosed after the withdrawal of the stalks but it is possible to place the stems exactly where required and they will remain fresh for at least two days without refilling. If the water is topped up and the block kept wet I find that blooms last at least as long as in water and probably longer. For the professional they are particularly useful for a large decoration may be built up with little display of the container in use.

While we are considering types of decoration, it is as well to remember that the rose itself offers an astonishing variety of material for floral design. One would probably rank 'restraint' very highly as a desirable character. To know when to stop is just as important as to know where to begin. Each bloom should 'tell', and be indispensable to the whole. This is particularly true of the large-flowered hybrid teas, with which I would class such tall-stemmed and full-flowered varieties as 'Queen Elizabeth', in whatever class they may supposedly belong. A few varieties are particularly dependable for length of stem. 'Uncle Walter' is useful in this way at all times, but in its climbing form, flower stems may be at least 75 cm (30 in) in length, and what a wealth of opportunity such stems offer! Useful too is 'Spek's Yellow'. One must not be discouraged by the small, almost green flower in the tight bud, for the bloom develops and colours well after cutting. Such all-important factors must be learnt by experience, but a notebook, where such details as length of opening, colour combinations, and other points may be put down before the flowers have faded, will have immense cumulative value. Little tips and points can soon be forgotten, and they may prove invaluable in a crisis.

Additional rose foliage needs careful consideration. Some roses have heavy foliage which acts as a perfect foil for the individual shoot as it grows on the bush. When the shoot is cut and placed with other stems the restricted area becomes overcrowded and the effect is heavy and dull. Not only is it necessary to strip off much of the original foliage in such cases, but if one substitutes a smaller and lighter leaf the effect becomes more dainty, especially if such foliage can increase the height and enhance the silhouette by changing the outline.

Such additional foliage comes from a limited number of shrub species. One of the most effective is *R. omeiensis* (*R. sericea pteracantha*). This has finely divided foliage, on the small side, but the wood is almost covered with red translucent thorns. A large bush of this sort with the setting sun behind it can be unforgettable. Each thorn is lit with a ruby glow, as if alight from within. The finest effect is with one-year wood, but if shoots are gathered in June they will be very soft and may fail to remain upright after cutting if put to too rigorous a test. Bearing in mind that much of the best wood in these decorative foliaged roses is growth of the current year, when pruning one should cut out old shoots, and by leaving room for light and air encourage such growths. *R. willmottiae* with small greyish foliage and long pendulous shoots is among the most graceful. A deservedly popular variety is *R. rubrifolia*, the red-leaved form of rose. This has reddish wood with wine-red leaves. The flowers are small and insignificant, but the bunches of purple-brown hips on short twigs may be combined in the decoration to good effect. Probably one of the loveliest with larger leaves than most of those advocated, is *R. fedtschenkoana*. Not only the grey foliage but the grey wood with its clean outline is very attractive. Certain ramblers produce some handsome growths, with a shining gloss enhancing their rich red, copper, or pansy-purple foliage. Caution must be employed in their choice, for immature growth soon flags under show conditions.

Rose hips are lovely in themselves and highly decorative. An autumnal bowl may well have rose fruits as the predominant feature. The *R. moyesii* group with their large, scarlet, urn-shaped fruits are outstanding. *R. pomifera duplex* (Wolley-Dod's Rose) has large, rounded, bristly orange-red fruits. Many of the single and semi-single roses, especially the floribundas, provide wonderful masses of rounded, brilliant red and orange hips. Good rosarians would probably remove the flower heads to prevent fruiting, but a few heads left on such varieties as 'Masquerade' can be both useful and delightful.

Both leaf material and fruits should be put in while the outline is being built up. What may look elegant and graceful at this stage may lead to overcrowding later, and one must not hesitate to thin out foliage by totally removing leaves which might smother the effect. The same is true of big heads of floribundas. These are one of the most difficult items to fit in, for one large head may disturb the whole symmetry of design. Better, as a rule, to build up the same effect with two or three smaller heads which are more adaptable. Flower and buds on the same stem are very picturesque, but seldom fit into the picture as a unit. It is often better to have one stem with flower and one with bud.

Pioneers trying out new ideas should be given every encouragement. There are so many unusual colours in flowers, so many varying forms of blossom, that a wide variety is bound to be used. Innovators are never popular, but without their experimental work we should soon degenerate into repetitive mediocrity. An early memory of mine is of hearing people saying of 'Golden Emblem', 'That's not a true colour for a rose, give me pink or red or perhaps white, but not that deep staring yellow.' Granted, some new colours may appear 'muddy' to the purist. The mauves and lilacs may be too close to the pinks for clarity, but a great advance has been brought about in a few years. Now there are the soft golden browns such as 'Amberlight' bringing new promise. During the last ten years much advance has been made especially in the mat types of colour, two of which, 'Vesper', a lovely self pastel shade of buff-orange, and 'Jocelyn', a deep mahogany with purple shadings, are a challenge and contrast to any ardent exhibitor. Now a 'new' colour in floribunda roses in varying shades of purple such as 'News' and clear lilac mauves such as 'Ripples' widen the horizon.

A new factor in colour is also to be found in the vivid clarity of some of the scarlets and vermilions which possess the ardent glow of living flames. Floral art demands that every new phase should be exploited and welded into the whole wide possibility of decorative work.

What is the object of decoration? Surely to convey a message to whoever will stop and stare and wonder, and maybe, give a word of thanks. Each item should be a picture in itself, but just as surely as we choose appropriate pictures for our different rooms, so too we should choose bowls, vases, or any receptacle to contain something suited to its environment. How often has one paused and looked and praised, and that should be the hope of all, who, learning the ways of the flowers they love, display them to the best advantage, so bringing the joy of achievement to themselves and giving endless pleasure to those who appreciate beauty in a lovely setting.

 CHAPTER X

Roses under Glass

As experience widens the horizon and capacity of the rose enthusiast, his thoughts will turn to the production of rose blooms long before the dormant bushes outside have put on their juvenile dress. There is a vast difference between forcing roses commercially, and growing early roses with some measure of protection. Forcing roses during the winter months, on the grounds of expense alone is impossible for most amateurs. To obtain roses at Christmas and the New Year calls for the expenditure of much fuel and is the specialist work of trained experts. Then, because the whole enterprise must be commercially sound, the choice of varieties is very limited, and therefore such production is more like a flower factory than an extension of gardening. Quantity, as well as quality, of bloom is of paramount importance, and considerations not applicable to the amateur decide production methods.

The approach for the amateur should be from a very different angle. While costs must be considered in their right perspective, it is the pleasure of anticipation and achievement to which he looks for repayment. The fact that the blooms are a harbinger of the longer harvest to be gathered later is a delight. With the protection from weather which glass affords he can obtain perfection of bloom for the fuller varieties which can seldom be achieved in the open air.

The only satisfactory way of producing early roses is to have a glass-house and before buying any kind of greenhouse we must consider its siting in the garden. Remembering that we shall want flowers when there will be little sunlight, at least during the early period of growth, we must try for the maximum of light. This is an argument for large panes of glass, if possible 45 × 60 cm (18 × 24 in) or even of Dutch light size. Wider glass means fewer sash-bars and so more light. The size of house need not deter us. A lady who has won prizes at the Royal National Rose Society's Spring Show has adapted an alpine house 3 × 2 m (9 ft 6 in × 7 ft 6in), with a maximum span roof height of 2 m (7 ft 6 in). By lowering the shelves to 15 cm (6 in) above the soil, enough room was left for the growing plants and for the accommodation of some thirty plants in 20-cm (8-in) pots and a few 23-cm (9-in) pots. This is a little too small where choice is possible and any house 3·6 × 2·4 m up to 7 × 2·7 m (12 × 8 ft up to 24 × 9 ft) is admirable. In the smaller house pot plants would be grown; and in the larger, I should advocate planting the bushes directly into the soil.

The smaller the house, the more difficult to control temperature in the summer, but one has to admit that larger houses can be very expensive to heat if one is not careful. Natural heat may well rocket a cool night temperature of 5° C up to 30° C (45° F up to 100° F) at midday, and some method of control becomes essential. There is much to be said for a lean-to where the supporting wall is north. The siting of the greenhouse should be controlled by two factors. It should be as near the house as possible for convenience and wiring costs, but far enough away to ensure sufficient light. Much will depend on the aspect of the house itself.

Some measure of heat is necessary if we need roses before early May, but good roses can be obtained from the second week in May in cold houses. If we decide on some heat, then electricity is the most trouble free, and provided we do not attempt high tempera-tures, costs are moderate. In the alpine house, two sixty-watt strip electric heaters set at 5° C (41° F) will give flowers in a normal year at about mid April. It is essential if electricity is used to bear a few facts in mind. Before all else, wiring and layout are an expert's job, and advice will be given by the local representatives of Area Elec-tricity Boards. The wiring should be carried out professionally. The method of heating should be considered, but on balance, tubular heaters made of aluminium to withstand humidity give the best results. These are made in various lengths and can be added to quite easily if further heat is needed. Remembering that the heat will be controlled by thermostat, it is wise to have more tubular heaters than the absolute minimum. No more current will be used, but it will be better distributed, and extra power will be available in emergency. It is essential to have a good-quality thermostat, for everything may well depend upon its reliability. We have spoken of 5° C (41° F) as a minimum regular temperature. To obtain this, a boost of 16° C (30° F) should be aimed at. This means that even if the outside temperature drops so low as to give twenty-eight degrees (Fahrenheit) of frost, the house could still be kept at 5° C (41° F). A 3·6 × 2·4 m (12 × 8 ft) span greenhouse can be kept at a minimum temperature 7° C (45° F) during the period from the 1st of October to the 30th of April for a consumption of about 2,200 units of electricity. It should be borne in mind that an exposed position might increase consumption greatly, also that roses would need heat for not more than three (albeit the coldest) of these months if April roses were our objective. By this method there could be trouble-free, clean, and comparatively cheap heating. While 2,200 units were quoted for a temperature of 7° C (45° F), yet raising the temperature a further 3° C or 5° F to 10° C (50° F) only will consume almost double the current. It is wise to have an oil emergency heater in case of accidents or power cuts.

If one is content to use the house for roses only, then planting directly into the soil is much simpler and involves much less work. Before we describe this method, it might be well to consider the height of the house. Undoubtedly a taller house with a 2·4 to 3 m (8 to 10 ft) high roof is a great advantage, but every height increase adds to heating costs. Usually one has to be content with a house giving headroom at its highest point, but with greater height better ventilation and more even temperature can be obtained. And with greater height, a climbing variety may be grown in the roof, but careful thought must be given to its selection, for a climber under glass can be three times as vigorous as the same tree outside.

A very modern method of protection is that given by polythene and two methods are possible. The first is to plant the bushes in the soil and let them grow without protection during the summer but closer to each other, as with a greenhouse, and limited to the size of the polythene house frame, leaving a centre path of 45 cm (18 in) and planting 23 cm (9 in) from the path. After Christmas the steel framework of the house may be erected over the roses and the polythene covering positioned. Good crops of roses may be had during May and then the frame can be moved to the adjoining area and a tomato crop followed by chrysanthemums may be grown after which the frame is again placed over the roses. This means much work and it is doubtful if the same polythene can be used twice but protection is given to a considerable area and the main cost, that of the steel, is halved. The house may be left over the roses all the time but ample ventilation through the doors is needed all summer and the air must be changed by leaving one door open during the spring when weather permits. Usually a house 7·4 m (25 ft) long is the longest advisable unless special fans are built in, an expensive operation. Plants grown under such conditions flourish and give good-quality clean blooms during the period of protection from May until November.

Before beginning any planting, one should decide what is wanted. Is it to be quantity, quality, or variety or is the aim to achieve all three? It is the outstanding advantage of weather protection which should be exploited to the full. Such full-petalled sorts as 'Baccara' may be brought to such perfection as cannot be seen outside. Those weathered, dirty petals, that washed-out colouring, or worse, the rotten flower head, are all insured against, and one perfect flower produced under glass is a joy and delight. One may grow 'Red Devil' well under such circumstances. For this reason it is advisable, if aiming at perfection of flower, to include some double, long-stemmed varieties. I would point out that such types, in which one would include 'Peace', 'Bonsoir' and 'Alec's Red', will take considerably longer to flower and produce fewer flowers per plant. For general use one will find sorts with twenty-eight to thirty-five petals more free-flowering and quicker to bloom. Of reds, 'National Trust', 'Fragrant Cloud' and 'Ernest H. Morse' are good. Of pinks, 'Lady Sylvia', 'My Choice' and 'Blessings' are a good choice. In bicolours, 'Piccadilly', although of few petals, is always free in flowers which last well when cut. Yellow roses are not so satisfactory but 'Ellinor Le Grice', 'Dr. Verhage', 'Grandpa Dickson' and 'Peer Gynt' are the best although secondary blooms of the last often have very short stems. The brick red 'Summer Holiday' and the tall vermilion 'Alexander' are unusual in colour and effective when cut. When one is planning such planting, the colour scheme in the home should be considered, and if there is a favourite colour, enough should be grown to ensure more flowers of that shade.

Before marking out the beds, the width of the path must be considered. This means valuable space unoccupied, and so the minimum should be used. A 45-cm (18-in) concrete slab path should be enough, provided that the first roses are planted not less and 23 cm (9 in) away from the path. In considering distance between plants, it should be decided whether large bushes or short trees are required. Large bushes will produce more blooms for a given area, but the light pruning needed will induce taller growths, and the bushes will soon grow 1·5 to 2 m (5 to 7 ft) high. Such size is usually unwise in a low house, as there will be insufficient head-room, and the space between bush and glass will not give free circulation of air. Under such circumstances disease and pests will multiply. Unless one has a tall roof, the better method is to prune hard and plant closely. This would mean 30 to 38 cm (12 to 15 in) between plants and 45 cm (18 in) between rows. Bushes pruned to 15 cm (6 in) in January will reach 1·2 m (4 ft) by the autumn.

Preparing the soil is a major problem, for this is to support the plants for a long while and must provide a regular and continuous supply of moisture. The subsoil should be tackled, but in such a confined area it is better to break up the top 30 cm (12 in), turn it over and forward, and then, clearing the trench left, thoroughly break up the lower soil. At the same time one should incorporate a liberal dressing of peat. By 'liberal' I mean a coverage of 7·6 cm (3 in) thick to which should be added 227 g (8 oz) of ground bone and 113·5 g (4 oz) of hoof-and-horn to the metre run. Having spread this, it should be worked into the trench as deeply as possible, which will mean 20 to 25 cm (8 to 10 in). The top 30 cm (1 ft) of soil should be treated in the same way. This will mean a very heavy dressing of peat, which itself should be of the best absorbent quality, for under the warm and moist conditions of the house, it will soon disappear. When it goes, however, it will leave the soil aerated and absorbent. It is essential to soak such peat very thoroughly before applying, or it will remain in its dry state for months and take the moisture from the plants when they are in need. If one is able to obtain good farmyard manure this should be used for the subsoil instead of peat. Experience compels me to admit that the quality of the soil greatly affects the growth of the bushes and where a choice is possible the site should have been well cultivated before the house is erected.

This preparatory work should be done in September, and when you have soaked the soil with the equivalent of 7·6 cm (3 in) of rain the ventilators should be left open and the ground left to settle.

Planting may begin in early October if the plants are procurable locally, otherwise it is better to wait until mid-November. One would prefer bushes with two well-ripened shoots rather than a proliferation of growth. The object should be to obtain a few strong, virile growths from each tree, rather than many shoots. When planting, begin at one end, working steadily down the strip. To obtain straight lines in planting it is easier, as with outside bushes, to plant each bush in a similar corner, spreading the roots in the remaining space, rather than to plant centrally and arrange the roots equally on all sides. Every care should be taken, by using fine earth and peat, to ensure soil contact for all roots. The soil should be firmed round the roots, but not trodden down so heavily as to prevent the ready access of air and moisture. The heavy watering which comes later should consolidate the soil sufficiently.

When planting has been completed there should be no attempt to hasten growth. Indeed, for the first season growth should follow the normal course which nature sees fit to provide for plants protected from the extremes of weather. To this end, windows and all ventilators should be left open even when there is a slight frost. No attempt should be made to start the bushes into growth until February.

In January, pruning may be done. This will need to be more severe than outside, for the tendency is for fewer eyes to break into growth. Pruning to two or three eyes is enough, and allowing for the fact that 2·5 cm (1 in) of the budded portion is below ground there should be 5 to 7·5 cm (2 to 3 in) of wood above. Ventilation should be continued except under very bitter conditions. Early in February, watering should begin. This is the most important task, for it awakens the plant, and for a continuous and healthy crop there must be sufficient water in the subsoil to ensure a regular supply of moisture while growth continues. The statement is simple but the application very important. The following method may be used for discovering the necessary quantity of water to be given. Dig up 0·028 cu m (1 cu ft) of soil. Allow it to dry slowly and completely, then add water slowly, keeping a check on the amount used. Saturation point is determined when the soil ceases to absorb any more. This can be further tested by squeezing the soil, and if moisture exudes it is sufficiently wet. It is useless to add more water than the soil will take beyond this point, for it cannot be retained, and will either be lost in the subsoil or waterlog the surface. By this method one can easily calculate how much water the top 38 cm (15 in) of the soil will take.

This heavy watering takes care of the moisture to be brought up by the anchor roots. Future watering will be done to promote a moist, growing atmosphere, and to dissolve the foods near the surface for the fibrous roots. The plant will depend for its regular, steady growth upon the deep watering carried out early.

It is after this first heavy watering that feeding the fibrous roots should begin. To apply soluble fertilizers before the watering would wash the food out of reach of the plant. The following formula makes a good beginning and should be spread at the rate of 56 g (2 oz) to the plant. It is the same as suggested for outside work, but one should remember that bone meal has already been used liberally, so that the overall availability of phosphate is higher. As phosphates promote early growth, this extra is needed, for the plants under glass have to make an early start.

1 part nitro-chalk	15·5	per cent N	4 nutrient ratio
1 part triple superphosphate	47	per cent P_2O_5	12 nutrient ratio
1 part sulphate of potash	48	per cent K_2O	12 nutrient ratio
1 part Kieserite about	24	per cent MgO	6 nutrient ratio

After application, the fertilizer should be hoed in and a 2·5-cm (1-in) thick mulch of wet peat applied. Choosing a warm day, the border should be watered enough to weld peat and soil, but not sufficiently to leave the bed sodden.

During February and early March little growth will appear. Odd shoots will seem to be making unbalanced growth, but towards the end of March the plant will settle down into steady progress.

Ventilation is a major problem which faces two hazards, cold winds and bursts of sunshine, the latter increasing in strength as the days lengthen. Where the house must be left unattended, some ventilation should be left on all day, and where the early morning rays strike before one rises, just a little at night. 'Sweating' due to a sudden rise in temperature without ventilation can be deadly. While a cold wind may produce powdery mildew which is easily controllable, sweating can produce more dangerous mildew. I have seen a house ruined by this latter type of mildew induced through a two-hour burst of sunshine getting the better of the owner in his absence. Within a few days the foliage changed and fell, and not a bloom was cut, where two hundred and fifty good blooms should have been ready at one time. If one can arrange ventilation away from the wind, so much the better, but if there is doubt, open on the west side rather than the east. Top ventilation is the ideal, and draughts from side ventilators should be avoided. Spraying with clean water is an effective deterrent to many pests and induces a moist growing atmosphere. When this is carried out do not be afraid to spray forcefully, and make sure that there is time for the foliage to dry before nightfall. As the plants grow, remove any blind shoots. These are leafy growths without flower buds. In the case of 'Peace' and a few others this often happens. If not crowding the other growth, these may be left, when they will make flower shoots later. There is little likelihood of too many growths, but if especially good flowers are wanted, reduce the number of shoots at an early stage by rubbing off the weaker growths. One flower to the branch should be enough. During April, the tiny flower buds will develop rapidly, and as soon as possible, side buds should be rubbed off and the main bud left. If especially good results are required, a foliar feed may be used. This is a highly soluble form of compounded fertilizer, including some trace elements which is sprayed on and absorbed through the foliage. Provided that the quantities recommended are used, results are very good. Foliar feed should be done once a fortnight and during the intervening week a spray of Epsom salts (commercial type) magnesium sulphate, of 28 g to 4·6 l (1 oz to the gallon) will be found beneficial. It is unwise to spray with foliar feed once the blooms begin to show colour, as red flowers in particular have their colour affected. Even clear water spraying should cease as well at that time, so that the opening flowers are unspotted.

Diseases are few, mildew is the worst enemy, but this may be controlled with green sulphur powder which can be dusted on from a small canister with bellows. If one is prepared for extra expense, excellent small electric sulphur heaters are available which burn very little current. They heat the sulphur in a canister which gives a fine powder of sulphur over the whole leaf surface. Quantities of sulphur used are very small, but the result is complete mildew control. This should be used during the nights only, when the bushes are flowering. A sharp lookout must be kept for caterpillars and grubs, especially if the plants have been brought in from the open. The finger and thumb method should be enough for their destruction. Greenfly is a major trouble: if not checked at once the pest spreads with alarming rapidity. Nicotine, as fumigant shreds or evaporated in a special lamp, is an effective cure. A small aerosol canister kept in the house will check the spread at once. Better to use these at once and prevent further infection. Red spider can be a major problem and once established is almost impossible to eradicate. A dry atmosphere is its best friend so one should seek to encourage a moist atmosphere which is excellent for growing cut roses. Where a dry atmosphere is essential, as in hybridizing, the pest is most difficult to control. Any spray used should be changed fairly rapidly as this trouble soon builds up resistance. Azobenzine smokes, if used with care are an excellent control while malathion is useful for a change. A new systemic which claims to give control for a considerable period is Temik 10G, a fully systemic carbonate pesticide which in moist soil is rapidly absorbed by the roots and moves upward into all the plant parts often beginning to act within twenty-four hours and continuing for from two to four months. It is active against red spider, aphides, nematodes (eelworm) and vine weevil. It appears generally to promote healthy growth. It is a highly poisonous material demanding most careful use. One of the essentials is cleanliness and at the end of the season all dead leaves and waste should be removed and the wood and other structural material scrubbed down with a strong disinfectant. A very harassing complaint, difficult to eradicate once it has a hold, is thrips. This minute insect causes the petals to be deformed and is especially virulent with the 'Lady Sylvia' group and many pink roses.

One source of danger for roses under glass is too strong sunlight. Much of the growth will be made during dull weather and will be very susceptible to burning if the sun breaks through. No doubt the ideal shelter is movable blinds, although the latest scientific achievement is the production of a green liquid controlled by the sunlight which flows over the glass as a continuous shading while the sun lasts, and ceases when the strength diminishes. Like self-opening garage doors, this is a luxury outside most people's purse range. A simple way is to whitewash or rather sprinkle the glass. By using ground chalk mixed with water, an adhesive covering can be made which lasts well. The glass should not be completely covered but sprinkled sufficiently to break the concentrated rays of the sun. Where the area is not large, green netlon fixed inside is excellent as it can be removed quite easily and reused.

The average time taken to produce a rose under cold-house conditions is twelve to fourteen weeks. The second crop will appear much more quickly, and it has been a matter for surprise that roses grown under glass during the summer with unshaded glass, leading to temperatures up to $38°$ C ($100°$ F), produce blooms which last longer when cut, than those from outside. The foregoing description of growing roses in the soil has taken a disproportionate amount of space, in view of the fact that the majority of those who possess a small greenhouse like to use it for other purposes rather than roses only. Fortunately roses are not difficult and can live and produce good blooms where other plants are growing if adequate ventilation is given. Better still is the method by which potted rose trees are grown in the house from January to May and then placed outside to grow and ripen until forcing begins again for the following spring. For this purpose the rose trees must be grown in pots. Two methods are available. Probably the best is to pot up rugosa stocks in 18-cm (7-in) flower pots. This may be done in the autumn or winter if some slight protection such as a frame can be given to induce rooting.

These stocks are made the previous season from 25-cm (10-in) shoots, from which all but the two top 'eyes' have been removed. This is done by cutting a nick, sufficiently deep to destroy the main eye with its two guard eyes. With properly made stocks no suckers should come, however old the plants.

In autumn, when rooted, the cuttings are lifted, and are trimmed clean of roots to within 7·5 cm (3 in) of the base. They are then potted in good soil. John Innes No. 3 potting compost of good quality is ideal. The flower pots chosen should be 18 cm (7 in) for stocks and 20 cm (8 in) for established bushes. Two or three large crocks should ensure drainage. These should be covered with 1·25 cm (½ in) of smaller pieces and finally a small lump or two of soaked peat placed in position to prevent soil washing through. The use of broken bones instead of crocks was a favourite tip of a keen chrysanthemum grower and it may be tried. Just enough soil should cover the drainage, and then the plant roots should be put in. This can present a major problem with an established tree. With care, most roots can be induced to conform by using a circular motion as one puts the rose into the pot. If it will not conform, then it is better to trim the root. This done, fill the pot with soil, tapping the bottom to shake the contents down. When the roots are covered, ram the soil between them with a stick. Try to get the bud about level with the soil, which should stop within an inch of the top. Too much soil means insufficient room for watering.

It is never easy to decide what to do with pot roses when these have to be placed outside. A little care in preparing a special position is well worth while. If the pots are placed on the open soil worms may enter through the drainage holes, and in a wet season fibrous roots will find their way into the soil beneath only to be torn off when the pots are moved. A concrete base large enough to take the plants is the answer. This should have a slight slope and may be surrounded by 19·5 × 2·5 cm (8 × 1 in) weatherproofed boards. When the pots are arranged on the base, damp peat should be pushed around them, but the peat should come up to pot level. All this may seem a lot of trouble, but if this is done, little watering will have to be done during the summer, and if they are well soaked before you go away for a holiday, the plants will be growing happily on your return. If the above is not possible the pots should be stood on a thick layer of ashes to prevent the entry of worms. When spraying your other rose trees, do not neglect these pot plants. It will save a build-up of troublesome pests for the following spring. (See plates 8 and 9.)

Where bush roses are potted up, forcing should not be used during the first season. Better to establish the plants in the pots during the first season by standing them on a hard base such as brick or concrete, covering the pots with peat, and keeping them growing normally during the summer. They may then be treated exactly as those budded on rugosa stems in their second year. Pot plants should not be placed on the soil in the greenhouse but are better either on slatted benches or on solid benches on which pea shingle has first been placed to ensure air circulation beneath the pots. To encourage the warm air to circulate there should be a space between bench and wall. If the heating apparatus is fixed on the side of the house a warm current of air will rise, passing the plants, circulating across the glass roof and coming down from the apex of the roof to the path, to be warmed again by the electricity. This free circulation will give the maximum heat where most needed.

The height of the benches will depend on the height of the greenhouse, but need be only 23 to 30 cm (9 to 12 in) above the ground. This will provide a comfortable working level. When spacing pots one must allow for the final growth of the plants and although they may require little space while dormant, all crowding must be avoided as growth demands space. A house $3 \cdot 6 \times 1 \cdot 8$ m (12×10 ft) should take about forty pots, quite a good supply. There is a great variation in the number of flowers produced per pot. Very full varieties, such as 'Red Devil' and 'Baccara', may provide only two or three, 'Sutter's Gold', which is unusually free, up to seven, while 'Lady Sylvia', used so much for forcing, will give considerably more, as will 'Piccadilly'. It is this variation in behaviour which will give added zest to the experiment.

Potted stocks should be treated as suggested for the pot roses and should be kept on the damp side to encourage growth. They must not dry out before budding. The stocks remain on the base until late June or early July when they should be budded. The sooner these can be budded after growth has started the better, provided that ripe budding wood is available. The stocks should be kept growing by adequate watering and by shielding from weed and pest. These budded stocks have the advantage of being well established in their pots and may be brought into a house in the early winter following budding where heat may be used if it is available. If there is no room in the house until the chrysanthemums or other crop has been removed, the pots should be given the shelter of a frame. When they are brought in, the top 2·5 cm (1 in) of soil should be removed and the plants gently tipped out of the pots when the roots should be inspected for worms or other troubles. A dressing of fresh soil, John Innes No. 3, should replace the removed earth. The stock should be cut down to within 2·5 cm (1 in) of the bud, as for outside stocks, and a 60-cm (2-ft) cane inserted. When growth begins, conditions should be as recommended above, and feeding may begin at that time. An excellent feed for this purpose is a stock solution of

113 g (4 oz) of potassium nitrate
113 g (4 oz) of ammonium phosphate
9 l (2 gallons) of water

This should be stored in a wooden or polythene container and may be used once a week at the rate of 0·28 l to a 9-litre can ($\frac{1}{2}$ pint to a 2-gallon) of water when growth begins. When growth is fast, a similar amount may be used at each watering. In addition, foliar feed may be given from the time the flower bud is at pea-size stage until colour shows, when watering only should be done. Avoid extremes of wet and dry. Carry out at least one foliage spray a day with clean soft water. As the flower head develops, make sure the stem is tied to the stake. The first year there should be one flower to a plant, but this method can produce magnificent flowers. The memory of 'Crimson Glory' flowers grown by this method, which won the Gold Medal at the National Rose Society's Spring Show in 1935, will be treasured, for this was one of the finest groups of that variety ever seen.

After these single shoots have flowered, they should be cut, if the bloom stems have not been cut already. If this has been done, one should try to leave at least 10 cm (4 in) of growth on the plant. Thanks to feeding and spraying with water the shoot will soon make several breaks. As soon as growth shows that the plant is happy in its new surroundings it may be transferred outside, where it should be kept growing during the summer and autumn. If heat is to be used and the plant is to be started early, it is better transferred to a frame in September, where growth can be checked by reducing the water supply and the wood hardened for early ripening. This ripe wood is an essential for good flowers, and to ensure it, feeding should cease in July. Before the plant is brought in for its second season of forcing, it should be tipped from the pot and the drainage should be examined and cleaned. The top 2·5 cm (1 in) of soil should be removed and fresh put in its place. After this, one should follow the natural course, and prune twelve to fifteen weeks before the flowers are needed. Beginning temperatures should be 4·4 to 7·6° C rising to 12·8 to 15·6° C (40 to 45° F rising to 55 to 60° F) in the daytime when the buds are coloured. It may be that these few plants have to take their place with other plants, and in that case they will accommodate themselves readily, but timing for the flowers will not be possible. One must be content with few flowers, but their lasting qualities will far excel the same variety cut from outside bushes. As the bush ages and grows, it may be planted into a 20-cm (8-in) or 22·5-cm (9-in) pot. While such large pots produce good results it must not be forgotten that these have to be moved about, and one's ability to shift weights must be taken into account.

The emphasis may appear to have been so far on large specimen blooms, but when one is going to the trouble of growing roses under glass the flowers should be as fine as possible. Where quantity is required a smaller-type flower may be used with advantage. 'Michèle Meilland', 'Blessings', 'Sutter's Gold', 'Ellinor Le Grice',

'Fragrant Cloud' and 'Peer Gynt' are the right types for such purposes. Extra flowers per main shoot may be allowed.

Floribunda roses are very amenable to such treatment but relatively few are really free-flowering. 'Copper Delight', with its rich depth of golden orange colour and sweet scent, flowers early and late. 'Iceberg' is particularly good. 'Circus' makes a large head of flowers on short sturdy stems but is later-flowering. 'Ester Ofarim' is very good for this purpose, a little late-flowering, and needs to have the centre flower of each cluster removed so that more blooms may be had at one time if the stems are needed for cutting.

'Allgold', although its stems are short, is very early and free-flowering. Probably 'Firecrest' is the most useful in its colour because of length of stem and lasting qualities.

A number of excellent small flowered roses for cutting, known as 'Garnette' types, are noted for their full flowers which are very long lasting when cut. These are primarily 'forcing' roses and usually require considerable disbudding, for their natural tendency is to come in clusters which are disbudded to one flower and are usually sold with comparatively short stems. Such varieties as 'Garnette' and its many sports, and 'Carol' and 'Zorina' are typical but the tendency is for named cultivars to be superseded rapidly on the cut-flower market.

Where there is wall space as in a lean-to type of house, standard roses, especially if planted out in the border, can give abundant bloom of high quality. Budding on 75-cm (2½-ft) stems is enough.

It is amazing to see roses grown in borders flourishing and flowering freely for weeks at a time without further watering beyond the heavy spring soaking. Little attention is needed, and although watering and feeding up to July will encourage more blooms, a bush pruned to 23 cm (9 in) in the spring will grow into a sturdy tree of 0·9 to 1·2 m (3 to 4 ft) by the season's end.

Few flowers are treasured as is a rose out of season, and a single bloom is not only a joy in itself, but as a harbinger of summer, is beyond price.

PART III

KNOWING ROSES

 CHAPTER XI

One Hundred Years of the Royal National Rose Society

There must be a number of contributory factors for a society to celebrate its hundred years successfully and to have become a vigorous centenarian. In the Rose Society's case two of those factors were outstanding. The first was, and still is, the personnel. By their unflagging efforts throughout the hundred years its members have built up a strong tradition of service, strengthened by specialist knowledge freely made available to all. The second was the common bond of love for roses, possessed in varying degrees and expressed in many different ways. Added to this the increasing development of the rose in colour, purpose and presentation itself increased interest in the rose. It would not be possible to analyse these inter-locking means of advancement. The Society certainly contributed to the improvement of the rose, but equally the increase in the introduction of new cultivars for a growing variety of purposes widened the scale of appeal to a larger and more varied member-ship.

As my next chapter describes the advance in rose breeding made by British raisers over the same hundred years I won't say much about that side now but I shall speak here of the work of other countries. Even if these allusions are brief, this should in no way detract from the important work done by many in other lands. Their achievements are outstanding, and without their initial successes the rose would have had far less appeal, for its purposes would have been far more restricted than they are today.

This story of the first hundred years of the Rose Society will be based on the personalities around which its advance was made.

The rose has always been one of the most popular flowers though there were limits to its appeal in the earlier years before this history began, one of its limiting factors being its short flowering season, another its reduced appeal for decoration largely because of its weak flower stem and its restricted life as a cut flower. Probably its outstanding characteristic was its rich perfume which lived on in the dried petals as potpourri, or in perfumes such as rose water or, more limited and costly, as attar of roses.

Growing roses in the earlier days was a haphazard affair. The tall shrubs produced many types of flowers and when they competed with one another at exhibitions there was neither rule nor precedent for judging.

There were rose societies older than the National Rose Society such as the West of Scotland Rosarians Society, whose first meeting was held at Helensburgh on 28th October 1768, and the Hereford Rose Society, founded in 1868.

In 1858 Reynolds Hole, later Dean of Rochester, with the special help of well-known nurserymen such as Thomas Rivers, William Paul and Charles Turner, started a National Rose Show at St. James's Hall, Piccadilly, to which two thousand people came. The following year it was staged in Hanover Square and in 1860 it went to the Crystal Palace by which time sixteen thousand people were attending. In 1861 through pressure of other work Reynolds Hole had to give up the organization, and it was passed on to the Royal Horticultural Society which was then at low ebb. The show was strangled by mismanagement and ceased. In 1856 John Cranston of King's Acre Nurseries, Hereford wrote in *Gossip for the Garden* advocating a national rose society. In the *Gardeners' Chronicle* of 1876 we read that a conference of rose exhibitors and rose growers was to be held at the Horticultural Club House (itself a conception of D'ombrain, a founder member of the National Rose Society). Items to be discussed were 'the formation of a National Rose Society' and 'to revive the National Rose Show which was merged into the Royal Horticultural Society' and which 'like most things connected with that *ill-starred institution* has fallen through' (italics mine). A report of the meeting is given in the *Gardeners' Chronicle* of 9th December 1876. The Revd. Canon Hole who presided, was made president and remained so until his death in 1904. Proceedings were very enthusiastic and decisions unanimous. The Revd. D. Honeywood D'ombrain and Horace K. Mayor were appointed joint honorary secretaries, and it was decided that a show should be held in 1877 at St. James's Hall, Regent Street. This show was not a financial success: at the first annual meeting there was a deficit of £300, despite subscriptions. The exhibitors were owed £127 and agreed to take half. D'ombrain did not prove himself a co-operative joint secretary and Mayor resigned within a year. The Revd. J. B. M. Camm left complaining bitterly and publicly that not all members had been notified of the annual meeting. The annual accounts could not be passed as some receipts were missing. In fairness to D'ombrain it should be stressed that he accepted secretaryship on the strict understanding that he had nothing to do with finance. It was at this juncture that Edward Mawley became co-secretary and from that moment the business and finances of the Society were dealt with adequately. It is to him that the Society owed its success for its first thirty-six years. Later, in 1895, D'ombrain wrote of Mawley, 'It is impossible to exaggerate the services he has rendered to our National Society.' He was a successful exhibitor of roses all over England. His meteorological knowledge was put to use in the *Rosarian's Year Book* with masterly clarity from the viewpoint of a most knowledgeable rosarian. One would in no way wish to belittle the work of D'ombrain, but if he were the Luther of the Society, Mawley was the Melanchthon.

Major-General Naylor in his excellent published lecture *History of the National Rose Society* (see the N.R.S. *Annual* for 1965) divides the periods by secretaryships, but I should like to divide this history into twenty-five-year periods. Moreover, what is written in this chapter should be considered in the light of life as it was then with the more emphasized divisiveness of 'society'.

While the work and success of the Rose Society in the early days rested with the secretaries, yet the presidency under the Revd. S. Reynolds Hole gave prestige and popularity to the venture which few, if any, could have emulated. As an author, especially of *A Book about Roses* (first published in 1869) which ran into many editions (my copy is the fifteenth edition in 1896), he spread the love of the rose and encouraged its cultivation to a very wide public. His early participation in the actual cultivation and showing of the rose became more restricted as his other duties increased, but he gave rose culture an aura of social respectability which lifted it into the conversation and interest of the drawing-room. This may sound snobbish, but it provided the impetus the rose needed then. To read the history of horticulture at that time is to become inextricably mixed with the clergy. Most local societies either owed their inception or continuance to the devoted labours of the country parson together with the squire to provide a site for the show tents, a challenge cup for the best exhibit and a wife to present the cup and give lunch to the visiting dignitaries. This was the way of life, and skills were fostered which might otherwise never have come to fruition.

The Rose Society with Dean Hole as its president, and the Revd. D. H. D'ombrain as one secretary was no exception and many of the outstanding rosarians such as Foster Melliar, J. H. Pemberton and F. Page Roberts were clergymen. All worked well for the Rose Society and a large number of rose nurserymen also gave it their blessing and support. It is always difficult and sometimes invidious to mention individuals lest one worthy of inclusion is omitted, but the risk must be taken for, as I have said, the history of the Society is the story of personalities who presented their gifts ungrudgingly. If at times they were somewhat overbearing, it should be attributed more to zeal than self-aggrandizement.

After the first uncertainties of initiation the Society went steadily on its way. The subscription of 10s and later an optional £1 brought in the minimum for its subsistence, and it would seem that any special charge had to depend on a friendly 'whip round' by the few. With so small a subscription, and so few members—there were only five hundred after fifteen years—little could be done to help with literature. For a long while the Society depended upon the *Rosarian's Year Book*, edited and published by D'ombrain personally at 1s but independent of the Rose Society. This contained a few good articles, including 'The Man of the Year' with photograph, a number of advertisements and after the first year the insertion of the annual report of the Society. It ran from at least 1879 to 1902. This was a permanent contribution to the Rose Society by D'ombrain and is his best memorial. Added to this, as a constant visitor to rose shows and associate societies, he encouraged many to join. His biennial visits to France kept the Society informed as to what the French were offering in new roses, and as a judge of a novelty rose his assessment was excellent. He was the first to note the most famous rose of the period 'Maréchal Niel', and later 'Mrs. John Laing'. Edward Mawley was a most self-effacing person, but he seems to have applied a clear scientific outlook with a pleasing friendly personality, as well as a shrewd application of business acumen.

The two secretaries worked together for many years, although it was Mawley who appears to have attended to the brunt of the work and built up the friendly comradeship which has had such a lasting influence on the Society. His wide outlook coined the phrase 'Roses for the millions'. One must remember that these words should be understood in their context. In the early years each was kept to his 'station'. 'The rich man in his castle, the poor man at his gate' (as Dean Hole quotes in his *A Book about Roses*) was the established order and the humble gardener was considered a necessary adjunct to most aspiring prize-winning members. At Perth there was a complaint that the Revd. A. Hill Gray was exhibiting *without the name of his gardener*. Not to have a gardener and exhibit was unthinkable! The average established nurseryman at the time had a background of training and education. There were a few firms of considerable distinction and longstanding, with great experience, who were responsible for setting the standards of the rose shows in quality and quantity of rose blooms. Without them there would have been no crowd-compelling attraction, a fact which one needs to remember at the present time. The shows at first consisted of rows upon rows of exhibition blooms, the greatest class having seventy-two distinct varieties.

Even in 1845 several names stood out as exhibitors and growers: Rivers of Sawbridgeworth, Paul of Cheshunt, Lane of Berkhamsted, Alex Dickson of Newtownards and James Cocker of Aberdeen. It is interesting to find that their subsequent success often came through having their sons trained at other nurseries by such great rosarians as Turner and Rivers.

It appears that successful showing led to success in business. Such was the case of Ben R. Cant, who in 1853 was introduced to Laffay's roses. An amateur, Mr. Penrose, who bought famous roses in France, sold Ben Cant 'Gloire de Dijon', 'General Jacqueminot' and 'Jules Mangollin', and from 1856 when he began to show, he immediately stepped into the limelight winning five Grand Challenge Trophies in rapid succession.

It was such firms who were the strength of the Society. By their consistent support they ensured a measure of success for the Society's ventures.

At this time showing was the main incentive for joining the Society, and exhibition roses were the sole competitors. This led to monotony. The hybrid perpetual reigned supreme and the colour range was limited to pink, red and white, as was the time of their appearance. It was men like Mawley who saw the need and encouraged the appearance of teas and decorative roses. The hybrid perpetuals with their proneness to autumn mildew held the field until the 1900s, to be gradually displaced by the H.Ts. with their longer flowering season and more pointed bloom.

1876–1901

The time from the Society's inception in 1876 until 1901 is probably an excellent period to consider on its own. This was a time of very slow growth. The small membership produced too small a cash balance to invest in publicity, but the Society's work was maintained and even grew slowly. These twenty-five years were when the Society was largely run for exhibitors by exhibitors, and so the horizon was limited by their needs. It was really a rose exhibitors' clique rather than a national concern. D'ombrain probably displays the opinion of most when in 1886 he declared, 'I should be glad to see the name "Hybrid Tea" expunged altogether from our list' (*Rosarian's Year Book*, 1886, p. 38). He could see no use for the H.T. class and considered that they would soon be put back into the H.P. class. Later he changed his mind, but there is little doubt that when Mawley's hands were freed he was able to guide the Society in a more statesmanlike fashion. This was to be possible when he became sole secretary on D'ombrain's full retirement in 1901.

Probably one of the greatest of the Society's achievements in its first twenty-five years was the bringing of order into the rose world. Before 1876 rules, such as they were, varied greatly in content and application. The Revd. Alexander Hill Gray, a prolific and amusing writer in the *Rosarian's Year Book*, speaks of using foliage other than its true leaves, going round the country to collect good rose blooms (where the postman had the advantage), over-dressing and bending the rules to suit special exhibitors. He instances a case where though the rules stated that staging must be completed by 8 p.m., some nurserymen did not stage until 10 the next morning. In many schedules any rose of any type or form might be mixed indiscriminately. J. B. M. Camm, who had resigned from the Society at one time, gives a series of excellent rules for judging in the *Journal of Horticulture* (7th February 1878) which cover the main rules to this day. In 1893 the Society for the first time limited the entrants of some classes to the number of roses grown, so preventing the growers of many roses from swamping growers who had few, a situation which had been to the latter's great discouragement.

By encouraging as many local societies as possible to join the Rose Society, some degree of uniformity gradually replaced the former chaotic uncertainties. In 1893 the rose selection of the year was introduced and a first step towards eliminating unwanted seedlings was made, ensuring that those put up for the award were real novelties.

Towards the end of this period the controversial class for H.Ts. became the major issue and these were accepted as a separate class. One can see the same uncertainties every time a new class is evolved. The coming of the Pernetiana, returning later to H.Ts., the hybrid polyantha merging into the floribunda and the floribunda into floribunda H.T. type, the modern shrub roses, the *kordesii* and perpetual climbers, all took time to be recognized, but the previous confusion of earlier days was avoided by the rulings of the Society.

The Society's Shows were held at the Crystal Palace, who gave the Society a grant of £115 a year. In 1901 the Society's Show moved from there to the Inner Temple. This immediately increased the gate money. The Shows themselves were becoming more attractive. The rows of exhibition boxes were being interspersed by other classes, for instance those of the lighter and more varied colourings of the teas and later of the decorative roses, the possibilities of which were seen by Mawley and which even in 1893 were making a useful contribution. It was the massive exhibition rose which still held the field. As I mentioned earlier an old exhibition hand who worked for a prominent firm of those days told me he had sold the champion bloom after a Show for what were then ten shillings. I think one should remember that in the earlier years of the Rose Society, before mass production lowered prices, many new roses sold for twenty shillings each! Their appeal was limited to the few, but who today would pay ten pounds for the privilege of having a new rose in its first year?

Before closing my discussion of this period, there are some rose growers who deserve special mention for their influence on rose production. The main stock used at the beginning of the period was 'la Grifferae'. This was not really hardy but was used for teas. With the rise of the hybrid perpetuals the manettii, introduced by Rivers of Sawbridgeworth, took the lead and was in constant use during this period as it was easy to propagate from cuttings and suited hybrid perpetuals. A serious rival in seedling briers was introduced by Mr. George Prince who found it more suitable for teas as they increased in popularity. This was also to be true of hybrid teas. The Colchester nurseries favoured brier cuttings. A painstaking survey, taken over a series of years by Mawley showed seedling brier to give the longest life and the best results. Exhibition roses were found to do best on seedling brier standards, grubbed in their thousands from the tall hedgerows of that time!

Only Dickson's of Northern Ireland used the multiflora seedling and cutting, although they used manettii for a large U.S.A. export trade. By the end of this period manettii was much less grown, although it was being used in small quantities in 1918, and is still being used for forcing roses as it is shallow rooted and responds to heat when forced.

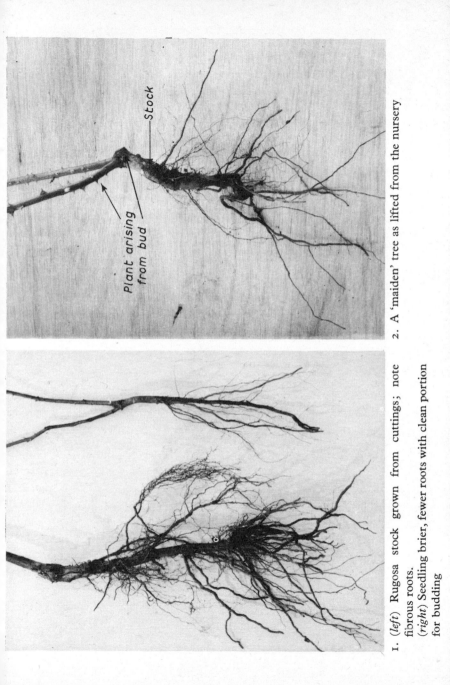

Stock

Plant arising from bud

2. A 'maiden' tree as lifted from the nursery

1. (*left*) Rugosa stock grown from cuttings; note fibrous roots.
(*right*) Seedling brier, fewer roots with clean portion for budding

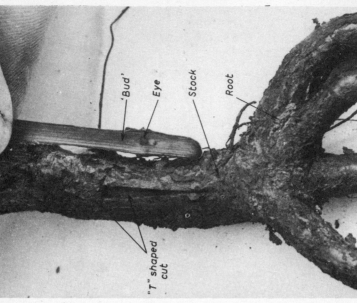

'Bud'
Eye
Stock
Root
"T"-shaped cut

3a. Selected budding wood prepared by shortening leaves and removing thorns

3b. 'Bud' prepared (reversed to show full 'eye') with "T"-shaped cut with bark opened for insertion of 'bud'

3c. 'Bud' inserted but not trimmed. Surplus to be removed level with 'T' cut

3d. 'Bud' tied-in after trimming. Note raffia presses 'eye' firmly to the stock

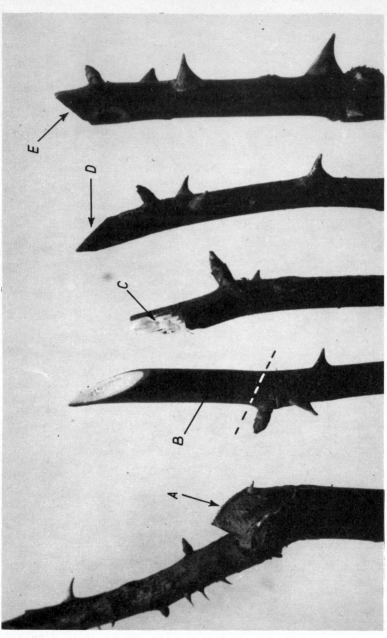

4. PRUNING: the difference between good and bad pruning lies in the way in which the cut is made. (*A*) A shoot damaged by bad pruning – note area of dead wood. (*B*) Over-long snag above bud. (*C*) Damaged wood with over-long snag. (*D*) Cut made with wrong slope. (*E*) Correct clean cut

5. PRUNING A BED. (*above*) A fifteen-year-old bed of H.T. 'Violinista Costa' before pruning. (*below*) The same bed after pruning – these bushes have been pruned hard to restrict them to a limited area

6a. A neglected rose bed; note weak and numerous twiggy growths

6b. The bush in the foreground pruned. All old and weak wood removed

6c. The same bush as in 6b, after first growth

6d. An unpruned bush in the same bed. Note the long, bare and ungainly shoots

7. PRUNING OF CLIMBERS. (*above*) A perpetual climber pruned. (*below*) The same perpetual climber after growth. A vigorous climber, if well trained, will give up to three hundred blooms in a year

8. A potted plant ready for plunging

9. A pot plant pruned

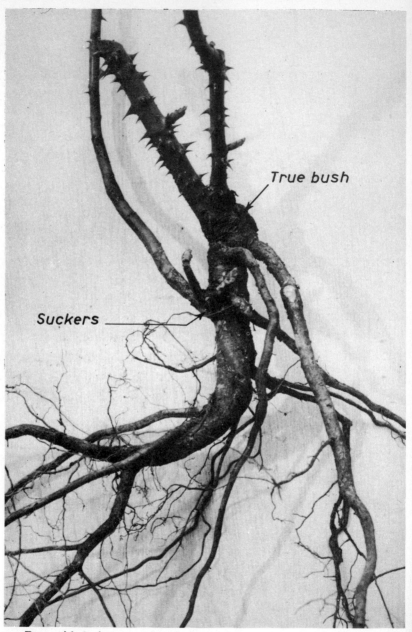

10. Rose with suckers

11. Of the sucking insects, the rose aphis is the worst enemy

(a) 'Vein banding'   (b) 'Vein Mosaic'

12. COMMON FORMS OF VIRUS

(d) Ringspot

(c) Line Pattern

13. Black spot is the biggest threat to the growing
of roses

14. The outdoor variety of mildew

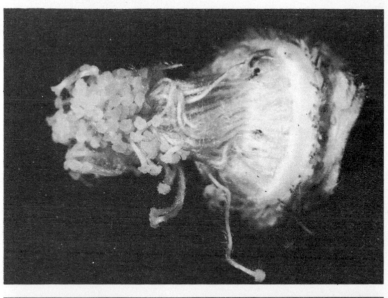

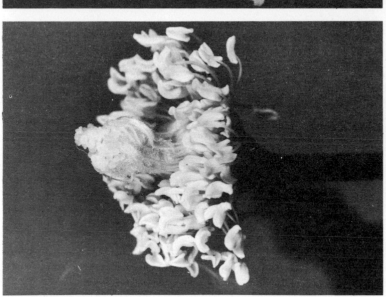

15. The practice of raising new roses. 'Emasculation', the removal of the anthers, takes place after the petals have been removed

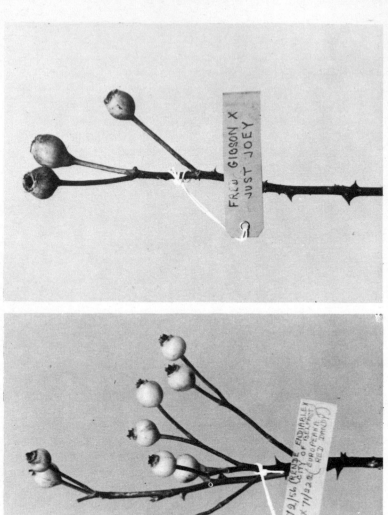

16. Labelling the flower head with the cross just made. (*left*) A head of floribunda fertilized. (*right*) An H.T. fertilized head

I have already spoken of John Cranston's work towards the establishment of the Society, but to make a regular impact on the London shows one had to find more men in or near London, especially when one considers the methods of transport. At that time Charles Turner of Slough was a great stalwart, especially for exhibition. His introduction of 'Crimson Rambler' in 1893 (the 'Engineer's Rose') changed the gardens of England, for everywhere in June this rose flourished for the next twenty-five years. Later, his forced pot roses were to be the finest ever produced.

An unusual circumstance of this time and one which led to considerable confusion was that firms were often related and often had the same names. The firm of Ben R. Cant which was founded in 1765 but became rose growers in 1856 was contemporary with the formation of the Society. A great exhibitor and loyal supporter of the Society, the firm is still with us, having since joined with Frank Cant & Co. which was formed much later.

Alex Dickson of Newtownards was probably one of the oldest firms, begun by George Dickson in 1819. They were raisers of more good new roses over a longer period than any other British firm. They were past-masters at exhibiting new roses. The firm of Hugh Dickson of Belfast began later, but on the death of the founder the firm died out.

It is probably with the firms William Paul and George Paul that the greatest confusion exists. Both were important firms. George Paul had a great influence on the Society and lived until 1923. He had exhibited at the first Rose Show in 1858 and at the first National Rose Show. His firm was known as Paul & Son of Cheshunt and he claimed to have raised the first British H.T. 'Cheshunt Hybrid' in 1874. This was strongly denied by Henry Bennett, the leading hybridist, as he considered this a chance cross not a deliberate hybrid. George Paul and Charles Turner were great rival contestants at the Rose Shows. William Paul of Waltham Cross was famous both for his book *The Rose Garden*, of which there were editions from 1848 to 1899, and for the great roses, 'Paul's Scarlet Climber' in 1916 and 'Mermaid' in 1918. The firm was succeeded by Chaplin Bros.

In seeking to sum up the progress of the Society in its first

F

twenty-five years one should place very great importance on the foundations that were laid then, rather than on any numerical and financial progress. That these foundations were solid has been proved many times. Whatever was achieved in later years was an extension of the early principles, based on the well-being of the rose in exhibition, cultivation and dissemination of knowledge.

By 1901 there were 750 members, an increase of 100 in ten years. Finances were sound but too limited for with a balance of about £50 a year little could be done.

The Society was recognized as of national importance, and the acceptance of the position of Patroness by H.R.H. Princess Alexandra, then Princess of Wales, gave it a publicity and status which was of great importance to it.

Publications were few and had it not been for the *Rosarian's Year Book*, there would have been a serious gap in its public relations.

Shows grew in interest and appeal and the support of the rose trade ensured success, while the increasing interest in new roses was fostered by the Gold Medal and Certificate of Merit given for the first time in 1883, the rose 'Her Majesty' being the first recipient, followed by the famous 'Mrs. John Laing' in 1885, both hybrid perpetuals and both raised by Henry Bennett. These successes were soon followed by those of Alex Dickson & Sons of Newtownards who then took the lead.

1901–1926

The second period under review was a time for expansion. The old order was passing. Both Dean Hole and D'ombrain died in 1904, the latter having retired in 1902. Fortunately, Mawley who had been largely responsible for the secretarial work apart from the *Rosarian's Year Book* continued as secretary and extended the policy he had advocated. Assisted by increasing funds he was enabled to place more stress on the importance of publications as well as developing the showing side. The Shows were made more varied and Charles E. Shea as president backed Mawley in urging a change in show layout, 'Rose Shows as at present are tiresomely monotonous.' As early as 1886 a class for decoratives was incorporated in the schedules. At the Society's Show at the Temple on 6th July 1901, 'there were two classes for blooms in vases in the Nurserymen's Classes and the superior effect that these have, compared with the old system of throttling the blooms in boxes should result in the system being extended to other classes another year.' In 1907 an innovation by the nurserymen of showing roses in tubes paved the way for the spectacular displays of the future.

It is more difficult to assess these years, but one would say on the whole that a major influence at the time was that of Edwardian wealth and Society. The former enabled some who had the means to make considerable contributions to the scale of 'amateur' exhibition. Heating and labour were cheap and plentiful, and at least one amateur member erected a modern block of greenhouses to compete in the Spring Show which had been instituted in 1913.

A further incentive in this period was the increase in types of roses. Among these were the polyantha roses with their small flowers and large trusses produced throughout a long season; the new types of ramblers from France and later the U.S.A., crosses with *R. wichuraiana*, widened the appeal, and above all the new crosses raised by Pernet Ducher from *R. lutea* produced a revolution in colour with yellow, apricot, scarlet and bicolours. To these must be added the shrub type 'Pemberton' hybrid musks and the 'Poulsen' type hybrid polyanthas, later to evolve into the widely grown floribundas.

Here was a most exciting time, when a great advance was made not only in the rose world, but even more in the vision of the hybridist, which resulted in rapid progress later.

Changes in the secretaryship were necessary when in 1915 Mawley became president. H. R. Darlington took over Mawley's duties and for the first time the Society had London offices. In 1916 Darlington was joined by Courtney Page as joint hon. secretary and in 1916 the latter took on the full duties and also became editor of *The Rose Annual*. Courtney Page was to serve for thirty years. He would have to contend with three very difficult periods, the two World Wars and the slump of the 1930s. He was a man of very

strong opinions and would brook no interference where he considered the well-being of the Society was concerned. He was well
aware that the publicity given by the Press was of great value, and
on one occasion when the judges had decided that no new variety
of rose exhibited at the show was worth a Gold Medal his instruction to them was, 'Have another look and find one, we can't have a
Show without a Gold.' Another time the judges were about to give
a Gold Medal when he intervened; 'You can't do that, there is a
better one on the way,' they were told. The Council had little to
do at that time beyond endorsing the decisions of the Finance and
General Purposes Committee. If it was a dictatorship, and it was
not far off it, it was a benevolent dictatorship where the rose was
regarded as supreme and everyone and everything was judged on
that basis.

That the love of the rose must have some therapeutic action
might well be gathered from the longevity of a number of prominent rosarians. At the turn of the century the ranks of the members
who had formed the Society began to thin, several of them dying,
mostly in their eighties, before this period ended; these were Dean
Hole, D'ombrain, George Paul, Alex Dickson, the Revd. J. H.
Pemberton and Edward Mawley.

As I have said, publications in this period assumed greater
importance. In 1902 Mawley issued the first *Select List of Varieties*,
in 1905 the *Handbook on Pruning Roses* and in 1908 *The Enemies of
the Rose*. These have continued ever since, although in some cases
in condensed form. The major advance lay with the production of
The Rose Annual, first brought out in 1907. This soon aspired to
coloured plates and became the most important link with the
provincial members.

The Society increased its membership and financial resources
during this twenty-five years, although the First World War reduced membership quite dramatically. In 1902 membership was
900, in 1914 6,000, in 1926 to about 16,000. Reserves grew from
£38 to £8,800 in the same period.

In 1901 the Summer Show was moved from St. James's Hall,
Piccadilly to the gardens of the Inner Temple. In 1904 another
move was made to the Botanic Gardens in Regent's Park. Roses

were exhibited in more than one tent and the smallest tent in which new seedlings were exhibited invariably drew its own specialist crowd, often resulting in an early queue awaiting the judges' decision. There were times when wind, dust and heat ruined the blooms before their first day was over, and one may be thankful that soaring costs caused the later abandonment of such shows under canvas. The Spring and Summer Shows became increasingly popular and indeed became social events. This brought in extra gate money and moreover wealthy visitors encouraged trade exhibits by placing substantial orders.

In 1905 the first Autumn Show was staged at the Royal Horticultural Hall, Vincent Square, which had been lately completed. That an Autumn Show was possible proved how greatly the flowering period of the rose had been extended by the introduction of the H.Ts. polyanthas and later hybrid polyantha roses.

In 1913 the first Spring Show was held for roses grown under glass. Still remembered are the famous exhibits of A.T. Goodwin of Maidstone who showed 'Maréchal Niel' (noisette, Pradel, 1864) in perfection such as no other yellow roses have ever attained. At the earliest period pot bush roses and specimen pot ramblers of a quality unlikely to be seen again were exhibited. The forced rose reached a peak of cultivation in the new seedling roses exhibited by Alex Dickson & Son, never to be repeated by others.

During this period the Provincial Shows, sponsored by the Society as an integral part of their original policy, and timed later than their London Shows brought the work of the Society into the provinces.

In this period the Society had presidents who both knew and grew roses to perfection. Each contributed to the Society's wellbeing. Charles E. Shea was the first president to succeed Dean Hole, and at his first Annual Meeting encouraged more adventurous showing. It was thanks to his suggestion that the Society moved their show to Temple Gardens, the beginning of their advance. To ensure success he suggested a Guarantee Fund against loss and contributed toward it. As chairman of the Finance and General Purpose Committee he inaugurated measures which greatly improved the Society's finances. A rule had been made limiting any future president's office to two years but he was elected to serve again in 1913–14. E. B. Linsdell of Hitchin (1909–10) had been prominent at the turn of the century and served the Society in many ways. The Revd. F. Page Roberts, who followed, was an able contributor to both *The Rose Annual* and the show bench. The Revd. J. H. Pemberton (1913–14), the first to receive the Dean Hole Medal in 1909, combined a delightful personality with great skill as a hybridist, and as one of the few who left his name to a type of rose, made his own memorial. In 1915–16 Edward Mawley, V.M.H., accepted the office, the crown to a lifetime's achievement on the Society's behalf, having received the Dean Hole Medal in 1910 but he died in the autumn before completing his term.

H. R. Darlington (1919–20), was a man of many parts who amid numerous other duties found time to serve the Society in difficult times. A prolific writer on roses and daffodils, he became honorary secretary and editor of *The Rose Annual* for 1915 at very short notice and continued in 1916 and, as joint editor with Courtney Page, in 1917. He was twice president, as was Sir Edward J. Holland too (1917–18, 1921–2) who served the Society as writer, exhibitor and administrator.

This was a very full period and opportunity brought out many great professional rosarians whose roses, produced at this time, are mentioned elsewhere. There were many who contributed to the advance of the rose. Alex Dickson & Son continued to add to their fame and Gold Medals, and were especially noted for their strains of good roses which every few years produced an advance. Of lesser calibre, but nevertheless a permanent contribution, were the hybrid musks as well as H.Ts. raised by Pemberton. Walter Easlea had many good varieties at this time, a number of them single or semi-double. Probably the most brilliant hybridizer at this time was Sam McGredy II. Many must still remember the cluster of eager rose growers, both professional and amateur, who waited while McGredy, that past-master of suspense, opened his cases to reveal the remarkable colour breaks he exploited so brilliantly from Pernet-Ducher's beginnings.

All the while there were the regular exhibitors who made the popular and brilliant displays which encouraged the sightseer and induced him to become a rose enthusiast.

The 1925 Report of the Council records the wording of a wreath card, 'In loyal remembrance of Her Majesty Queen Alexandra, who was for 37 years Patroness of the National Rose Society' from the members of the Rose Society.

1926–1951

Although I had been a member and small exhibitor before this period, it is from this point that I can write with some personal knowledge. Looking back at this time when I was a beginner I can appreciate even more the friendly help given in a world of fierce competition and dwindling income. The early part of this period was one of unremitting toil for very little reward, at least financially. The 'slump years' affected all, and one of the great nurserymen characters at this time was Sydney Cant who, with the assistance of Courtney Page, formed the Association of British Rose Producers. Fierce foreign competition had made England a dumping ground for over-production, and in 1931, eleven million rose trees were imported annually, against a home production of eight million, many of which had to be burned. A small tariff charge on imported bushes resulted from the Association's work, and slowly the rose growers became solvent, just as the Second World War cut short all production. A bi-product of this alliance was the formation of the Queen Mary Rose Garden, the major portion of the roses coming from the newly formed Association of British Rose Producers. The close association between the amateur Rose Society and the professional rose growers was strengthened, to the mutual benefit of both. One result was the growing friendly association which encouraged all to work for the benefit of the Rose Society.

Throughout almost the whole of this period Courtney Page reigned, dying at the age of eighty in 1947. From a 16,000 membership in 1929 a dramatic fall took place in the slump and war years. It was 11,500 in 1940 but rose to 15,000 by 1947. In many ways the thickness of *The Rose Annual* indicates the numerical and financial position of the Rose Society through these years better than any analysis of figures. It achieved its thickest—three hundred pages—in 1939 at which time reserves stood at over £23,000.

During this period society itself was changing. The number of smaller owner-occupiers was increasing rapidly and usually the first plants for the new home were roses, while the owners of larger gardens faced by labour and other problems were less able to purchase. With the increasing flowering period and better bedding effect, public gardens brought in far greater quantities, so production increased to meet the need. Today, many of the foremost amateur exhibitors of the finest flowers are growers of hundreds rather than thousands of roses, and few have paid assistance.

Undoubtedly one of the great factors in the popularity of the rose was its recognition as a bedding plant, so that the hybrid polyantha roses (later to be called floribundas) came into their own. It is hard to realize how much prejudice had to be overcome. At a small stand during a Summer Show I exhibited a grand bowl of 'Karen Poulsen' when new. A lady judge passed by, tossed her head, and with scorn said, 'Hybrid polyanthas!' For my temerity in staging these I received no recognition but that of a good supply of orders!

Few periods could have seen such rapid changes as these twenty-five years. The earlier war had destroyed the life of leisure to which rose growing and showing had been geared. The slump years stunted the growth of membership which might well have increased otherwise. Slowly this improved as the financial crisis passed, but almost at once the nation was plunged into another war and rose growing gave way to the 'Dig for Victory Campaign'. This was carried to extremes such as no other country knew. While he was away in hospital one hybridist had all his seedlings ploughed under, unknown to him. The result was disastrous for British raisers after the war, for this policy put them ten years behind their world competitors and lost the country much-needed foreign currency. Occupied territories, on the other hand, had been encouraged to continue. Before the Second World War the greatest advance had come via the Poulsen family, who did more to increase sales by raising the strain later called floribundas, so widening the purpose of the rose, than any other raiser. 'Kirsten' and 'Else

Poulsen' (S. Poulsen 1924) and later 'Karen Poulsen' (1933) made an amazing impact on the rose world. W. Kordes's 'Crimson Glory' 1935 and 'Orange Triumph' 1937 were but two of the successes which continued after the war years, and the very fine *spinosissima* hybrids, the Frühlings group, of which Frühlingsgold is the most popular, suggested a new dimension for shrub roses.

It was not until the end of this period that 'Peace' (Meilland 1946) set a new standard for H.T. roses. It was this variety which was to have as profound an effect on the habit of the rose as Pernet-Ducher had in the previous twenty-five years on colour.

It was during this period that the Society took one of its most important steps. Earlier, a demand had arisen for somewhere to test roses before they came on the market, but expense proved the main obstacle. This was overcome by Courtney Page offering a piece of land adjoining his home and garden in 1928. He also offered to act as supervisor, again reducing costs. One should always associate the success of this venture with the Rose Foreman—later Superintendent of the Trial Grounds—E. Baines, whose long association with it lasted from the original 'Haywards Heath' through the 'Oaklands' period and finished at our present trial grounds at Bone Hill, St. Albans, the toughest assignment of all. He was retired at the age of seventy-two having won the esteem and respect of both raisers and Committee as one of the greatest rosarians of his generation. He was fittingly awarded the Dean Hole Medal. It was typical of Sydney Cant that he spared his own foreman for this world-important work. While the Gold Medal and Certificate of Merit were still given on the show bench, the winning of a Trial Ground Certificate was not at first considered essential for obtaining a Show Award. This came later when confidence in the Trials had been established.

During this period much good work was also done by British raisers, whose work is recorded in our next chapter.

It was at this time that rose growing became a business as well as a way of life. Mechanization entered into the work and costs became paramount for survival. It is worth comparing the prices of new seedling roses which in the 1870s were fifteen to twenty shillings each and had by now become three-and-six to five shillings, although grafted plants could be purchased in the year of introduction for fifteen shillings each.

Showing continued and in 1927 the great Summer Show was moved from Regent's Park to the Royal Hospital, Chelsea where it remained until 1939. All Society shows were held in the R.H.S. Hall after this, but the Spring Show ceased in 1939. Costs had risen so that few could afford the necessary labour and fuel. One should record the importance attached to the awarding of the Gold Medal and Certificate of Merit at the shows. This was undoubtedly the highlight. What's new at the Show? was the constant question, and much of the wider interest excited came through the wide Press publicity. The abandonment of this method may be justified, but it also removed one of the great publicity points of the Show.

The great tradition that Society affairs were in the hands of those who could both grow and show their roses, continued. In many cases Council members could write about roses too, and the members were fortunate in the calibre of their presidents who were often not only great rosarians, but also men with fine records of personal service in other walks of life.

At the beginning of this period Her Majesty Queen Mary became Royal Patroness and showed a keen interest in the Society's Shows which she often visited. In 1926, the Golden Jubilee of the Society, the membership rose to 14,105. The Spring Show was a delight and there were outstanding amateur exhibits by Sir Edward Holland, H. R. Darlington, Sidney F. Jackson and J. N. Hart, all either past or future presidents and usually with keen rosarian gardeners behind them. Two roses always showed particularly well, 'Mrs. Foley Hobbs' (1910 Alex Dickson & Sons) and 'Maréchal Niel'. A great feature of the Shows at this time and for many years were the decorative tables though bowls and baskets and the tradition of floral art have reached new dimensions and provoked even greater interest since then. At this time pot plants were still a feature of the shows, although, like the exhibition boxes, there were smaller areas and fewer exhibitors.

At the Summer Shows in this period Elisha J. Hicks dominated the major classes, although Alex Dickson & Sons more than once wrested the Championship Trophy from them. Competition was keen, for there were ten entries in this 10 × 8-ft table class. The Jubilee year saw six shows, the Spring, Summer, New Roses and Autumn Shows in London, a Provincial Show at Leeds and a further Show at Southport where the Trades Exhibits were divided into Northern and Southern sections, for at this time of year Northern exhibitors were at their peak, and Southern growers were over their main blooming period.

In 1928 an 'International Rose Conference' was held, but all speakers were British.

In 1930 the 'talk of the show' was 'Dainty Bess', the crowning achievement in single H.T. roses. From time to time these lovely single roses, such as 'Irish Elegance', 'Irish Fireflame' and 'Isobel' had given a special elegance to the decorative classes, and Miss Archer, the daughter of the raiser of 'Dainty Bess', showed the single roses to perfection in her table decorations of that time.

In the great Summer Show of 1932, amid fierce competition, R. Harkness & Co. won the Championship Trophy. The contribution of Willie Harkness to the Rose Society went far beyond the magnificent massed groups, mostly of exhibition blooms, in which he excelled, for his happy personality won him the highest esteem everywhere. His contribution to the Society at times of difficulty can only be acknowledged; they will never be excelled.

This show was indicative of the abilities of the great amateurs. The area of Potters Bar seemed to encourage rose experts. J. N. Hart and H. R. Darlington excelled in their classes. Bertram Park, W. E. Moore and Charles H. Rigg won their respective classes and were all important contributors to the work of the Society in other ways.

It is impossible to do justice to these crowded years. A unique feature of 1935 was the cancellation, for the first time in fifty-nine years, of the Summer Show, owing to exceptionally adverse weather conditions. This was followed by extremely good Provincial and Autumn Shows.

1936, the Diamond Jubilee year, saw the membership at 14,000. In 1938 an excellent International Conference was held. Among the papers given, those by M. Jean Gaujard and Herr Wilhelm Kordes on the cross-fertilization of roses gave the key to future rose development.

Here one should pause, for many would look on this year as the end of an epoch. Here one said good-bye to the professional gardener employed by the amateur, and bade farewell to the activities of some nursery firms for whom the future years proved too bleak. After this too, the Society, beset by wartime difficulties, would have to face recession and retrenchment. It was now that the carefully husbanded reserve fund of the Society was invaluable in continuing a policy temporarily slowed down but not deflected.

In 1939 Shows were limited to the Summer Show in London and the Provincial Show in Leicester, while 1940 saw a big drop in receipts and there were no Shows. There were no Shows in 1941 and no Council Report was published in the attenuated annual, and this continued until 1948, when a larger annual under new editorship became possible. In 1942 both Summer and Autumn Shows were held, although greatly limited, as they were the following year too. The Shows were cancelled in 1944 owing to damage to the Halls by enemy action. The Summer and Autumn Shows were held in 1945. The Summer Report ends: 'Looking backwards and remembering all the loveliness that was displayed that day . . . the Summer Show of 1945 is but a foretaste of the beauties and achievements to come.' From then on many pre-war exhibitors, especially famous nursery firms, were missing from the shows.

The Summer Show for 1946 was postponed from 28th June to 4th July and in 1947 the last *Annual* was sent out under the name of Courtney Page. He died on 8th September 1947, having been a member for fifty-four years. He had lifted the Society from a membership of about 1,000 in 1915 and a debt of £1,500 to stability both financially and numerically.

The time had come for change. In 1948 T. T. Leach became acting secretary, but H. Edland, who had been trained under Courtney Page, was given the post the following year. Bertram Park, O.B.E., was appointed editor. One should remember that a publications committee was in operation and took some of the responsibility for all publications. The financial position was reviewed, and with rapidly increasing membership under peacetime conditions, the possibility of a new trial ground with the resulting upheaval could be viewed with equanimity. A site was found at Oaklands, the Hertfordshire Institute of Agriculture. Work was started on 17th June 1948 and the first roses planted the following autumn. The site was excellent and was the happiest home for rose growing the Society has yet had.

In 1950 the first Provincial Show since the war was held at Wolverhampton, and the trial grounds were officially opened on 26th June 1950. We were fortunate in that both the Principal, Mr. J. Hunter Smith and the Horticultural Superintendent, Mr. A. H. Lugg were keenly interested in roses and assisted the Society in every possible way.

1951 closed this period on an optimistic note. Having endured great difficulties and major changes in leadership and policy, the forward look of all was encouraged by increasing membership and revenue, and above all by the widening outlook of the Society. The Council were beginning to feel the important part they had to play in advancing its interests.

Before we close this period, a glance back at the very difficult time through which the nurserymen passed during the early war years would help us to gain a right perspective for that sombre period. Very much depended upon the agricultural committees of the area, but many rose growers found themselves compelled to destroy their stocks of roses without compensation, and to begin again as small farmers or vegetable growers, reduced in labour and capital. The most severe blow was to the raiser of new roses who often was compelled to destroy his carefully selected stocks, so that when war was over he had to begin again and was, as I said, ten years behind his more fortunate foreign competitors. That these raisers did begin again is a tribute to the persistent determination of those for whom rose raising was more than a profession, it was a vocation.

1951–1976

The last twenty-five years of the Society's history have been years of great expansion, though threatened toward the end by some contraction enforced by the demands of inflation, but even so they are years of which any society could be proud. They began with a new full-time secretary, a new editor and a little earlier, a new and excellent treasurer. The earlier part of this period saw a record rate of increase from 27,500 members with 249 affiliated societies in 1951 to over 90,000 with over 800 affiliated societies by 1963. 1963 was the last year Bertram Park edited *The Rose Annual*. In 1951 Royalton Kisch induced a somewhat reluctant Society to apply for recognition as a 'charity'. By this act of foresight he greatly helped the finances of the Society for income tax was eased immediately. He always placed his acute legal mind at the service of the Society, and served as president from 1961 to 1962.

On the death of Queen Mary in 1953, Her Royal Highness the Princess Royal honoured the Society by becoming its patron. In memory of the late Queen's long association the Queen Mary Commemoration Medal for successful British hybridists was established, and seven hybridists were awarded this honour at that time. In the 1952 *Annual* the death of Gulliver Speight is recorded, one of the oldest and best-known exhibitors. For many years his spare figure bent over his precious 'box' exhibits was a part of the shows.

In 1955 the Summer Show brought a gentle criticism of the heavy massed effect of the average stand. It took many years to achieve an improvement but the interest and beauty of the stands of John Mattock Ltd. show that firms are now learning to avoid overcrowding. The massive banks of majestic flowers are giving way to a display where the grace and natural character of the rose in its charm of flower, foliage and fruit portray its possibilities in the modern garden throughout the growing season.

In 1956 a brave attempt was made to revive the showing of roses in the Spring by exhibiting in special classes by permission of the R.H.S.

In 1957 A. Norman became president. Few men have had so wide a knowledge of or success with the rose. As an hybridist he reached his zenith in one great leap with two of the greatest roses of that period 'Frensham' and 'Ena Harkness'. Although he never attained such heights again he produced many good cultivars later. As an author, as an exhibitor and above all as a judge of a new rose, he has had few equals.

In 1958 another International Rose Conference was held in London when speakers from Australia, Germany, the U.S.A. and Britain gave excellent papers. A noteworthy paper by Wilhelm Kordes was given on 'Breeding for Hardiness'. The Conference Committee under the able chairmanship of B. W. W. Sampson set a new high standard for later conferences.

In the 1959 *Annual* a new position, that of Honorary Scientific Adviser, was ably filled by the enthusiastic and knowledgeable E. F. Allen, M.A., Dip. Agri. (Cantab.), whose work and influence has since been at the service of the Society. His presidency was from 1975 to 1976. In 1959 the Society decided to move its by then inadequate headquarters from 117 Victoria Street, Westminster, and eventually bought Bone Hill at Chiswell Green, St. Albans. During this period, and both before and after, the Society was greatly indebted to Mr. H. G. Clacy who used his skill and professional knowledge in the purchase, upkeep and extension of the Society's property. One of the prime instigators of this move was Mr. F. Fairbrother, M.Sc., F.R.I.C. He did much to encourage the difficult search and bring it to a successful conclusion. An outstanding exhibitor, especially at the Spring Show, and an author of authority, his keen wit and meticulous accuracy were seen best when the annual report came before the Council for adoption. The Society owes much to him throughout the years, and he is still unflagging in his attendance as New Seedlings judge. He was elected president from 1959 to 1960. His genial and kindly personality is typical of the helpful spirit which pervades our Society.

A further innovation was the beginning of a series of Rose Gardens where award-winning roses could be grown under other climatic conditions. The first two were in Cardiff and Harlow Car to be followed later by a number throughout the British Isles. Membership was advancing rapidly, and was 72,000 in 1960. In 1961 the Society decided to move the Show to Alexandra Palace which although away from the centre of London provided excellent car parking, and thanks to careful planning, transport to and from the Underground was equally easy. In the succeeding years despite catering and other difficulties with increased expenditure, the greater accommodation was well used. At the same time the Society was settling in to its new headquarters and membership was given as a record 79,712. In 1962 membership rose to 86,400 and in the same year extensions were made to the Trial Ground accommodation. The first Show at Alexandra Palace saw an attendance of 60,000.

1962 recorded the deaths of two past presidents. The passing of John N. Hart who had joined the Society in 1906 severed the tenuous link with the early days. He had been a great exhibitor winning the highest awards at the Spring, Summer, Provincial and Autumn Shows. He was president during 1939 and 1940 and honorary treasurer from 1949 until his death in 1963. His was a happy personality enjoyed by many. In the same year Oliver Mee, O.B.E. died. He had been president from 1955 to 1956. A very keen exhibitor he became a successful hybridist, winning a Gold Medal for his H.T. rose, 'Ethel Sanday'. He was a north-countryman and applied his official training to produce the briefest Council meetings I can remember. The third loss was Gilbert Burch who died in his first year as deputy president.

The new headquarters of the Society were sufficiently advanced in 1963 for its official opening by the Royal Patron, Her Royal Highness the Princess Royal.

In 1964 the Society, in line with many enlightened employers, established a Supplementary Staff Pension Scheme. Mr. Leonard Hollis, a vice-president well known for his articles in the *Annual* was appointed editor and produced his first of many excellent *Annuals*. He retired in 1975, much to everyone's regret. On 15th December 1964 Harry Edland died suddenly. He had served the Society most worthily from junior to secretary for forty-two years. The service he gave is best seen in the growth and strength of the Society. The pavilion erected in the Society grounds and the Medal Award for fragrance perpetuate his memory. He grew in personality and stature with the Society he loved and served. During these years the Society was honoured in its presidency by Major-General R. F. B. Naylor. He served in two periods, 1963 to 1964 and 1967 to 1968. Few people have had so great an impact on the Society. He was almost passionately attached to its well-being, and Bone Hill might at times have been his second home. Not only was he a keen yet humble rosarian, but those who later attended his memorial service realized how simply he carried the deserved honours he had received in a full and dedicated life of service in many spheres.

It was on 26th February 1965 that the Society changed its name to the Royal National Rose Society, by gracious command of Her Majesty the Queen. Much preliminary guidance and work had been carried out by Mr. Gordon Edwards, C.B.E., to achieve this happy conclusion.

In recording a membership of 109,500 members in 1966 the first warning note is sounded. The Society was losing money on new members who paid the lower sum of 10s 6d per year, a trifling sum for the many advantages received. It was because many members were paying the higher rate of £1 1s that the Society managed to pay its way. At this time, 1965–6, Mr. F. A. Gibson was president and ably guided the Society in its many problems.

In 1968 a fourth International Conference was held when a Federation of National Rose Societies was advocated by our Society. The objectives were stated as: 'To co-ordinate any activities of an international character which have as their object the development and knowledge of the Rose. To disseminate information of a scientific and cultural nature. To regulate and standardize as far as may be possible in the light of different national needs such matters pertaining to Conferences and other International meetings or assemblies.' Membership was to be open to all recognized National Societies. The Council agreed to participate, and accepted responsibility for the Secretariat for the first three years. Thanks to an excellent and painstaking sub-committee under the chairmanship of B. W. W. Sampson, an expert and truly international panel were chosen for a very representative programme which included such subjects as Rose Propagation, Disease Control, a study session on Rose Classification, Flower Photography, Feeding Roses and Rose Breeding, the Value of Shrub Roses in the Garden, Rose Viruses, Informal Gardening with Roses and Climbing Roses.

Contributors from France, Germany, Holland, Israel, New Zealand, Poland and the U.S.A., as well as the United Kingdom took part.

In this year the difficulties of finance led to a resolution to level the subscription to £1 per member. When this was implemented in January 1970 the membership fell to 103,000. For the next few years this drop was to continue and the Society, like others of a specialist nature, was to face the effect of inflation driving up expenses and pulling down membership. A further contribution by the Society to rose showing was the introduction of examinations for rose judges.

An innovation was the *Bulletin* in 1970, a rose magazine to maintain interest in the Society's work the year round. The First International Rose Convention was held in Hamilton, New Zealand in 1971 when twenty-five British members attended. The inaugural meeting of the World Federation of Rose Societies was held during the week. Dr. R. C. Allen of the American Rose Society became president and F. M. Bowen, deputy president. The secretary of the Federation was our secretary L. G. Turner. Frank Bowen has served our Society in very many ways, as treasurer from 1964 to 1968 when he became deputy president and as president in 1971 to 1972, but his interest in the international aspect was shown in Australia, and again at the New Zealand Conference, when his tact and forbearance, as well as diplomacy, helped to launch this new international venture.

In 1972 we were reminded that the Spring Show which had languished was beginning to appeal more widely, and fresh blood among the stalwarts was bringing new life and stronger competition. At the end of the year two great rosarians died. One, Bertram Park died on 25th December 1972; he had been editor of *The Rose Annual* and other publications from 1947 to 1963. He had many qualifications for this onerous duty, but was also a well-known exhibitor, author and hybridist. The other was the much loved John Clarke who held office from 1969 to 1970. He died suddenly on 22nd November 1972. He had been a fount of inspiration on committees and all work of the Society and it was sad that his boundless, compulsive energy burnt itself out in willing service to so many, so soon. It was a delight to see John Clarke and Frank Naylor working together in harmony on their many projects.

In 1973 the Summer Show returned to the R.H.S. Halls, partly for economy and partly because trade exhibits were filling less space, as they too were hit by soaring costs and falling sales. That the Society was filling as important a role as ever is shown by the fact that there were now 1,300 affiliated societies. During these latter years the presidents, including Frank Bowen and Dick Balfour, visited European and other Rose *Concours* helping to weld all rose growers in international accord.

A special General Meeting was held on 29th June 1972, when the president, Dick Balfour, took the meeting into the confidence of the Council, and in a lucid statement explained the unhappy position in which the Society had been placed by having to pay Value Added Tax on its already shrinking revenue. The annual subscription was raised to £1.75. This led to a very considerable drop in membership. Most unusually, but understandably, a small loss was sustained on the year's working.

After many years the Society moved their Provincial Show from Leeds to Holker Hall near Grange-over-Sands. Mr. F. E. Owen became Amateur Champion for the fifth year in succession.

Although Leonard Turner, who succeeded Harry Edland as secretary, has received little mention throughout this period, he has played a most important part in the efficient running of the Society, both in its organization and in implementing the instructions of the Committee and Council. Few people have responded to demand as he has, and his integrity, business acumen and happy personality have had a profound effect on the Society's well-being. His judgement and opinions, given without fear or favour, have won for him the high regard and deep respect reserved for those who prove themselves completely competent.

In previous periods some personalities among the nurserymen have received special mention, but the difficulties of selection at the moment may be realized. Probably one who has done much for the Society, both as exhibitor and Council member, is the nephew of Willie Harkness, Jack, whose stands have followed in the true Harkness tradition. One who held a unique position in the affection and respect of members was John Mattock, whose modesty was only matched by his efficiency and good judgement. Little wonder that his firm continues as past-masters of exhibition. Still flourishing and maintaining their good name are Cants (who celebrated their first two hundred years in 1965), with Mr. Pawsey to guide them; Alex Dickson with A. P. C. (Pat) Dickson maintaining the good name and reputation of his great firm; a more colourful nurseryman is Sam McGredy IV, now of New Zealand, whose epoch-making roses, including his hand-painted varieties, are known and grown throughout the world. The flamboyant Harry Wheatcroft Roses, built on salesmanship, had an amazing effect on the rose trade, and no one could beat Harry at spotting a winner. Of other great firms Gregory's have a deserved reputation and C. W. Gregory gave time and his shrewd judgement to the Society's affairs.

A quiet and lovable character who served the Society in many ways, especially as a shrewd judge of a good rose, was Ernest H. Morse whose namesake rose gained a Gold Medal in 1964, the year of his death.

Of necessity many honoured names have had to be omitted, but one is mindful that however good leadership may be, much depends upon the many and the importance of the formation of local rose societies and the band of experts who by their lectures, advice and encouragement make new recruits and weld the mature membership into a harmonious whole. Nor should the work of scientific endeavour be forgotten, for by grants for research and publications and by the appointment of a scientific adviser, the Society has helped to make real advance possible.

In conclusion I would remind readers of the broad work of the Society. There are three Shows held in London; there are rose competitions at the end of April or early May; there is a full Show occupying the two R.H.S. Halls for two days at the end of June or early July and an Autumn Show in mid September. There is a Northern Show now held at Holker Hall but for many years at Leeds. There are also special R.N.R.S. classes held at many Provincial Shows. There are numerous display gardens to be visited. There are International Conventions to be encouraged, and the special Convention to be held in Oxford to celebrate the centenary of the Society in 1976. There are many publications, many free to members, such as the *Rose Bulletin, The Rose Annual,* the *Cultivation of the Rose,* the *Select List of Roses.* There are judges' examinations, and a panel of lecturers, as well as films and slides available. There is a valuable library for the use of members, a Rose Variety Directory, and special Members' badges and ties. In addition there are the Society's gardens which offer all the best varieties on display, as well as the Test Garden which supplies information and awards for outstanding new roses.

There are many awards and trophies for outstanding exhibits. There is a president who holds office, for two years usually, followed by his deputy president who has served the previous two years. There is an elected Council of thirty-six members, some of whom retire in rotation, and sixteen vice-presidents elected for long and special service to the Society. In addition there is a short list of honorary vice-presidents. The highest award for personal service is the Dean Hole Memorial Medal. The Finance and General Purposes Committee controls the business. The New Seedlings Judging Committee of twenty-one members with an elected amateur chairman makes the awards at the trial grounds. A member having an interest in a rose withdraws from the assessment. An exhibition committee prepares Show schedules. The Gardens Management Committee sees to the running and general management of the gardens at present under the competent Superintendency of Donald Maginnis. Finally there is a publications committee to assist the editor. Those who have worked on the Council for many years are amazed at the amount of voluntary effort and skilled advice given so readily for the well-being of the Society.

It is to be hoped that with such firm foundations the succeeding years may strengthen the Royal National Rose Society even more and extend its influence.

 CHAPTER XII

One Hundred Years of New Seedling British Roses

1876–1901

One might say that the National Rose Society began its life at just about the right time from the point of view of raising new British roses. The French had largely monopolized the production and marketing of new roses from the time of the Empress Josephine, who really popularized the rose by encouraging the work of rose raisers. There was one great difference between the multitude of seedling roses raised in France during this period and the few roses beginning with Bennett, the first true hybridist in Britain, in 1882. The French relied upon their climate to produce thousands of seed pods by natural fertilization, the crossing being carried out by natural means and the variation encouraged by planting the roses in mixed groups. This seed was collected, sown and the resulting seedlings allowed to flower in very large numbers. The better seedlings were then selected, named and marketed. They were sold largely on the embellished descriptions of their owners. Such a method led to much disappointment, and as there was little difference in colours—they were mostly red, pink and white—variety was lacking. It is interesting to note that the famous 'Maréchal Niel' (noisette, Pradel 1864), a vigorous climber, was at first dismissed as 'only a yellow rose'.

It is difficult to know why this haphazard method was used when cross-fertilization with chosen parents was well known. Possibly the French raisers of that time were less literate—they have been described as 'of foreman type'—and the keeping of records was unlikely to appeal. There were, of course, exceptions and although William Paul had advocated the keeping of records in his *The Rose Garden* (1848), the Englishman Henry Bennett, who first advocated and indeed pioneered the method of deliberate hand pollination from known parents for commercial use, owed his initiation to Jean Sisley of France. Bennett, of Manor Farm Nursery, Stapleford, Shrewsbury, saw the possibility of a new race and chose teas for his seed parents and hybrid perpetuals for his pollen parents. One of his first was 'Beauty of Stapleford' (1879) 'Mme Bravy' (14) × 'Countess of Oxford' H.P. (28). The genuineness of his claim to know the parentage of his seedlings was challenged. He demonstrated the truth of his claim before the Scientific Committee of the R.H.S., chaired by Sir Joseph Hooker, demonstrating his method and giving examples of the resultant seed pods and seedlings. He proved his seedlings to be true H.Ts. He strongly disagreed with Paul & Sons of Cheshunt who said that their 'Cheshunt Hybrid' was the first deliberate H.T., arguing that this was a chance seedling fertilized naturally in a greenhouse where 'Mme de Tartas' and 'Prince Camille de Rohan' were growing together. The chromosome count of 21 does agree with this putative parentage.

Once Bennett's method was used, the resulting seedlings were a great improvement on those produced by the chance methods used previously and Britain began to take the lead in rose raising. The proportion of good roses raised by the new method was amazing. About this time Mr. Dickson said he usually made about 300 crosses and raised some 3,000 seeds.

Records are not easy to obtain for the first few years but 'Sultan of Zanzibar' (1876) was raised by George Paul of Paul & Son. Two more noted in 1880 were 'Duke of Teck' (G. Paul) and 'Crown Prince' (H.P. W. Paul). The next year W. Paul sent out 'Pride of Waltham' H.P.

Now came the real break by Bennett with 'Lady Mary Fitzwilliam' (H.T. 1882), from 'Devonensis' and 'Victor Verdier' (H.P.). This became a famous stud rose. He sent out two further cultivars in that year. These were followed by 'Grace Darling' (1884), 'Her Majesty' (1885), 'Viscountess Folkestone' (1886) and finally 'Mrs. John Laing' (1887). The last was still listed in the 1910

Rose Annual as one of the best roses. The year 1891 records Alex
Dickson & Son as raising 'Margaret Dickson' ('Lady Mary Fitzwilliam' × 'Merveille de Lyon'). This is the first H.T. recorded as
having 28 chromosomes. In 1893 Bennett introduced 'Captain
Hayward' (H.P.). In 1894 William Paul sent out 'Clio' (H.P.) and
Alex Dickson & Sons 'Mrs. R. G. Sharman Crawford'. In 1895
Alex Dickson raised the famous 'Mrs. W. J. Grant' (H.T.). They
followed this with 'Killarney' (H.T. 1898), which with its sports
was popular for many years and in 1899 introduced 'Bessie Brown'
and 'Mrs. Mawley'. I am indebted to the present Alexander
Dickson for a note of the personalities involved in his firm's
hybridizing successes: his father, Alexander, began crossing and,
after producing 'Mrs. W. J. Grant', handed over to his brother
George in 1893. He continued until 1927 although the present
Alexander had been crossing from 1922 and continued until his son
A. P. C. (Pat) Dickson took over in 1956.

In 1900 one of the most famous Dickson seedlings made its
appearance. This was 'Liberty' (H.T.), a child of 'Lady Mary
Fitzwilliam' and a parent of the famous forcing rose 'Richmond',
and of many others. The final year of this period was noted for
another Dickson introduction, 'Mildred Grant'.

Looking back over these twenty-five years we note the increasing
progress made through controlled crossing and the accumulating
knowledge of pedigree parentage brought considerable acceleration
in results. Bennett had guided the rose world into a more controlled
approach to breeding, and Dickson's use of the famous 'Lady Mary
Fitzwilliam' was producing roses which were far superior in health
and freedom of flower to the previous H.Ps., the last of note of this
type being the famous 'Frau Karl Druschki' (1900 P. Lambert).
One of the great factors encouraging fertility was that the H.Ts.
from being infertile triploids had become fertile tetraploids.

1901–1926

This second twenty-five years of the Rose Society was probably the
most exciting period ever known in the raising of new roses. Firstly,
there was the break produced by Pernet-Ducher, see page 229. By

his introduction of new blood through *R. lutea* the colour range was dramatically increased. In 1901 Jackson & Perkins introduced the new type of rambler 'Dorothy Perkins' (*R. wichuraiana* × Mme G. Luizet). Barbier continued with this strain, as did Van Fleet. The polyantha rose came into its own with 'Orleans Rose' (Levavasseur 1909) and its many sports including the first orange-scarlet. This strain was upgraded by the Poulsen family by the production of 'Rodhatte' ('Mme Norbert Levavasseur' × 'Richmond'), but it was not until the two roses 'Else' and 'Kirsten Poulsen' (S. Poulsen 1924) that the floribunda rose became a recognized strain, although it was known at first as a hybrid polyantha. At the close of this period the only British contribution came in the form of so-called hybrid musks, raised by the Revd. J. H. Pemberton, although the initial work was done by P. Lambert in 1904, when he raised 'Trier'. This strain was to be used later by Wilhelm Kordes.

The above recital may seem strange when writing of British raisers, but no raiser works independently, and is himself greatly indebted to other raisers for their research and the resulting seedlings. Having noted this, we plunge into a rapidly increasing number of raisers and their results. The next rose of lasting importance was 'Hugh Dickson' (H.P.) raised by Hugh Dickson of Belfast. In 1904 'Lady Ashtown' and 'Dean Hole' were sent out by Dickson's of Newtownwards. In 1905 the same firm brought out 'Irish Elegance', a five-petalled flower of surpassing beauty. In the same year S. McGredy & Son began to win awards for their new roses. These were bred by McGredy II who won his first N.R.S. gold medal in 1905 with 'The Countess of Gosford' (H.T.).

The artistic appeal of such lovely flowers with their long shapely pointed buds, influenced raisers until the more free flowering floribundas took their place. Probably the culmination of these beauties was found in 'Dainty Bess' (H.T. W. E. B. Archer 1926). In 1907 'Dorothy Page Roberts' was introduced by Alex Dickson. From now on the task of making a selection of those cultivars vital to rose progress becomes harder, although with the advent of the *Rose Annual* there is a more reliable source of information. In 1908 'Molly Sharman Crawford' was sent out by Alex Dickson.

This was unusual as it was a tea. In 1909 Messrs. J. Veitch & Sons introduced *R. moyesii* from China. While not a British-raised rose, it was to influence rose lovers by reminding them of the possibility of roses as fruit as well as flowering shrubs. It is to be regretted that the wide range of *moyesii* seedlings raised by Hurst of Cambridge were never put into commerce. They were grown for some years at Doncaster's Nurseries in Cambridge and were of great interest. In 1909 Hugh Dickson sent out 'Lady Pirie', a beautiful rose of slender petalage and in pastel shades, for which he obtained the Gold Medal. In 1910 McGredy II introduced two great roses, 'His Majesty', a red H.T., and 'Mrs. Herbert Stevens', a very popular white for many years, with long slender stems and exquisite pointed blooms. The parentage 'Frau Karl Druschki' (H.P.) × 'Niphetos' (T.) is of interest, showing that McGredy went back to the source for H.Ts. and produced less fertile triploids at his early attempts.

It is interesting that in the same year, 1910, two teas were introduced, 'Lady Hillingdon', unique for its pansy purple wood and foliage. This was introduced by Lowe and Shawyer and was a cross between 'Papa Gontier' × 'Mme Hoste'. The other, 'Mrs. Foley Hobbs' was sent out by A. Dickson. This is probably the last time teas made an impact on breeding. 1912 saw the introduction by William Paul of one of the greatest roses, 'Ophelia'. It is noted for its perfume and forcing qualities especially in its deeper sports, 'Mme Butterfly' and 'Lady Sylvia' which were sold in millions as under-glass cut roses. In 1913 a hybrid polyantha, 'Susie', was introduced by Easlea. This was an important period for Pernet-Ducher whose introductions at that time included 'Rayon d'Or' (1910) and 'Mme E. Herriot' (1913) and 'Constance' (1915), all contributing to the material for British raisers. In 1914 Pemberton's roses 'Danae' and 'Moonlight', both registered as H.Ts. came out. This was a heavy year for A. Dickson's introductions, as they sent out seven sorts including the famous 'Red Letter Day' (H.T.), a semi-single red and 'Mrs. Wemyss Quin' (H.T.), a creamy yellow bedding rose. 'Augustus Hartman' (H.T.) was raised and introduced by B. R. Cant. Here we note the increasing number of raisers making their contribution to the swelling tide of types and varieties.

1915 was a vintage year, with five raisers contributing their roses. There were 'Gorgeous' (H.T.) from Hugh Dickson of Belfast; 'Cupid', a lovely semi-single pastel peach semi climber from B. R. Cant; 'Paul's Scarlet Pillar' from Wm. Paul, an outstanding contribution to climbers; 'Paul's Lemon Pillar' (Clg. H.T.) from George Paul; 'Isobel (H.T. single) and 'Golden Emblem' (H.T.) from McGredy, the first deep yellow raised by a British raiser but very prone to die-back, as were most of that colour for some years to come. 1916 was another great year despite the war, when Dr. A. K. Williams, an amateur, raised 'Emily Gray', a yellow rambler; Alex Dickson brought out the very popular bright red semi-single 'K. of K.', while McGredy introduced 'Christine' and 'Miss Willmott'. In 1917 the 'neap tide' period persisted. McGredy brought out 'The Queen Alexandra Rose', a most striking bicolour, as well as 'Emma Wright', clear orange-salmon; Alex Dickson had 'Sunstar', of few petals in yellow splashed scarlet. William Paul produced his most famous rose, 'Mermaid', Pemberton another of his 'musk hybrids' 'Pax', Easlea his unusual cadmium 'Lamia' and B. R. Cant a popular red in 'Covent Garden' as well as one of the best forcing roses in 'Golden Ophelia'. A wonderful year to which six firms contributed roses which remained in commerce for many years, with 'Pax' and 'Mermaid', and particularly the latter, unsurpassed. 1919 saw the introduction of a number of good roses, 'Mrs. Henry Morse' (McGredy), a bicolour pink which, despite its mildew, was grown in thousands for many years. 'Prosperity' continued the Pemberton line, while Bees came to the fore as raisers of good roses with 'Independence Day', sunflower-gold stained apricot. In 1920 came 'Mrs. Charles Lamplough' and in 1921 the deep yellow 'Mabel Morse' (McGredy), but a poor growth measured by reluctant inches. Alex Dickson introduced 'Betty Uprichard', a bicolour pink which then had a luminous glow, unequalled since. B. R. Cant continued with a short sturdy gold shaded carmine in 'Revd. Page Roberts' (H.T.). Murrells showed 'Coral Cluster', one of the few outstanding of the many 'Orleans' sports which sold in thousands especially as forced pot plants. The year 1922 continued fruitful. Alex Dickson showed a magnificent pair in 'Lady Inchquin', a bright cerise, and 'Shot Silk', which is still with us. B. R. Cant showed 'Sovereign', and Chaplin Bros. brought out the tough 'Mrs. Henry Bowles', one of the best pink roses ever staged. The next year 1923 was quieter, but 'Florence L. Izzard' was a popular yellow, and improvement in growth and hardiness. 1924 was noteworthy for 'Else' and 'Kirsten Poulsen' by Poulsen's of Denmark and from then on floribunda roses edged their way on to the market. In 1925 'Marcia Stanhope', a white scented H.T., was the premier rose. Unfortunately the raiser, George Lilly, had little stock to supply an unfulfilled demand. So we come to the final year of this period, 1926. McGredy's brought out three very good roses that year, 'Mrs. A. R. Barraclough', an enormous self-pink, 'White Ensign', a small perfectly formed white, with excellent foliage, and 'Norman Lambert', yellow with orange and scarlet. This was to be the last time McGredy II exhibited for he died in 1926 having become famous throughout the world as a great raiser of new roses. Born with opportunity which was knocking at the door of success, he flung it wide open to delight the rose world, and with Dickson's brought Britain to the forefront as raisers of famous roses. Alex Dickson showed the perfect exhibition rose in deep pink, scented 'Dame E. Helen', but never a bedding rose. Dobbie's of Edinburgh introduced 'Duchess of Atholl', a most unusual colour, burnt orange, a tribute to a great raiser, whoever he was. Last, but not least, was the newcomer, W. E. B. Archer, whose 'Dainty Bess' with silver pink, five-petalled blooms with chocolate anthers, crowned the series of beautiful and very artistic five-petalled H.Ts.

Looking back over these twenty-five years, I would repeat that this was probably the most exciting period ever to be known in the history of seedling British roses. In this time the rose took a leap forward in colour, growth, freedom of flower and variation of form, which it has never surpassed since. Even so, great roses were rare, as they always will be, and hybridizing is more important for the general raising of standards than for the few flashing comets which cause a fleeting stir for a few brief years in the world of roses.

1926–1951

The next twenty-five years might be called years of consolidation, leading to the great advance achieved in 1945 by the coming of 'Peace'. Of interest too, as the forerunner of the so-called perpetual climbers was 'Guinée' (Mallerin 1938). To Kordes one owes the later interest in shrub roses with the raising, towards the end of the period, of the Frühlings group, during the 1940s. This group brought in the species *R. spinossima altica*, opening the way to another group in the final twenty-five years. It was largely because of the British Government's wartime policy of halting work on hybridization that most of the advances in this period came from abroad where growers did not suffer the same handicap.

Three varieties introduced in 1927 should be mentioned. The first was the rambler 'Thelma', a distinct advance in quality of flower on the older roses of this type. Walter Easlea raised a great many good roses, although few, if any, made a lasting impression. The next rose, 'Bedford Crimson' (H.T.), short petalled, deep red and scented, was for a time a very popular bedding rose, and but for the untimely death of the raiser Edward Laxton of Laxton Bros. during an air-raid, he might well have become one of our best hybridizers, for he raised a number of sorts including the strawberry-red 'Mrs. E. W. Laxton'. The third introduction which should have special recognition as one of the most interesting and useful parents of famous roses is 'Charles P. Kilham' (McGredy). This was introduced by the firm Geo. Beckwith & Son who, at that time, acted as a clearing house for a great many new roses each year, offering at least thirty to fifty sorts a year from world-wide sources. Charles P. Kilham was foreman there, one of a large band of little-known men whose contributions enriched the rose world. One might mention in the same breath Tom Beatty of B. R. Cant, whose seedlings brought prestige to that firm for many years, including this period. His contribution in 1928 was one of the best roses he ever sent out, 'Lady Forteviot', a lovely orange-apricot H.T. Bees sent out their brilliant red 'J. C. Thornton' and W. E. B. Archer won most of the publicity that year with his deep red, sweetly scented 'Daily Mail Scented'. Easlea introduced 'Aphrodite', a lovely semi-single, shell-pink H.T.

In 1929 it was Alex Dickson's turn with 'Lucie Marie', a very fine yellow shaded carmine, and 'Barbara Richards', a beautiful white shaded fawn, of exhibition form, very popular for many years, but the rose of the year was undoubtedly 'Mrs. Sam McGredy' of similar but deeper colouring, fading to salmon. Its young foliage was a beautiful foil, and its climbing form which arrived later produced some of the finest flowers imaginable. In 1930 'Lilian' (B. R. Cant) completed their sturdy race of shaded yellows with a clear deep yellow slightly stained carmine. This was probably the most hardy rose of that colour yet bred. In 1932 McGredy brought out one of their finest bedding roses in the short growing pink 'Picture', aptly named. Another worthy rose was 'Sir Henry Segrave', pale lemon yellow (A. Dickson). 1933 was a year of variety. McGredy sent out 'Rex Anderson' (H.T.), huge exhibition flowers in pale creamy yellow, Alex Dickson distributed 'Lord Lonsdale', shown surpassingly well, a deep buttercup yellow, magnificent in flower but paltry in growth. Two new raisers appeared, D. Prior and Son. They introduced 'Betty Prior' (Fl.), a very free-flowering pink with masses of small flowers in large heads, which is still popular for massing in the United States, and a little later the deep red 'Donald Prior' (Fl.). These were two of the best floribundas ever produced.

So we come to a quiet year, 1934, noteworthy for the deaths of two great rosarians, Miss Willmott, and Sam McGredy III whose premature death cut short the fulfilment of a great promise for his rose, 'Mrs. Sam McGredy', which was one of the finest roses ever produced.

1935 is noteworthy for the appearance of a great hybridist whose work had covered pyrethrums and delphiniums up till that period. Herbert Robinson possessed the flair and used very limited resources with unique results. With the sudden death of McGredy III it was a number of years before active hybridizing started up again under McGredy IV, and Dickson's decreased their output at the same time. It was fortunate for both the Rose Society and rose growing as a whole that Robinson's productions kept up interest until the Second World War brought a full stop to new roses. One should mention here the firm of Wheatcroft Bros., who introduced Robinson's sorts, and with their usual acumen and publicity forced these excellent roses on the public's attention. The first pair of roses and probably the most popular, were the clear yellow 'Phyllis Gold' and the brilliant red 'Christopher Stone'. That same year Chaplin Bros. contributed 'Crimson Conquest', a large once-flowering rambler; Laxton Brothers' 'Mrs. Edward Laxton'; Dickson's the pale pink 'Leading Lady'; W. E. B. Archer one of his loveliest five-petalled cluster H.Ts. in the cream 'Ellen Willmott' with its lovely pink edge, and last but not least the bicolour pink, 'Lal' of Easlea's. In 1936 some very fine foreign roses were introduced including Kordes 'Crimson Glory'. Herbert Robinson sent out 'Percy Izzard', a very good deep yellow. 1937 saw 'Sam McGredy', a large deep cream of perfect exhibition form and, speaking personally as well as historically, this year saw the introduction of 'Dainty Maid' (Fl.) (E. B. Le Grice). This lovely brier pink single maintained its popularity, especially as a medium-height hedge, for over thirty years. In 1938 one foreign rose of interest was Poulsen's 'Yellow' (Fl.), the first yellow floribunda of note, though its great fault of fading has been a fatal tendency for many yellow floribunda roses since. Robinson introduced his 'Walter Bentley', a great name among wholesale rose growers. It is a beautiful exhibition rose when well grown, but is not of bedding quality. The colour coppery orange shaded salmon could fade to a dingy salmon. A less spectacular rose, but one which stood the test of time was the sweetly scented 'Hector Deane' (McGredy), an attractive colour orange, carmine and salmon-pink, fading somewhat with age. These two roses did show that the exhibition roses of 'Walter Bentley' type were appealing to a very restricted public. It was the free-flowering, dependable, sweet scent, with attractive colouring which demanded increased production. From 1940 to 1945 rose growing gave place to the all-demanding production of food. Only McGredy's 'Salmon' and 'Cynthia Brook' were worth recording. The latter was of an unusual cadmium yellow and gave rise to good seedlings at a later date. This was a heart-breaking period for the hybridist, and Herbert Robinson returned from hospital to find his seedlings ploughed up by zealous officials. As I said earlier, such blows dealt in Britain alone to hybridists of the world put us back ten years in our recovery after the war.

1946 saw a resurgence of new roses. Most of these were of pre-war vintage, but awaiting introduction. Abroad this was the year of 'Peace' (Meilland) which was to have a profound effect on all rose breeding everywhere, giving a new standard in growth, health and size of bush and flower. At home it was the year of the greatest amateur success ever known. A. Norman, although a diamond cutter by trade, was a most knowledgeable rosarian, publishing an excellent book, and proving a successful exhibitor and an outstanding rose breeder, whose small resources were most skilfully used. He raised a number of good roses, all introduced by Harkness and Co., some posthumously. Two great roses of his were sent out in that year, one, 'Ena Harkness' (H.T.) ('Crimson Glory' × 'Southport') the finest red since 'Crimson Glory', but retaining its vivid red overlaid maroon. Well scented it produced a great number of good blooms, many of exhibition quality. Its one great fault was its weak flower head, an unforgivable sin among those who wanted flowers for cutting. This cross had a unique quality in that two other roses similar, but of more exhibition type, were said to be raised from the same seed pod, certainly the same cross. These were 'William Harvey' and 'Red Ensign'. But this triumph was not enough, and a floribunda destined to be grown in hundreds of thousands was distributed the same year, 'Frensham' (unknown seedling (rambler × *polyantha*) × 'Crimson Glory'). This vigorous, free-flowering crimson was massed everywhere until superseded by a less mildewy rival. Norman raised a number of good floribunda and hybrid tea roses later, but none rose to the stature of his first two. His once-flowering rambler was probably unique, for 'Crimson Showers' flowered at least a month later than other ramblers. In the same year McGredy's began again with 'Mrs. C. H. Rigg', a large exhibition bloom of pale lemon yellow, but easily damaged by rain. This was a characteristic trouble of many roses of that time and earlier, possibly inherited from the old tea rose, for here the pointed bloom depended on the petals wrapping themselves around their inner fellows, often enclosing the point which soon 'sealed' with wet. One of the greatest advances of the next twenty-five years was the pointed bloom of sturdier petals which did not overlap at the tip. Dickson's also introduced 'The Admiral', a useful multi-purpose H.T. in shades of pink.

In 1947 'Dusky Maiden' (E. B. Le Grice) was introduced, one of the few deep red floribunda roses with the damask perfume, a legacy of its pollen parent ('Daily Mail Scented' × 'Étoile de Hollande') × 'Else Poulsen'. This was one of a number of single and semi-single roses raised by myself to receive awards in the next few years.

In 1948 McGredy's introduced 'Rubaiyat' (H.T.), cerise crimson. This was a trouble-free rose and became a great seller in the United States.

In 1949 McGredy's sent out 'Dorothy Anderson', a grand bicolour pink for exhibition, as those who saw Mr. Allen's (Senior) bloom at Taunton will remember. It was one of the finest flowers ever seen anywhere. In the same year 'Ellinor Le Grice' (H.T.), golden yellow, came on the market. It will be remembered by myself as it was named after my wife and brought in much needed royalties in dollars during the early post-war years. It later became the parent of 'Allgold'. In 1950 McGredy's produced 'Lamplighter' (H.T.), a multi-coloured rose, and Dickson's 'Hebe', one of their long pointed bicolour pinks from a series produced over many years.

1951–1976

In 1952 'Wellworth' (H.T. E. B. Le Grice) was brought into commerce. I was warned that an award was imminent and that I must find it a name. 'Greatheart' had been turned down, and breaking my holiday on the way to the trials at Haywards Heath, I composed 'Wellworth'. Naming has always been a problem for raisers, and every year it becomes increasingly difficult.

1953 saw a change in Dickson's roses, which was to have far-reaching results. For the first time, I believe, they released a floribunda, and 'Nymph' ('Fashion' × unnamed seedling), a very double, large, pale salmon-pink, became the forerunner of many

G

highly successful varieties of floribundas. Here one should remember how interdependent raisers are on each other. Boerner of the
U.S.A. had produced 'Fashion', one of its parents, and he in turn
had depended on 'Pinocchio' (Kordes). The following year 'Anne
Letts' (H.T. Letts) deserves mention, though other good roses were
produced then too. Letts was a new raiser and this was his first and
last good effort, an immense full exhibition bloom in pale pink.
Missing 1955 we come to 1956, a year for me to remember for
'Allgold' ('Goldilocks' × 'Ellinor Le Grice') was introduced then.
This floribunda is still unbeaten for stability of colour and health
of foliage. 1958 saw three good roses by three different raisers. 'My
Choice' (H.T., 'Wellworth' × 'Ena Harkness') (E. B. Le Grice), a
lovely pink with straw-yellow reverse, won many awards both in
Britain and other parts of the world. The second was 'Teenager'
(H.T., 'Ena Harkness' × 'Sutter's Gold'). The raiser, Mr. Arnott,
produced a few excellent roses, but I believe 'Evensong' was his
last in 1963. It is to be regretted that circumstances prevented him
from adding to the few very good roses produced by British raisers
during that time. The third was 'Dorothy Peach' (H.T. H. Robinson). This very good yellow H.T. was one of many excellent roses
covering a period of over forty years of rose raising by Herbert
Robinson.

The year 1959 is memorable in that it was when the present
Sam McGredy began his range of successes, which have continued
up to the present and have contributed greatly to the advance of
the rose. In no way has this been more apparent than in growth and
health. Certainly his 'Chanelle' (Fl.) with its large healthy foliage
and delightfully restful colouring was a great beginning, enhanced
by the Gold Medal his vivid single 'Orangeade' (Fl.) received. A
rose of sterling quality in the H.Ts., was 'Silver Lining' (H.T.
Dickson). Here was a grand exhibition rose of good bedding quality.
The dearth of results British raisers had been suffering was over
and there was a flood of good new roses produced by seven
different raisers—probably an all-time record.

1960 saw 'Piccadilly' (H.T. S. McGredy IV), an all-time best in
bicolours; 'Dearest' (Fl.), a sweetly scented product of A. P. C.
Dickson; 'Lady Sonia', a shrub by Mattocks; 'Westminster' (H.T.)

by H. Robinson; 'Fervid' (Fl.), a large single unfading scarlet by Le Grice; and 'Wendy Cussons' (H.T.), an introduction of Gregory & Son, a popular forerunner of other good roses of equal merit. Finally, the posthumous 'Red Dandy', raised by Norman, almost a forerunner of floribunda-H.T. types. 1961 was far less spectacular but interesting for the first attractive lilac-mauve floribunda 'Lilac Charm' (Le Grice), and for the beginner's luck of S. A. Cobley with 'Woburn Abbey', a striking colour but with insufficient health to stay the course.

As the number of introductions increase, I shall mention only those of outstanding merit or with unusual characteristics. In 1962 'Paddy McGredy' (Fl.) was introduced; short in growth with a hybrid tea flower, it was a most interesting break. From the same raiser came the famous 'Evelyn Fison' (Fl.), whose brilliant red trusses even now bedeck many thousands of homes. The first great contribution made to exhibition roses by Sanday's Ltd. was their 'Gavotte'. The use of 'Marcel Bourgouin' and other old-type roses led to some unusual colours. 'Amberlight' (Fl.) Le Grice, not only produced the new colour, 'Egyptian Buff', but a new perfume of intense sweetness.

Among many good roses for 1963 two at least should be mentioned. The first, 'Uncle Walter', remarkable for its vigour and beauty, was raised by McGredy, and 'Scarlet Queen Elizabeth' (Fl. Dickson), is a rose which has become better and more popular as its purpose and qualities are appreciated. Both are good roses for hedges.

1964 deserves to be remembered for 'Schoolgirl' (McGredy), the first of the new climbers, which produced large flowers over an extended season. An added attraction was its orange-apricot flowers. Dickson's produced 'Sea Pearl' (Fl.-H.T. type), a typical type of their breeding with the large H.T. flowers in grouped clusters such as they introduced during that decade. At their best they were outstanding, but the large flowers brought problems in wet weather and affected their popularity especially for massing.

1965 was a quiet year. Dickson's brought out another floribunda H.T. type 'Scented Air', and McGredy's brought out a new tall yellow floribunda 'Arthur Bell' with a sweet scent. Unfortunately this faded, and its too-tight cluster of flowers have been passed on to numerous progeny. Of more lasting beauty was the lovely 'Handel' (McGredy), one of the recurrent climbers with a unique ivory flower, flushed on the outer edges with deep carmine. Gregory's, in the same year, produced a stronger growing and freer-flowering climber in 'Pink Perpetue'.

In 1966 one of the most popular and widely grown H.Ts. of the decade was produced by Dickson's. 'Grandpa Dickson' made a special niche for itself, for although the colour is pale, and at times the bud almost green, the mature flower is freely produced and is of perfect formation. This year is interesting for a unique happening when Messrs. Harkness and Cocker showed a large number of seedling roses in perfect condition and from then on continued to introduce a large number of cultivars. After the first optimistic exuberance when thirty-five were sent out in three years, the numbers decreased with greater constraint, but they had by then secured a position as leading raisers. Three roses should be mentioned for 1967. A large exhibition red by Dickson's, 'Red Devil', which, with weather protection, can give all an exhibitor demands. Another delightful rose of quite different character was the multi-flowered, semi-single floribunda 'Escapade' (Harkness). An unusual mauve-pink, this delightful plant is ideal for massed bedding. The third was 'Vesper' (Fl. Le Grice), a flower arranger's rose in a delightful pastel brown, it had character and colour to commend it. In 1968 at least two roses should be mentioned: 'Blessings' (H.T. Gregory), a lovely salmon-pink, noteworthy for its freedom of growth and flower, a true bedding rose in the best tradition; another, 'City of Belfast' (McGredy), with its brilliant scarlet-red and compact growth is now losing to its rival 'Evelyn Fison', largely on growth.

Two roses were noteworthy in 1969. 'Molly McGredy' (Fl. McGredy), one of the finest plants one could wish for, but the mixed red and white colours prevent it from becoming a rose of top popularity. The second rose was a novel break in colour: 'News' (Fl. Le Grice) was the first time the purple shades of the old garden roses had been blended with the free-flowering qualities of the floribunda.

The rose of the year in 1970 was 'Alec's Red' (H.T. Cocker), for despite the number of red roses introduced, there was and still is a need for a top-quality cultivar, combining perfection of shape with colour, perfume and growth. 'Alec's Red' was the best multi-purpose rose so far, and with its qualities combined with publicity and good showing leapt to the fore.

Of the good roses of 1971 which included 'Mala Rubenstein' (H.T. Dickson), and 'Chorus Girl' from Robinson, 'Summer Holiday' (Gregory) proved a welcome addition. Its strong and bright, almost brick-red flower grew on an excellent free-flowering plant, appearing good in all weathers. 'Mala Rubenstein' was a very large, sweetly scented exhibition bloom, deep salmon.

1972 saw a brilliant very tall H.T. more suited to a hedge than for bedding, an intense-coloured 'Super Star'. 'Alexander' (Harkness) has made a great start. 1973 saw the introduction of a change in colour from the brilliant restless shades so indicative of the times. This was 'Just Joey' (H.T. Cants), described as coppery orange veined red but fading on the outer petals. This rose is of great promise and should remain for many years.

1974 had four different roses, 'Sunsilk' (Fl.-H.T. Fryer's), a clear yellow paling with age, 'Compassion' (Clg. Harkness), sweetly scented in light salmon-pink and 'Yesterday' (Fl.-poly. Harkness) a mauvy-pink, small flowered low shrub, offering a new type for experiment. A further advance in deep purple was the full-flowered 'Great News' (H.T.-Fl. type). The colour has yet to be fully accepted, but the increase in colour range is very desirable where so many excellent roses are close replicas of those already in commerce.

Here is the place for an explanation why many excellent British roses of sterling merit are not mentioned in the foregoing list. They make their special contribution to certain types of rose growing. Dickson's, and later Sanday's, contributed many excellent exhibition roses with limited appeal to the connoisseur. McGredy offered a selection of outstanding roses especially noteworthy for their contribution to health and stamina, but their real advance in hybridizing is their 'hand-painted' roses beginning with 'Picasso', followed by 'Old Master' and 'Eye Paint' and 'Matangi'. Here is another instance of the public shying away from the rose in a new form, but the delay in full recognition may be in part due to the fact that mixed colours do not make a happy contribution to the colour scheme in garden or park.

So this review comes to an end. What has been accomplished in the hundred years? We should remember, as I have already stressed, that the advances made were not due to British roses alone, far from it. Breeding is a co-operative matter. A raiser in one country may begin a new strain as Pernet-Ducher did in France, but it takes the raisers in many parts of the world to perfect the work he so ably began.

Briefly, one may mention at least six great improvements. When the period began the average rose was a shrub with single, semi-single, or double flowers growing in clusters with weak pedicles, so that most roses hung their heads. The only way to judge the rose was by the symmetry of the outer petals of the flower (see pages 291 and 292). With the deliberate crossing of the hybrid perpetual with the tea rose a new pointed bloom, often carried singly on a stem, became the accepted form, although later the polyantha, and after the floribunda, produced large flower heads with many single, semi-double or double blooms over a long period. One of the greatest changes was in the increase in hardiness and growth of the plant. There were many tall shrubby bushes with lax growth and much mildew on the one hand, and weak thin growth in the 'teas'. Hardiness was so lacking in the latter that they were often potted up and put in cold frames for the winter. A good maiden bush of 'Mme A. Chatenay' might have one shoot 46 cm (18 in) high with a second shoot of 15 cm (6 in). One has only to think of 'Peace' to realize the vast difference that has come about. One of the most spectacular changes has come in the colour ranges. Nearly all were at first red, pink or white. Now, in addition, we have yellow, flame, scarlet, bicolours, mauve, brown and purple. Another great change has been in the increase in the flowering period, and in the quality of the petal, leading to a longer life for the individual bloom.

For the first twenty-five years of the Society's life an Autumn Show was an impossibility, there were so few roses flowering after the first early flush. In the *Gardeners' Chronicle* of 20th December

1902 we read that a second show day when advocated was turned down 'as it is the rose makes a sorry display at the end of a day'. Now, one of the difficulties is to check the bushes from flowering so they may be lifted on the nursery. A mature bush these days needs help to finish flowering to be lifted in November.

The great increase in the various uses of the rose has led to far more bushes being planted. Now the floribunda types are favourites for bedding, especially in parks where their long flowering season and great variety of colours make them a popular bedding plant. Climbing roses are now flowering for a longer period. These and many other uses have become apparent as changes in growth, health and freedom have widened the field (see Chapter I). The length of flowering period has been mentioned already but with this has gone stiff flower stems, improving the decorative purpose of the rose, added to which the present rose bloom lasts a great deal longer now when cut.

Today one might say that rose bushes are over-produced, for during this period the rose stocks were changed to hardier and more productive forms, which in their turn permitted proportionally cheaper plants.

Here then lie some answers to the question 'Why produce new cultivars?', and we can use Wren's epitaph 'Look around you' if we wish to assess the results of the hybridists' work. It would be well to remember that raising new varieties is an increasingly expensive business and fewer of those produced bring adequate returns.

There have been many encouragements to produce better roses, and some of these come from the Royal National Rose Society. Their Trial Ground Awards such as the Gold Medal, President's Trophy and Edland Memorial Medal are all encouragements to produce roses which conform to present accepted standards of behaviour, and to a lesser degree, colour.

What does the future hold? Throughout this hundred years there have always been those who could declare, 'We have arrived at the end of the road', but the rose has continued to advance. I should like to play the prophet but we may be sure that the unexpected is more likely to occur than the anticipated. It is lamentable that with millions of seedling roses being raised throughout the world so few struggle to the light of acknowledgement and fewer still endure the glare of publicity.

As in every walk of life the pressures of modern inflation with its high costs compels the professional raiser of modern roses to sell his wares or perish. To introduce new species into the present rose genetic bank demands years of costly experiment and this must be the work of the subsidized scientist. There is room for the dedicated amateur to explore the possibilities of one of the hundred and more remaining species to be tried but he would need to begin young to achieve results. Even so, by pooling such results much information could be obtained and one would hope that advances in all directions might be possible. This would mean giving us more healthy, sweeter perfumes, a wider colour range and a more shapely evergreen, ever blooming bush. There is no other flower more widely grown or more deeply entrenched in the affection of the world.

CHAPTER XIII

The Genetics of Hybridizing and Cross-Breeding

This is a subject bristling with technical difficulties. To seek to define these operations in a few words invites informed criticism but an accurate, detailed description would not only be beyond the writer's capacity but probably beyond the average reader's ability and interest. This chapter, therefore, is an attempt to inform and help those interested in the art of breeding new roses. This breeding is loosely called 'hybridizing', although a hybrid is the progeny of two different species. This occurred in the earlier stages, as when *R. chinensis* was crossed with *R. gigantea*, but now most of the work is cross-breeding, using two parents from the same family, such as crossing two hybrid teas together. To avoid confusion all this breeding will be described as 'hybridizing'.

Whatever growth there may be of plant or animal, it is dependent upon the living cell from which its simple or complicated mass is built. Each living cell has a similar basic structure: an outer casing or wall, a food supply and a vital centre. This centre, the nucleus, is the part which concerns the hybridist, for it is in its structure, content and method of reproduction that his hope of success lies. With rare exceptions, which can be ignored at this stage, the nucleus of every living cell of the same species of plant has the same composition. Each nucleus has a fixed basic number of pairs of chromosomes, which are rod-like bodies, bearers of the hereditary material. Chromosomes are distinguishable when the cell divides, and owe their name to the fact that they take up colour on staining and so can be traced in their movements.

From now on we will consider the genus 'Rosa' only. Examination shows that the basic chromosome number is 7, and as chromosomes occur in pairs it means that every cell in the simplest rose plant has $7 \times 2 = 14$ chromosomes; the plant is referred to as a diploid. Many of the early garden roses were diploids. Higher chromosome numbers appeared very early as tetraploids (7×4), while more complex forms appeared as hexaploids (7×6). Not only were roses found with even numbers of pairs of chromosomes but from causes which we will study later, triploids (7×3) and pentaploids (7×5) occurred.

Growth can take place only if cells are able to multiply, and build up new tissues. When division of a cell occurs, each of the fourteen chromosomes in the nucleus will double by dividing lengthwise, forming two new ones. In each case the two new chromosomes thus formed are exactly like the original one except for size. At this stage they are crowded into the centre of the cell, but shortly afterwards the newly formed halves draw away from their 'partners' and begin to move to opposite ends of the cell. When this segregation has taken place a partition (a new cell wall) grows between them. The two groups of chromosomes round off to form new nuclei so there are now two identical cells, smaller than the original but in all other respects exactly like it, and after accumulating more food these will be ready when mature for another division (mitosis).

It is always possible, though unlikely, that such division can meet with some slight mishap, and this will give rise to a 'sport' or mutation, changing some character of the plant to a certain degree.

This cell division, leading to formation of new tissues, can and does take place repeatedly, especially when the plant is in full growth. It is this ability of a plant to produce new tissues that makes asexual reproduction possible by such means as budding, grafting, or cuttings. When we come to sexual reproduction, which the hybridist uses in his work, the process is more complicated. To obtain some insight into the action which takes place we must understand the importance and function of the sexual reproductive parts of the flower.

The male organ, called a stamen, consists of two parts: the stalk or filament by which it is attached to the rest of the flower, and the

Diagrams showing essentials of chromosome behaviour when a cell divides
(Only two pairs of chromosomes shown)

Initial stage is similar—
network breaks up into individual chromosomes

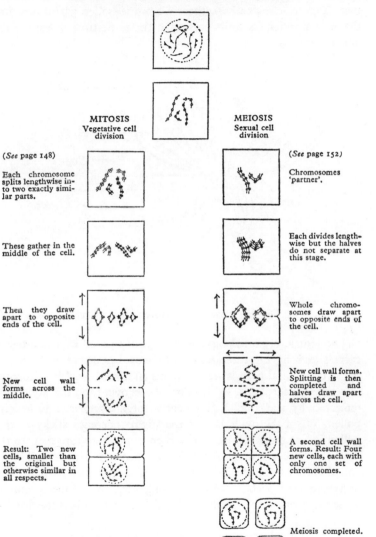

MITOSIS
Vegetative cell
division

MEIOSIS
Sexual cell
division

(*See* page 148)

Each chromosome splits lengthwise into two exactly similar parts.

(*See* page 152)

Chromosomes 'partner'.

These gather in the middle of the cell.

Each divides lengthwise but the halves do not separate at this stage.

Then they draw apart to opposite ends of the cell.

Whole chromosomes draw apart to opposite ends of the cell.

New cell wall forms across the middle.

New cell wall forms. Splitting is then completed and halves draw apart across the cell.

Result: Two new cells, smaller than the original but otherwise similar in all respects.

A second cell wall forms. Result: Four new cells, each with only one set of chromosomes.

Meiosis completed.

anther which surmounts it. The anther produces male cells or pollen grains which are usually heavily coated with wax, making them able to withstand weather. When the pollen grains are ripe, the anther splits, its walls curling at the same time to expose the pollen.

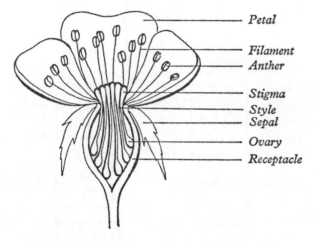

                — *Petal*

                — *Filament*
                — *Anther*

                — *Stigma*
                — *Style*
                — *Sepal*

                — *Ovary*

                — *Receptacle*

Diagram showing structure of rose flower

The female organ, the gynaecium, is composed of a number of carpels each having three parts. The most important is the ovary, the swollen basal part, which contains an ovule, capable of turning into a seed if fertilized. Each ovary has its own tube-like style, surmounted by the stigma, a receptive organ prepared to receive pollen. When the ovule is ripe the stigma becomes sticky so that pollen falling on it will be held and encouraged to function. In the roses there are a number of ovaries attached to the inner wall of the cup-shaped receptacle (enlarged top of flower stalk) which after flowering may become very enlarged, brightly coloured and, in some members of the family, highly decorative—this is the familiar 'hip'.

Even before leaving the anther, the nucleus of a pollen grain divides to give a vegetative and a generative nucleus. When the ripe pollen grain falls on a receptive stigma the vegetative nucleus induces action and a pollen tube is formed, growing down through the style and into the ovary where the vegetative nucleus disintegrates. The generative nucleus which has followed down the tube, enters the ovary and joins with an ovule to fertilize it. This later develops into a seed.

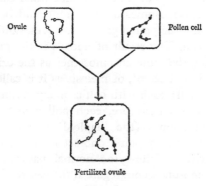

Ovule   Pollen cell

Fertilized ovule

Fertilization

These facts are to be borne in mind when hybridizing. It is a remarkable achievement for the male cell to travel such a distance and complete what is really the very complicated process leading to fertilization. Suitable air and temperature conditions are also important; these do not occur as regularly as one could wish, and the hybridist knows from sad experience that much of his effort will be unsuccessful. He can, by observation, find which male parents produce the best pollen, and which female parents produce the best set of healthy seed pods. Even so, weather and other factors beyond his control may cause failures. Little attention seems to have been paid to the physical character of the pollen, but the practical hybridist will soon realize that the type of pollen used makes a great deal of difference to the fertility and vitality of the seedlings produced, and to the health of their progeny.

To return to the fertilized ovule; it will be plain that in fertilization two nuclei, a male and a female, fuse together to form this fertilized ovule from which a new plant may develop. It has already

been stated that all cells in a rose plant carry 7 pairs of chromosomes or a multiple of 7. If it is a multiple of 7 the same principle
will be true although the numbers will be increased. By this token
the fertilized ovule should now carry 14 pairs, 7 from each parent.
If this continued, the doubling would go on indefinitely, each
generation having twice as many chromosomes as its parents. In
fact this does not happen. The new individual carries the same
complement of chromosomes as its parents did because the cell
divisions producing the pollen grains and ovules differ from those
of the ordinary cell. The result of mitosis is the production of 2
new cells carrying the same chromosomes as the original, but the
result of 'reduction division', or meiosis as it is called, is the production of 4 new cells, each with half as many chromosomes as the
parent cell. In roses, therefore, each pollen and ovule nucleus
contains 7 chromosomes (the 'haploid' number). Fertilization
restores the number to 7 pairs, one set from each parent. Subsequent cell divisions follow the normal pattern. In reduction
division the chromosomes congregate at the centre of the cell where
they become closely entangled with their 'partners'. Complete
chromosomes then draw apart and only when they have travelled
to opposite ends of the cell do they split lengthwise; the split is
followed by a second drawing apart, this time across the cell. When
new walls have formed there are 4 new cells, each containing one
set of chromosomes.

While the essentials are shown in the diagram on page 203, it is
really an over-simplification and two other important facts are to
be noted.

(a) During the pairing and splitting stage, chromosomes often
break and rejoin, frequently 'changing ends' with the correspond-
ing piece of the partner chromosome

This results in rearrangement of the genes (see below) in different combinations. Several breaks and rejoinings might occur along the length of one chromosome.

(*b*) Whole chromosomes can become reshuffled.

A plant might receive from one parent chromosomes represented

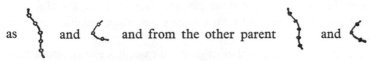

as   and   and from the other parent   and

When in turn this plant forms pollen and ovules it could hand on any of the following:

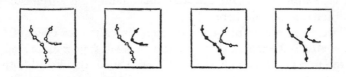

The process is really even more complicated than has been suggested above. While the chromosome has been described as rod-shaped, it is seen under high magnification to resemble a thread thickened at intervals along its length—some writers have likened it to a string of beads—and this is a convenient way of thinking of it. The 'beads' are genes, which separately, or in combination, represent qualities which are inherited by the plant, e.g. one gene could carry the factor (quality) for magenta flower colour, and for scent of a certain kind, and for a long flower stalk. On the other hand, a gene on a different chromosome might carry another factor intensifying the flower colour, or perhaps modifying the scent. It is convenient, however, to think of one gene carrying one factor.

The extra complications referred to in (*a*) and (*b*) above mean that genes can be combined in a great variety of ways as they are fairly thoroughly 'shuffled' during meiosis, leading to a bewildering possibility of variety in the progeny. Nevertheless, while some qualities appear more or less in accordance with the laws of chance, others do not seem to behave in this way. Plainly the closer together genes are on a chromosome the lower the chances are of a break occurring between them. If the 'string of beads' genes are considered as in the order A, B, C, D, E, F, then breaks are 5 times more likely to occur between genes A and F than between A and B. Certain qualities, therefore, almost always appear together simply because their genes are close to each other on the chromosome, or even controlled by the same gene. Such qualities are said to be 'linked'.

I do not think the number of genes in roses has been counted but in maize, which has 10 pairs of chromosomes only, there are known to be over 400 genes. Roses of the present day have 14 pairs of chromosomes so the number of genes should be far more than is the case with maize. One can well understand what a tremendous field for research lies here.

Two terms are in frequent use when discussing the effect of the genes after fertilization. Certain characters will appear more readily in the first generation (F.1). These are termed 'dominant'. Other characters which appear to be lost in the first generation (F.1) appear in the second (F.2). These are termed 'recessive'.

A hybridist might prefer to work with dominant characters only: his work would be easier, but such qualities are not always desirable. Dominant characters are very much harder to eliminate than recessives. In some strains proneness to mildew and petals which rot in rain are dominant characters. With some genes, incomplete dominance occurs, and in a plant carrying a dominant and recessive gene for a certain character, an intermediate result is shown which may be valuable as an alteration of character in hybridizing.

The commercial hybridist must be content to take a short cut for results, or, by using self restraint, look elsewhere for results. To acknowledge that he has reached the end of a strain is a necessary point for a hybridist. He must be content to lay aside a quest which may have taken years, and begin again along another path with his eye still on the same goal.

Generally speaking chromosomes in breeding behave in a normal and regular fashion. There are times when an entirely new character suddenly arises in a species. This is known as a mutation and will be found to act as a simple dominant but much more frequently as a recessive character. Such alteration is probably due to a single gene and is thought to be accounted for by some modification of its molecular structure. An instance where this occurred is in the new colour break among roses, first in the polyantha rose sports from the red 'Orleans'. This appeared in 'Paul Crampel', 'Gloria Mundi', etc. This fiery orange was due to a new colour. Normally the base material in red roses was cyanidin, but here the new colour pelargonidin appeared. Startling as this colour change was, it was only a minute but vital alteration of one oxygen molecule lost from an hydrogen-oxygen (Hydroxyl) group. This same change occurred in a seedling raised by Wilhelm Kordes, who claims that 'Baby Château', little known as itself, became the forerunner of vivid roses such as 'Independence' and many others. This mutation or 'sport' has proved itself capable of breeding a whole race of brilliant colours in hybrid tea, floribunda and shrub roses. Actually pelargonidin is always present with cyanidin so breeding results are not predictable.

For those in search of the blue colour it is a hopeful thought that the addition of one oxygen atom, turning one hydrogen molecule into an extra hydroxyl group, would cause the formation of delphinidin, the blue so much desired by hybridists today. Unfortunately there are many more adverse factors preventing this and while I would not like to say it is completely impossible one might say it was highly improbable. The first is that most if not all sports are due to a loss of factors not an addition, and another factor may be that there is insufficient iron in a rose to permit this to occur. It is interesting to note that the intense purple-blue of the cornflower is due to cyanidin, the same base material in the rose, but the reaction is only possible because of the iron which is much greater in the cornflower than in the rose. Any lilac, brown or purple effects are due to the combination of many primary colours both on the inner and outer sides of the petals being 'greyed' by the addition of other pigments.

Many major changes which are desired cannot be brought about by rule-of-thumb methods, but conditions can be made more promising by the elimination of factors which prevent, and the addition of factors which may bring about the hoped-for results.

There are other qualities which may discourage or encourage the raiser. One of these is the fact that a complex hybrid may be much more sterile than a simple species. Crane and Lawrence in *Genetics of Garden Plants* state that, 'Sterility is often associated with the offspring of wide crosses as in the rose "Mermaid" for example. In such extreme classes (*R. bracteata* × double yellow tea rose) the two sets of chromosomes derived from their respective parents work in harmony throughout the somatic life of the hybrid but are unable to pass successfully through the more intricate process of germ-cell formation.' This is proved by the numerous species which have evolved during the life of the rose. From simple diploids (7×2), very complex polyploids ($7 \times$ many) have been built up. This could not lead to complete sterility or the species would cease to exist. It has also brought about special methods of fertilization where *R. canina* (the dog brier) (7×5, pentaploid) employs only 7×4 of its chromosomes in fertilization. By this means cross-fertilization is cut out and breeding true is possible. This is important in the breeding of named types of briar stocks.

Remembering that the more complex hybrids are less fertile, the hybridist does not lose heart when a cross which he has contemplated does not mature at first. Indeed there is much truth in the fact that where hybridizing is difficult results are more likely to be worth while when they are finally achieved. Pernet-Ducher's raising of yellow roses is an illustration of this (see page 229).

Some genes are of themselves difficult to trace, but without their aid and interaction, some results would never be apparent. Apart from the fact that few scents are made up of one perfume only, it appears that more than one, perhaps many genes, may make up one scent. One would hesitate to say that any gene for perfume was dominant. Degrees of perfume of the same type may be found in the same parentage. Some genes may simply be there to intensify or inhibit certain qualities.

One of the most frustrating events in hybridizing is failure in a cross due to poor growth leading to death. This appears particularly in the crossing of white polyantha roses with other whites. Seed and even seedlings can be produced, but the result is eventual failure and would point to the possibility of there being 'lethal genes', which because of their make-up, inhibit normal growth. It is encouraging for a hybridist to realize that such failures are not due to lack of skill on his part, either in cultivation or hybridizing, but he should accept such warning and devote his time to other more remunerative crosses.

The physical factor has been mentioned, and one might well consider if pollen from a tiny type of flower, a miniature for instance, would have sufficient growth energy to penetrate and grow down the style of a full size hybrid tea. Such matters are worth consideration, and when a hybridist is making his programme, possibility and probability should sway him when he chooses his parents. It is possible to obtain a fertile cross by reversing the parents in a few cases within my experience, where the cross the other way has failed.

It is stated that choice of male or female parent in a cross makes no difference and that a 'My Choice' × 'Super Star' would give the same results as the reverse 'Super Star' × 'My Choice'. A very great weight of less informed opinion holds that growth comes from the female and colour from the male. Scientific evaluation denies this, and it may be genetically untrue. There are, however, what I would call physical factors, and the chance of a healthy child from a healthy mother is naturally greater than from an unhealthy mother. The best seed with the greatest viability would come from the healthiest parent. We should not misinterpret this term. Health does not necessarily mean coarse growth, and nature often provides remarkable viability for the little but tough.

Some crosses do differ, when the male or female used change places, and this is well known. It holds good with variegated varieties of some plants where the female only passes on the variegation, and other characteristics might well be increased by the use of one parent either as male or female; these changes are not within the nucleus, but are the effect of certain genes on specialized cells, producing the necessary enzyme which promotes the change.

Colour is the next inheritance factor to be considered. At the outset one may recall that colour may be due to pigmentation of all the cells or it may be of two pigments one over the other. The well-known example is the tomato; the dark red variety is a red flesh with a red skin, the bright red form is the red flesh with a yellow skin. There are many examples of such bicolours in roses. These do not have to be bicolours to the eye. Like the tomato, the colour the eye sees may be bright red, although two colours are actually present. By a blending of two separate layers of colour, we may get salmon and orange shades, and the substances causing the colours may vary in their lasting qualities. A variety beginning as clear yellow may with age change to salmon. These changes are most notable in varieties such as 'Masquerade'. With this variety the gene or genes causing the colour change are dominant, and there seems little hope of raising a pure yellow, which will retain its colour when ageing, from such a cross.

In all colour backgrounds there are at least two factors present, an 'absence of colour' factor and a factor for colour. Experiment shows that white roses may be due to either of these factors, for some whites prove dominant in a cross, although another factor, which give a green tinge, may be due to an entirely different cause. Many white roses are really creamy white and this ivory factor may be checked by a repressive factor which causes the change in colour. Again it may be caused by a repressed magenta factor, which, with the ivory, leads to apparent greenness as in 'Message' ('White Night').

It is considered that at least six factors go towards the making of the yellow colour alone. But this is only part of the problem, for if the rose in question is a tetraploid (7×4) it would be possible to have one of the six factors represented four times, so excluding others. In the yellow colour make-up there are (1) a gene for yellow, (2) a gene for repressing yellow, (3) a gene for red-blue colour, (4) a gene for intensifying that colour, (5) a gene for deciding the strength of the red-blue and another for increasing (6). This seems complicated enough, but in addition there is thought to be at least one gene for ivory colour and one for intensifying the yellow. When all these factors are worked out it would appear that in eighty yellows raised, only five would be intense, even if both parents appeared intense yellow.

It is obvious that a working hybridist must find some method by which he can get some idea as to the purity of colour in the strain on which he is working. Two shades of deep yellow are available.

The first is a mustard yellow such as 'Lydia', which owes its intensity to its greenish tinge, showing that the red-blue factor is present and active. The other, such as 'Allgold', is a clear deep yellow with no green shade. By studying the whole flower one can see the difference. In the first case somewhere in the stigma, style, anther, or filament the red or green or both red and green will show. In the second case the pure colour extends through the whole flower; stigma, style, anther, and filament are of the same shade as the petal.

Colour in itself is insufficient to produce a marketable rose. The history of one yellow rose may help to define the limitations a self-imposed standard may enforce. Pernet-Ducher brought out a series of very fine golden yellow hybrid teas (then called pernetianas) of which 'Mrs. Beckwith' (1923) and 'Souvenir de Claudius Pernet' were outstanding examples. They had one serious drawback in the English climate. In cold weather their golden colour did not develop, and at their first flowering they were usually turnipy white. To eliminate this failing I began various crosses and in 1935 introduced 'Yellowcrest', a pure yellow which retained its colour. But alas! Immediately after flowering its foliage fell. After a short rest period, growth began again, a normal autumn crop was produced, and the foliage fell once more. How was the colour to be kept and the foliage retained? At that time Mr. Beatty, of B. R. Cant & Sons Ltd., was producing a series—'Constance Casson', 'Sovereign', 'Mrs. Beatty'. Parent to the first two had been 'Queen Mary', canary-yellow shaded red. These bushes were short, almost squat in growth, with large globular flowers, but most important, they had heavy large foliage. 'Mrs. Beatty' was a clear yellow, and promised to be the needed parent. 'Yellowcrest' was crossed with 'Mrs. Beatty' and one seedling provided three plants as the Second World War broke out. Fortunately, a flower was seen while the rose beds were being cleared for food and the rose 'Ellinor Le Grice' survived. It carried its unfading gold yellow into its progeny 'Allgold' ('Goldilocks' × 'Ellinor Le Grice') together with one of the healthiest foliages we have. This patient search brought its reward, but it also brought out the fact that the pure yellow colour is linked with the globular bud brought in by the rose 'Mrs. Beckwith' all those years ago. Breed back or forward, every time this colour appears so does the globular bud.

It is this practical side which the hybridist must weigh up. Is the quality I need free for the getting? Or, with it, shall I obtain both curse and blessing? The fine range of yellows now appearing show very clearly by the red tinge on the outer petals of the bud, that they have the red-blue factor firmly in their composition. To breed a pure yellow, long in the bud and with vigorous, free growth and good foliage, seems as far off as ever.

If we consider the red colour in roses we shall find that the great difficulty is in eliminating the weak neck, while retaining the colour and perfume. 'Perfume' here should be limited to the damask perfume.

At least six types of red roses may be found. There is the pinky red, the easiest to obtain and as a rule one of the easiest and healthiest to grow. 'Rubaiyat' and 'Wendy Cussons' are good examples of this type. Usually the flower stem gives adequate support for the flower. The colour is not so popular.

There is the clear currant red. Here the flower is held upright but usually it is rather short petalled. Scent is either lacking or is of a sharp lemon. Growth and foliage are good and varieties can force well in this group.

There is the red with the inner side of the petal clear bright red but the outside dull red; with this goes a maroon edge to the petal. Such varieties, of which 'Red Devil' is an example, have petals with poor resistance to wet conditions.

There is the bright red with a golden base. This strain is usually on long thin stems with small, but healthy, foliage. There is some perfume but not of the damask type.

The smoky red, with deep but dull colour, provides an upright stem for the rose. It has damask perfume without intensity, growth is variable, but many good varieties such as 'Chrysler Imperial' and 'Alec's Red' may be included. Under good weather conditions they can be much brighter in colour. They die off to a bluish red.

The remaining, but very popular type, is the bright red, heavily overlaid with blackish maroon with a strong damask perfume: a large, well-built, pointed flower, every attribute except the one quality demanded—a stiff flower neck. This weakness appears to be caused by the over-long flower stem. By breeding a semi-double flower without weight this weakness may not be so marked, but varieties such as 'Ena Harkness', 'Étoile de Hollande', and 'Crimson Glory' are cursed with this trouble. Here appears one of the insoluble problems of the hybridist: of obtaining a damask scented, bright red rose overlaid with deeper shading, of good growth and upright flower stem.

It is these combined problems which play havoc with the hybridist's schemes and dreams. Colour? yes. Scent? yes. Growth? yes. Health? yes. Forcing qualities? yes. But to combine these qualities is a gargantuan task unlikely to be accomplished in our lifetime.

Two colours only have been mentioned and yet similar problems are associated with the other colours, with the quest for a free-flowering white untroubled by mildew, for the perfect pink for the mauve, purple, and blue shades.

Other new colours may well be produced (see Appendix 'Unusual Colours in Roses', page 341). Of these, brown, in rich golden shades such as the bronze of pansies or chrysanthemums, is a possibility. Experiment shows that such colours may be bred by using the purples of 'Tuscany Improved' and other old-fashioned types. This is a long task for the flowering of this type is on two-year wood, and at least 80 per cent will breed their normal type and most of these will be pinks and reds without character. Only one out of many hundreds will contain even part of the desired character.

We have been reminded that in the creation of most of our present garden varieties few of the many species in existence have been used. This is true, but much long preparatory work would be needed to alter this. Such breeding demands the time and resources of scientists rather than of the hybridist of commerce who has to meet the present demand of a clamorous public and the heavy wage bill of the moment.

Sufficient has been written in the foregoing pages to show the possibilities as well as the need for more careful hybridizing. When one considers that well over a million new seedling roses are produced annually, and yet the need is as urgent as ever, a challenge is presented which may well be taken up by professional and amateur alike. The practical application of these principles will be set out in the next chapters.

 CHAPTER XIV

The History of the Present-day Rose

In a biography, the opening chapter often appears to ignore the very person whose life story is to be told. Happenings in the remote past, ancestors long since dead, old events which have become facts of history, are marshalled together and analysed. It is realized that the past has much to do with the present. One may wish to plunge into the exciting parts of the story at once when the full stature of manhood has produced notable results. If we did, much of the hero's character would appear inexplicable, and we should not be able to assess with any degree of certainty his real achievements or the reason for his apparent failures.

To attempt to describe the building up of the modern roses from their parent stock is as complicated as preparing a family tree and appending armorial quarterings. The diagram on page 217 can point out only from what parentage the type was derived. In what proportions those typical qualities were handed down or how much appears visible and how much is latent, must vary as much as in the child who, while deriving its life from its parents, may inherit and display qualities from its diverse ancestry of many generations. All that is certain, is that the strain is completely assorted, as cross-breeding with any two modern roses will prove.

It is for a similar reason that we should seek to discover the forebears of our present roses, and the way in which present advance was made possible, by discovering and making use of latent qualities for the improvement of all types. Only then shall we be able to apply such knowledge to our practical needs of today.

The rose family is very widely distributed throughout the Northern Hemisphere. Over the ages, species have arisen which

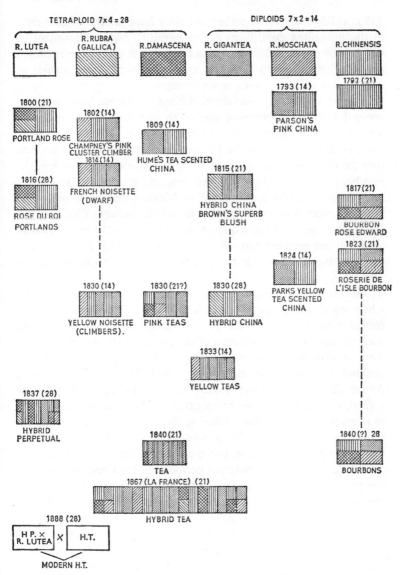

The parentage of the modern H.T. Rose

217

differ widely from one another, for they have adapted themselves to the prevailing conditions of temperature and environment in which they are found. From dwarf types, a few centimetres high, to giant climbers up to 12 m (40 ft), they present a wide variety of foliage, flower, fruit, thorn and growth.

Because of this wide variation, differing opinions have been expressed as to the number of species to be found. Some botanists were inclined to give every variation a fresh name, others were more conservative. With the increased knowledge of genetics, the rose family has been reduced to fewer species, and today the number is placed at about one hundred and twenty. These inhabit regions from Alaska and Siberia to Mexico, and some are to be found in every country of the Northern Hemisphere. That they are confined to north of the Equator may be due to the fact that rose seed will not germinate at over 26° C (80° F). This is offered as a partial solution, although there may be other reasons so far not advanced.

We need to rid ourselves of our modern ideas of the rose bloom when we consider the rose species. Some of the characters we consider most desirable are positive dangers for the rose in its natural state. The fierce thorns of the prairie roses preserved them from destruction by grazing animals. The large hooked thorns enabled the climbers to reach air and sunlight in the forest glades. Above all the single flower was essential. Doubling of the petals is a grave fault in nature, for every extra petal means one less anther to provide vital pollen for fertilizing the seed, which is essential to the future existence of the species. The more flowers, and the longer the period of bloom, the greater the chance of setting seed.

The duration of the flowering period has also a marked effect on the purity of the species. The farther north we travel the scarcer the suitable weather for flowering, so that the differing species are apt to flower either at the same time or to overlap one with another. This leads to the appearance of more hybrids, so that there is greater variety in the northern, cooler areas than in the south.

Although there are about one hundred and twenty species of roses, only five have played a major part in the production of the modern rose. A further seven species have contributed slightly to our present roses. This means that of the one hundred and twenty species known only fifteen have contributed to our modern roses.

It is a fair question to ask, why trouble to hybridize? Surely the wild rose in its natural beauty and variety should provide all that we need? It is my hope that neither side in such a controversy would hope to strengthen its position by belittling the other. Undoubtedly there is room for all types in the right place, but man demands variety, and change, which is not always synonymous with progress.

Some of the reasons for attempting hybridizing and cross-breeding are as follows. Very few species flower over a prolonged period. This character of continuous flowering is a recessive feature, but by breeding the flowering period of the garden rose has been increased, until we can have roses from May until the frosts. By breeding, desirable qualities have been added, such as hardiness, freedom from disease and ease of cultivation. Roses have been produced with growth suitable to special purposes, so that whether we desire a short, continuous-flowering bush, or a vigorous climber, our wishes can be satisfied. Colour especially has been made the servant of man, and new colours, adding greater variety to our choice, have been produced. Apart from these facts, one has to realize that to ensure a succession of healthy progeny, one must go back to seed-produced stock, to revitalize the plant, which, after generations of vegetative propagation, loses its vitality.

As we turn to the early ancestors of the rose, we must realize that the choice of the original parents was not fortuitous. The parents were chosen because these types had been in cultivation for thousands of years, and during that period they had travelled far from their original wildling state. In present terms they were 'cultivar', not species. The Chinese gardeners, with consummate skill and care, had built up stocks which enabled the hybridist to begin far along the line of advance. So too in Europe and the Near East, a different order of roses had been in cultivation, and were ready to hand to blend with the Chinese garden variants of species.

There has been much loose writing on the subject of hybridizing, and it is a very difficult subject on which to offer any certain facts. One may admit that the principles of hybridizing were known at least a hundred years before this knowledge was put into practice with roses.

Certainly until 1800, and often after that, advance was made by noticing and propagating natural hybrids. At first cross-pollination was the work of insects, and the raising of seedlings a natural chance. Only after this stage had been reached, did the gardener, by discovering the variety, seeing its possibilities and propagating it, preserve it for the benefit of himself and posterity. The next stage was the deliberate bringing together of roses from other areas, planting them together, collecting and sowing their seed, raising the seedlings, and selecting from them. Much activity along these lines occurred at the end of the eighteenth and beginning of the nineteenth century (see Chapter XII, 'One Hundred Years of New Seedling British Roses').

Parallel with these methods of introducing new roses was the discovery of sports. Because of the rarity of distinct breaks, small variations were treasured and propagated.

The function of pollen as an essential to fertility was accepted and used, if not understood, in the pollination of the date palm at least as early as 2000 B.C., and the function of pollen appears to have been understood in the learned world in the sixteenth century. Nehemiah Grew in 1676 had *The Anatomy of Plants* printed. These were a series of propositions put before the Royal Society. He deals at length with sex in plants. In Chapter 5, 'Of Flowers', page 173, he declares 'every plant is male and female' and goes on, 'Wherefore as the Seed-case is the Womb, so the Attire (which always stands upon or round about it) and those parts of the Sap hereinto discharged, are as it were the Menes or Flowers, and by this Sap in the Womb is duly qualified for the approaching generation of the Seed.' He goes on to say that as the early Attire (as he appears to call both stamens and stigma with styles) 'answers to part of the Female so it is probable, that afterwards when it opens or cracks, it performs the office of the Male'. It is clear that he is uncertain how or why pollen acts as it does, believing it fell in some way 'and so touches it (the Womb or Ovary as we call it) with prolific virtue'. There is considerable confusion as to the function of stamens, stigma and styles. These appeared to confuse him, as they performed, so he thought, similar functions. He becomes thoroughly tied up in trying to find parallel parts and functions between plants and animals, and finally has to admit that if all functions and organs were the same then plants would be a branch of the animal kingdom.

It is claimed that Radolphus Jacobus Camerius, in a work published in 1664, clearly set out the function of sex in plants, but as this work is in Latin, I have been unable to confirm this, although I know that he again is obsessed with the attempt to find exact parallels between the animal and vegetable kingdom in their reproductive processes.

Robert Bradley in 1717 in his *New Improvements of Planting and Gardening* . . ., Chapter 2, page 11, writes: 'I shall proceed to offer another discovery . . . which I conceive will be of extraordinary use to such as raise plantations of nuts [seeds?]. Moses tells us in his account of the creation "That plants have their seeds in themselves", that is, every plant contains in itself male and female powers (because they cannot move).' Bradley goes on to say that the first hint had been conveyed to him several years earlier by Robert Ball, who had had this notion for about thirty years 'that plants had a mode of generating somewhat analogous to that of animals'. In addition Samuel Moerland has given us to understand how the dust of the Apices in flowers (i.e. the male sperm) is conveyed into the Uterus or Vasculum Seminale of the plant by which means the seeds therein contained are impregnated. He gives details of the lily flower and then goes on to say, 'On the other hand the uterus of the Rose is without the flower at the bottom of the petals.' How long it was before this theory was put to practical use in the production of roses is at present impossible to say. The fact of cross-pollination was accepted at the turn of the eighteenth century and roses were probably deliberately planted near one another to induce cross-pollination. The actual accomplishment was probably left to natural means and the resulting seed pods were collected and sown in great quantities.

The lack of definite information may be due to the fact that those who knew about and practised hand pollination were anxious to keep the knowledge to themselves.

Although these facts were known, we have to go for an exposition to William Paul, who wrote on hybridizing in his outstanding work *The Rose Garden*. In the first edition of 1848 he writes, 'By hybridizing is understood the bringing together of individuals of different species, by cross-breeding individuals of the same species with a view to raising up new beings, differing from and superior to, those already existing.' He goes into detail as to the best method of preparing the blooms, crossing, treating the seed pods and raising the seedlings. He also gives an extract from his notebook used for keeping a report from his work:

1846	*Female*	*Male*	*Object in view*
No. 17	Harrisonii	Austrian Copper	A double copper Austrian.
No. 21	General Allard (Hybrid Chinese)	Mme Laffay (Hybrid Perpetual)	To invigorate the habit and perfect the tendency of G. Allard to flower in the autumn.

He states that he began hybridizing in 1840. He gives much interesting information on the hybridizing carried out by French amateurs, who appear to have been among the first to do such work. They were centred round Paris. I am indebted to Monsieur J. Gaujard for the following information which takes the matter as far as is possible at present. The Empress Josephine had collected one hundred and twenty varieties of roses obtained throughout Europe when she withdrew to Malmaison. Most of these were botanical types of roses. By 1815 her gardener Descemet had three hundred varieties of roses.

Many mixed species were growing side by side at Malmaison including repeat-flowering roses, of Kamchatka, Persia and China. Descemet intended to raise these types from their naturally fertilized seeds. To his surprise he obtained some varieties which were totally different from their parents. This came as a revelation to Descemet, who entered into an agreement with a Monsieur Vibert to become the first 'artificial' hybridizer.

William Paul, who devotes a page in his work to Monsieur Descemet and Monsieur Vibert, speaks of the former having an establishment at Saint-Denis and believes the stock was sold to Monsieur Vibert and moved to Chenevières-sur-Marne in 1815 when English troops entered France.

Monsieur Vibert was one of the most celebrated cultivators in France. He founded his establishment in the vicinity of Paris in 1815, and claims it to be the first of the kind in France. He removed later to Angers, where conditions were more favourable. In a catalogue of 1846 he speaks of thirty-five years of practice in horticulture, although he speaks of founding his nursery in 1815 and at that time (1846) was going into semi-retirement, but says, 'I shall always continue the cultivation of my seedlings; I shall never renounce them, and shall propagate few others.' He specialized in the raising of French and Provence roses, and at the end produced also a few moss and hybrid perpetuals.

Monsieur Laffay was a great raiser of roses, specializing in hybrid chinas and hybrid perpetuals. William Paul speaks of his raising two hundred to three hundred thousand seedlings a year. Possibly these figures suffered a little from 'poetic licence', a failing not unknown among raisers of today! Amateurs in the same area, among them Monsieur Hardy (raiser of the famous 'Mme Hardy') was Superintendent of the Jardin du Luxembourg of Paris, but did not sell his roses. It is considered that most of the first French hybridists were amateurs, but William Paul writes, 'Both M. Vibert & M. Laffay, the former especially, have engaged in the cultivation of roses for many years, and their enterprise and industry have brought them a full reward. They *now cultivate more for amusement than profit*,* confining themselves chiefly to the raising of seedlings, and the propagation of them for distribution.

'Having realized a comfortable independency and attained to the highest eminence in their profession, they seem inclined to recline beneath the laurels they have so peacefully won.' I think we may safely conclude that both Vibert and Laffay (the latter offered William Paul in about 1847 some moss hybrids which he had

* Author's italics

raised from a thousand seeds he had sown previously) were professional rose growers as well as hybridists.

By 1835 a small number of rose raisers round Lyons had begun
the search for new roses by artificial hybridization. They were
J.-B. Guillot, Père François Lacharme, Claude Ducher (founder
of the firm Pernet-Ducher), Liubaud, and Luizet. In 1844 both
Lacharme and Claude Ducher offered rose novelties.

With this information I feel we may safely assert that the first
artificial hybridizing was carried out in France before 1820.

I am informed on good authority that most of the new early
varieties known in Holland were imported from France, although
the moss roses first originated in Holland as sports.

To return to the events which led to deliberate hybridizing artificially, we must study the few varieties which inspired rosarians
to begin their work, for it is a very interesting fact that almost all
our present vast number of cultivated roses owe their existence to
a very few original sources. The majority of species have contributed nothing of their many qualities to the present garden varieties.
Many consider this a matter to be deplored and they may be right.
We would be wrong, even so, to think that those varieties used
came straight from the wild. Far from it, for those parents used
were as little like their wild ancestors as the city man of today, with
his bowler and umbrella, is like the ancient Briton with his woad
and club. True, both are basically the same, but the veneer of
civilization has accentuated some qualities and reduced others. The
parents of the present hybridized roses owed the very qualities to
be bred from them to the guiding hand of an ancient culture.

In far-off days in China, men had tamed the wild rose, and by
cultivation and observation had already produced qualities in the
strains which had been deeply-hidden as recessive factors in their
original forebears' blood. Single, coarse, once-flowering climbers
had, at least a thousand years ago, become many petalled, or dwarf,
or remontant (repeat-flowering). Colours had been selected, inten-
sified and fixed by the guiding hands and minds of skilled gardeners
over the centuries.

Two varieties were originally responsible for the roses which
brought this breeding stock to the Western World in the late 1700s

and early 1800s. The first was *R. chinensis*, the second *R. gigantea*. *R. chinensis* was the 'China' or 'Bengal' rose. The flower was about 5 cm (2 in) in diameter, not or only slightly fragrant. In colour crimson or pink, rarely white, usually with several, less often with solitary flowers on long stems, blooming more than once a season. The foliage was evergreen or partly so. Genetically it could be triploid or diploid. It is a native of China. The second rose for breeding stock from China was the cultivated form of *R. gigantea*. This was a diploid. Although a native of South-West China and Burma the wild form was not found and introduced until 1889.

It must be clearly understood that neither of these two varieties in their native form was used, but hybrids selected over many centuries were crossed.

Bearing these descriptions in mind, we come to four varieties which, bred with European sorts, started the modern rose. It is not claimed that these were the first roses introduced from China, such is not the case, for similar types were known in Italy many years earlier. They were the first which came when the gardening world was sufficiently skilled to appreciate their possibilities and use their qualities. This has been, and always will be, the test of a hybridist. The qualities needed are always there. It is his skill which is challenged to draw them out.

The first of these Chinese varieties was 'Slater's Crimson China' of 1792. This was dwarf, a perpetual-flowering semi-double variety with dark red flowers. It was a triploid (21 chromosomes). This could produce a limited progeny for it was not completely sterile. There were also diploid 'Crimson China' varieties. Its great importance lies in the fact that from it came the clear red colour.

The second, 'Parson's Pink China' of 1793, was sent to England to the famous Sir Joseph Banks. This, like 'Slater's Crimson', was soon used in France for breeding, and from there was sent to North America (1800). A diploid, the 'Old Blush China' of today is probably the same rose.

The third, 'Hume's Blush Tea-Scented China' (1809) was called *R. indica odorata*. Hurst considered it a cross, *R. chinensis* × *R.*

H

gigantea, with *R. gigantea* predominating. This variety became an important ancestor of the tea roses. It has been lost, but from its descendants one assumed it was also a diploid like the two original species.

We owe the fourth, 'Park's Yellow Tea-Scented China' (1824), to a plant-hunting expedition sponsored by the Royal Horticultural Society. It too is extinct, but was reliably drawn in 1835 under the title of *R. indica sulphurea*. This is also believed to be a diploid from *R. chinensis* × *R. gigantea* cross, with the latter again predominating. It extended the range of known rose colours, and was the only source of yellow until 'Persian Yellow' was used almost a century later.

These four were the 'China Stud' which brought in colour variation, especially yellow and its shades, remontancy (repeat-flowering), cluster-flowering, and climbing, also the pointed shape, now the ideal for rosarians. The principal faults, also introduced, were lack of hardiness and the weak flower stem with a tendency to throw rampant climbers.

Until nearly 1900, all roses of European origin depended upon a small section of the wild ancestors of the rose of the order Gallicanae. They were predominantly summer-flowering only, and were hardy shrub roses. *R. gallica*, the French rose, is an ancestor of them all, in the final reckoning. Its cultivation goes back further than we can trace. Originally of not more than twelve petals, variants appeared naturally, and were increased artificially by suckers, cuttings, and later by budding. As far as known, all *R. gallica* progeny were tetraploid. The damask group, also tetraploids, were derived from *R. gallica*, while their other parent was probably *R. phoenicia* (one of the musk group). This produced the summer-flowering type only. There was a variety of damask sometimes called *bi-fera* which gave a few autumn flowers as a second crop. This was believed to be derived from *R. gallica* × *R. moschata* (the musk rose). This increased period of flowering was much prized, and was exploited even in Roman times. The cabbage or centifolia roses were of late origin (early 1700s) and were very double. These too were tetraploids. They were too double to breed from, until a single-flowered 'sport' in the early 1800s made crossing possible.

From this group came the moss roses, again as 'sports' until one of their number 'sported' a single flower, when breeding for moss types became possible.

Another small group, the albas, were unusual in being hexaploid (7×6). The cross was probably *R. canina* × *R. gallica*.

Here then was the mainspring of Europe's contribution to our modern rose. The qualities introduced were perfume (damask type), colour (vinous red, white, and pink), hardiness, and in some cases a stiff neck. The flowers were carried single or in clusters and were largely tetraploids (7×4).

Where the Eastern and Western types of roses had been hybridized the first crosses had resulted in less fertile triploids (7×3). After a time seedlings had appeared which produced fertile tetraploids. This important pattern was to be repeated again and again when the diploid Chinese roses and the tetraploid European roses were crossed. A triploid would result in a distinct hybrid. This would lead to a period of progress which was slow because of infertility. Then a tetraploid would appear, leading to increased fertility with rapid progress.

Briefly the noisettes were: *R. moschata* (7×4) × 'Parson's Pink China' (7×2) producing 'Champney's Pink Cluster' (7×2), a climber. In the next generation, called French noisette roses, the recessive dwarf factor reappeared. This was continued in the noisettes which, crossed with 'Park's Yellow' in 1830, produced the yellow noisettes (climbers), and recrossed with 'Park's Yellow' in 1833 produced yellow shaded dwarf teas. More crossing produced the climbing yellow teas such as 'William Allan Richardson' and 'Maréchal Niel' (both diploids, 7×2).

Further alterations took place when the bourbon group came into being. A chance seedling between the pink 'Autumn Damask' and 'Parson's Pink China' was found in 1817 in the Réunion Islands (then known as l'Île de Bourbon) by a French botanist named Bréon. On its being sent to France, a variety was raised in 1822 and called 'Rosier de l'Île Bourbon'. This was a vigorous plant with bright rose-pink, semi-double flowers, damask perfume and autumn flower. Originally the bourbons were triploids, but widely grown and much crossed with gallicas and damasks, they became tetraploids. Another group, the pink tea roses, came from crossing a bourbon with 'Hume's Blush Tea-Scented China'.

By crossing the yellow noisette teas with the pink bourbon teas a wide variety of forms with large, beautifully shaped flowers were produced between 1840 and 1890. Unfortunately these varieties lacked hardiness. Their very mixed parentage led to a great assortment of diploids, triploids and some tetraploids. Most of the breeding stock used was diploid.

(*R. damascena* × *R. gallica*) × 'Slater's Crimson China' resulted in the 'Portland Rose' of about 1800. This was a triploid, but the 'Rose du Roi' raised in the gardens of Saint Cloud in 1812 was a tetraploid, and other tetraploids followed. *R. gallica* × 'Hume's Blush Tea-Scented China' produced the hybrid Chinas. By breeding these two strains Portlands × hybrid Chinas with bourbons, the hybrid perpetual (*circa* 1837) arose. This new race was certainly hybrid but 'perpetual' was a more hopeful than exact designation.

Here then emerged two groups, both owing their inheritance to China and Europe, but each possessing good characteristics and bad faults. The good qualities, beauty of form and hardiness with freedom, demanded admission. Lack of hardiness and lack of freedom called for early elimination. Perfume, even then an elusive quality, fell by the way. It was treated as a useful extra but unessential.

It fell to the French breeder, Guillot, to produce 'La France' (1867), which was recognized at some future time as the first hybrid tea. This was a triploid (7 × 3). Here was combined the vigorous shrub form of the hybrid perpetual with the fine shaped buds and free-flowering character of the tea roses.

For a long time these triploid derivatives prevented easy crossing, as they led to sterility, but ultimately, as before, tetraploids were produced and hybridizing became easy and abundant. The colours in the hybrid tea group were largely white, red and pink, the yellow appearing as a golden zone at the base of the petal or as a mother-of-pearl sheen.

The introduction of the golden-yellow colour is due to the persistence of Pernet-Ducher. He conceived the idea of introducing the colour into the roses of his time by using *R. lutea*, the double form of 'Persian Yellow', which had been known for a thousand years. He patiently and persistently crossed thousands of flowers with this variety. It was a most infertile pollen and all crosses failed except one with 'Antoine Ducher' which became the grandmother of the Pernet seedlings. This cross gave a few seeds in 1888. Two hybrids were raised and flowered. One was interesting in the preponderance of its paternal *R. lutea* character but being sterile and a climber was useless. The other plant first flowered in 1893 but it was 1894 before its possibilities were recognized. It showed characteristics of both parents. Crossed with a hybrid tea it produced the first Pernet rose, 'Soleil d'Or'. With this break came not only golden yellow, but the brilliant bicolours with which we are now so familiar. There were grave faults as well, such as extremely thorny and pithy wood; a badly quartered bloom (a flower which had a broken centre); lack of hardiness and proneness to black spot.

Soon the group, by interbreeding, was merged with the hybrid teas and many major faults are even now being eliminated. Because they were tetraploids, no difficulty was found in breeding, beyond the fact that the tendency for all highly bred roses is to sterility, and it also becomes more difficult to segregate and pass on desirable qualities.

It was at this period that many may have thought that further novelty and improvement were impossible. Yet this was far from the truth, as events were to show.

In the beginning of this new race, the diploid *R. multiflora* appears. Seeds from Japan sent to France about 1860 produced some double-flowered climbers which flowered once. In the second generation raised by Guillot, there were some dwarf-flowering, double, perpetual types including 'Pâquerette' (Sisley 1879). Probably the cross had arisen from *R. multiflora* × 'Dwarf Pink China'. 'Pâquerette' was a white variety; 'Mignonette' from the same lot of seed, was pink. The 'Orleans Rose' (1909), a derivative, was grown by the million and produced sports in all colours from red to orange and pale pink to salmon. These dwarf polyanthas had many admirable characteristics, being bushy, of hardy growth, with abundance of truly remontant flowers over an extended period.

Here was the background and the parent promising a great advance. The Danish raiser Dines Poulsen required a hardy but more showy rose than the polyantha, and he began to cross the diploid polyantha with hybrid teas. Called 'Hybrid Polyanthas' these roses showed how effective they could be for carefree bedding and colourful massing. All these early hybrid polyantha roses were triploids and were difficult to cross, although most of them produced useful progeny. Again came the movement from triploid to tetraploid progeny, and the field for hybridizing was enlarged. From mass of flower, the aim has changed to quality of flower, and it is for the present-day hybridist to decide whether quality of flower shall be considered more important than quantity. What has made the present-day floribunda (so-called because of the very mixed blood) so popular, has undoubtedly been the mass of flower over a very long period. To retain this quality should be the aim of all hybridists.

Besides these main classes, other minor branches of hybridizing have been carried out, with climbers, ramblers, large specimens and hybrid musks, while latterly the 'miniature' classes have become increasingly popular through the work begun by John de Vink and carried out by many leading hybridists especially Mr. Ralph Moore.

Before considering the actual task of hybridizing, one must pause to consider the even more important task of carrying out a planned programme.

Sufficient has been said in the foregoing short history of the present-day rose to make it clear that hybridizing under these conditions, with this material, is not likely to give spectacular results in the near future. Apart from the very remote possibility of a colour break, and with the production of the blue colour delphinidin, the advance is to be along the lines of a steady but gradual improvement. As a first suggestion: it might be wise to work on one type only. For the amateur, perpetual climbers and shrub roses, although yielding little financial reward, do offer an excellent field. Recent advances have shown the great need for and possibility of producing perpetual-flowering, climbing roses with large blooms. The shrub roses too are most rewarding in their beauty, but for these considerable room is needed for testing; then there is the time factor, for they take longer to mature.

Suppose one settles for hybrid teas? The question of colour, shape, constitution and purpose will need careful consideration. Far better to concentrate on one colour at first, and work out what likely parents you have available. Are you to try for an exhibition-type rose, with quality before quantity? Will perfume be high on your list? Or will you strive for roses for bedding and cutting? In any case, one needs to have an ideal for each of these types, choosing parentage for that purpose. It is only as one begins to prepare such a programme that a realization of the many details involved begins to come home, and we begin to look at roses from a new angle.

An analysis of some of these needed characters may help us to appreciate the difficulties to be overcome, and also to appreciate what has been achieved. There will be certain basic qualities needed in all progeny whatever their ultimate purpose. Before flower must come growth, and before growth, health. One should place this resolutely before all else. It is suggested that the following qualities are dominant and dependent upon one gene: glossy leaves *v*. dull, mildew resistance *v*. susceptibility, climbing habit *v*. dwarf, double flowers *v*. single. Even these would vary greatly in their proportion in the second generation. Two only of these qualities would come into one's general list of requirements, glossy leaves and resistance to mildew.

General health cannot be decided on the evidence of the greenhouse specimens we are to use for hybridizing. Artificial conditions may well prevent certain spores from germinating, while on the other hand another strain of disease to which the roses are immune outside may prove damaging inside. All evidence for health and growth must be collected from outside experience with roses growing under normal conditions.

We shall discuss very briefly, later, the needs for forcing roses. The requirements are fundamentally different, proportionately difficult to obtain, and when obtained and exploited, greatly rewarding.

Included with general health will come growth. Is the variety to be bushy and spreading, i.e. short-jointed, or is it to be tall and upright? Each time such a decision is made the number of putative parents is drastically reduced. The final reduction will come with the consideration of colour.

There is much to be said, when planning a programme, for beginning with as large a number of different crosses as possible. By carefully watching the results, an indication can be seen as to what may be a useful cross. It is then advisable to concentrate most of one's energies on these possibilities, rather than further to dissipate one's resources over a wider field. This is how 'Allgold' was achieved. A preliminary cross gave promising colours. The next year something like eight thousand seedlings were raised from this 'Goldilocks' × 'Ellinor Le Grice' cross, and of the resulting seedlings nearly forty were carried through for further test. Careful notes were kept on all these, including colour, petalage, foliage and growth. Of this number, four were finally put into commerce: 'Honeyglow', 'Copper Delight', 'Golden Delight' and 'Allgold'. The copper shades revealed the grandparent of 'Goldilocks' as the table below will show. The dates given are the year of introduction. Parentage was:

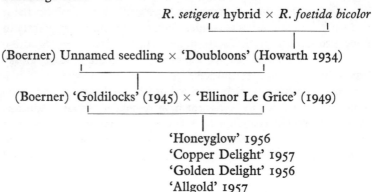

R. setigera hybrid × *R. foetida bicolor*

(Boerner) Unnamed seedling × 'Doubloons' (Howarth 1934)

(Boerner) 'Goldilocks' (1945) × 'Ellinor Le Grice' (1949)

'Honeyglow' 1956
'Copper Delight' 1957
'Golden Delight' 1956
'Allgold' 1957

The production of roses for forcing, as stated earlier, is a much more difficult task, for two reasons: the actual parentage must be different, and such varieties are bred for underglass-work only, and the method of testing is more exacting and is specialist work. Two distinct types are evolved for forcing, those which produce a great number of easily induced blooms which fetch a low price, but because of high turnover, pay their way, and those with full flowers, long stems and great lasting qualities, which produce few flowers, but which make high prices and so again pay their way. Another factor which greatly influences the choice of variety is the ability to flower when light is reduced in winter. Such flowers, coming at that time, can fetch high prices, and so pay high dividends per bush. It is all a matter of finance. Great experience is needed in such production and progress is slow. Until recently, 80 per cent of production of forced cut roses in the U.S.A. were of 'Columbia' and its sports, a rose raised by E. G. Hill in 1916. In Europe much more variety is acceptable. 'Lady Sylvia' is still grown in great quantities as a heavy producer of cheap flowers in England, but 'Baccara' is the most popular on the Continent.

A full rose which opens and develops in water will last longer, and here a rose like 'Baccara' excels. The fuller the petalage, the slower the development, but also the longer the bloom remains useful, and if these qualities are present, a higher price will be paid, so compensating for the fewer flowers such a plant produces. A good forcing rose must show its true colour in the early stages, so that the buyer catches a glimpse of future promise. Such qualities limit the field for experiment, and only the expert, after careful trial, can make the necessary assessment. There is great need for other good forcing varieties, especially in reds and yellows, but if one needs to raise one hundred-thousand seedlings to obtain an outstanding rose for outside, one would need treble that quantity to get a good forcing rose. If one is so fortunate to raise such a forcing rose as 'Baccara', it not only pays the hybridist, but by improving the demand for forcing roses, improves the whole industry.

Because these tests have to be carried out over an extended period under commercial conditions, cross-breeding for forcing is likely to remain the province of the specialist professional.

Having said this much on selection, I would like to add that if the amateur wishes to hybridize, he may just cross anything he feels like crossing. Whatever the result, it will be a new rose for him, and though it may not be of commercial worth, it will give him the delight of having produced something unique.

The real difference between amateur and professional hybridizing is that the former is for immediate results, the latter for the production of a strain. Such a strain should lead to good results because the parentage has been built up through generations of proved worth. It may well take twenty years to establish such a strain. Those who knew the strains produced by the Dicksons in pre-war years could follow their improvements through the rose generations.

The greatest advance is not made by spectacular leaps. Such events occur perhaps once in ten years, and progress depends upon the gradual improvement of better qualities and the elimination of small weaknesses.

RAISING A NEW SEEDLING

This is not difficult and can prove just one more delight for rose enthusiasts. Nothing spectacular may result but he may claim such a seedling 'a poor thing but mine own'. This sense of personal achievement is not only valuable in itself, but the quickening of our perception and shrewder evaluation of the qualities in a rose are clear gains.

 CHAPTER XV

The Practice of Raising New Roses

With the preceding chapter well digested, the time has arrived to deal with the method of pollinating and raising the seed. Before we do so, the treatment of the parent plant should be considered.

In our English climate one should always work under glass. The main reason is that our weather conditions are too uncertain to allow the hips to set, develop and ripen in time out in the open. The other reason is that insect pests and cultural conditions, especially watering, can be controlled more easily under glass.

When preparing the plants, either for pot or soil culture, one should remember that rank growth has to be avoided at all costs. Nitrogenous manure should not be used, although phosphates, potash and magnesium are essential. A retentive soils will be useful, but a mulch of peat on pots or top soil will prevent undue evaporation and keep watering to a minimum.

Where plants are in the open ground they should be given a maximum watering when beginning growth, and all watering should stop when flowering begins. Experience shows that plants will flourish under such conditions and the air remains dry and buoyant.

Some prefer a few large plants with many flowers, all pollinated. Others prefer small plants, confining their efforts to two or three flowers per plant. Whichever way is chosen, restricted root run is advisable.

When the plants begin to flower, zero hour is approaching. Under glass, one will have to provide pollen and flowers for hybridizing. With most roses the pollen ripens well before the stigma (female part), but this does not happen usually until the petals are well coloured, and the bud is sufficiently advanced for the petals to be stripped off with ease. Some varieties (certain polyanthas) ripen very early, and the anthers must be removed while the bud is quite tight. The petals are taken away by peeling off cleanly and at the same time cutting or breaking off the green sepals, avoiding damage to the remaining green parts and making sure that all the petal is removed. Otherwise, tiny bits of petal may decay, and set up what is the worst trouble of all, botrytis. This mould can cause rapid decay, although its worst effect is often delayed until the seed pod has become well formed. Then decay begins where the petal was only partially removed, and the whole pod rots.

At this point one's policy is to be dictated by the absence or presence of insects. My experience has been that where ordinary insecticides are used regularly in the greenhouse there is little likelihood of cross-pollination by bees or insects. If this trouble is feared, the prepared flower should be covered with a paper cone.

'Emasculation', the removal of the anthers, takes place after the petals have been removed. This is a more delicate and tedious job. If one decides to keep the anthers to produce pollen for other crosses they should be saved, labelled, and stored in a warm, dry atmosphere when the pollen will be free to use a day or so later. Probably the simplest and quickest method of emasculation is to use a pair of slender, curved manicure scissors. Anthers should be removed by cutting through the filament where it joins the flower and levering out if the anthers are still embedded round the pistils. While the majority come away easily, some varieties are more difficult, and it is essential to see that every anther is removed so that the receptive stigma does not receive any pollen from its own flower (see plate 15).

It is not possible to give the time in hours when the stigma will be ready, but with normal weather, a flower head prepared one morning should be ready the following day. A very sunny day may hasten matters, a cool day may delay or even prevent the stigma from becoming receptive. This state can be seen quite easily, for the stigma will appear shiny and sticky if it is ready.

Now comes the time for transferring the chosen pollen. Some use a small paint-brush which has the disadvantage of needing cleaning. Some use a piece of dark, rough-textured cloth. The black will show up the golden or brown pollen, and its removal will be easy. The forefinger makes a simple tool for the job, and if the work is done gently, can be very effective. Where flowers are plentiful the pollen-laden flower may be removed, the petals folded and held back, and the anthers placed against the stigma of the chosen flower. One pollen-laden flower should pollinate at least three prepared heads.

Whichever method is used is of little importance, so long as the stigma is well dusted with pollen. The next item is to label the flower head with the cross just made (see plate 16). The paper cap can be refixed to exclude insects. It is advisable within a few days to dust the treated heads with dry Captan as this reduces the risk of botrytis. On no account should the plants be watered from above, and the aim should be to produce a dry buoyant atmosphere. Trickle irrigation is used when hybridizing on a large scale, so that the surface soil remains perfectly dry.

It will be some weeks before the results will be apparent, and one must not be disappointed if a large percentage of crosses fail to take. It will be possible, under glass, to catch a batch of later flowers if first results have been poor. Results may not then be as good, but they can be very useful. So much depends upon the weather when the plants are in flower. Sunshine is a great asset, but if the sun is too fierce a slight sprinkling of whitewash scattered on the glass will prevent a too strong concentration of heat on the exposed stigma.

The ripening of the pod is a long, slow process, and that is one reason why fertilization carried out in the garden, even if successful, cannot usually produce a ripened seed pod in time.

Pods should be collected and sorted by parentage. From then on a wide variation in methods of 'after ripening' is employed; 'after ripening' is probably the most important factor in successful germination. When the pod leaves the plant the seed is only partly ripe, and when one examines a ripened seed the contrast between the thick hard outer shell and the tiny seed within is most marked.

How can this tiny seed break through such a hard coat? The answer lies in the period between ripening and germination and is called 'after ripening'. Undoubtedly the rotting of the seed pod, with its acid reaction, softens the seed coat, so that a period of storage in the seed pod is indicated. These should be stored in a material which, while remaining damp, allows ample air, so damp peat or vermiculite are excellent materials in which to store these pods. From now on two methods may be employed. For simplicity the amateur is well advised to store his seed pods outside in a northern aspect where the peat can be well weathered, but protected from pests. A temperature of 1° C (34° F) is considered ideal, but in a winter where temperatures see-saw around freezing-point, results are generally good. A mild winter can give poor immediate results.

At this stage one should be warned against the arch-enemy of the rose seed. These enemies are mice, especially field-mice, which can play havoc in a night. They will come a long way for such a feast. Beside using a protection such as perforated zinc, a few traps should be kept in position to destroy these marauders.

It is now maintained that if possible after ripening should be in two stages. The first a period of heat for about six weeks when the temperature should be 15·6° to 21·1° C (60° to 70° F), and then a period of chilling at 1° C or 40° F.

Where adequate uniform treatment by temperature is possible seeds may be sown at a temperature of 15·6° C (60° F) in November. This is not practical for the amateur who is advised to wait, and in mid or late February the seeds should be removed from their pods and they will show various degrees of ripening. All normal rounded seeds should be sown 2·5 × 2·5 cm apart (1 × 1 in) in either new seed boxes or sterilized flower pots, according to the number of seeds. The coverage of seed should be 1·25 cm (½ in) of sterilized soil with a surface covering of sharp grit or very coarse sand to prevent the formation of moss at a later date. If possible they should be given a temperature of 13° to 17·5° C (55° to 65° F). Hybrid teas germinate better at slightly higher temperatures than floribunda roses. If temperatures cannot be kept as high, one need not worry. Germination will be slower and more erratic, but the final results may be as good. Plants may be grown on after germination, or as soon as the true leaf shows may be transplanted into 5-cm (2-in) pots which need to be buried in damp peat to keep uniformly moist. On no account should one allow the temperature to rise to 26·7° C (80° F), as it can well do on a sunny April day if not checked by screening or ventilation. Germination will cease under such conditions. From this stage the expert must diverge completely from the inexperienced amateur. The expert may weed out all unsuitable varieties when the first flower blooms, and bud the tiny rose bush when 10 cm (4 in) high, getting up to four eyes. The safer method is to destroy useless varieties, but after nipping off the flowers of the remainder to the first leaf, feed with foliar feed, and so encourage thicker growth which will give better blooms and thicker budding wood, which will be ready for budding in August. The initial soil should be John Innes No. 1 with a quarter extra in bulk of sharp sand. Fast drainage is essential.

'Aftercare' is a problem which can baffle the most skilled at times. Heat is not essential for rose germination. Seed will germinate at very low temperatures, and in the early stages will not be damaged by frost. As the true leaves appear and unfold, they become prone to mildew, and here heat helps to keep them growing. Dusting with green sulphur powder keeps the trouble in check. There are electric heaters which evaporate sulphur very slowly; these are ideal. Damping off is a great enemy which can be controlled by dusting with Captan. The third trouble is aphis, which can be checked by burning nicotine shreds, or using a good insecticide as a powder or spray.

After the crop, such as it is, has germinated, a very great number of gaps may indicate that there are many more plants to come. The boxes, if placed in a cool frame, will often germinate in the autumn, a most undesirable happening, as it is most difficult to bring them through the winter. If you have removed the germinated plants or propagated from them, dry off the boxes and keep them dry during the winter, watering thoroughly in the following spring, when they may be brought into the greenhouse again and may germinate freely. Many consider this second chance a waste of time, but some very good results have disproved this.

One must remember that raising the seedling is only the beginning, although a very interesting start to a long journey towards success.

When the first flower of the seedling has appeared, some assessment of the possibilities can be made. The colour will change little, but the stages through which the flower will pass from the coloured bud to the falling flower are many and important. Is the colour clear, pleasing and above all stable? If the colour is good in the early stages and the fading shade pleasing, there is nothing to prevent this from being useful. Some shades, especially the salmon-orange, invariably fade in age. The fading bloom can tell much. If the ageing bloom is displeasing, that is, if an orange flame takes on a purple tinge, or a shell-pink becomes white or spotty, a 'Masquerade' type becomes blotched or uneven, then this should be discarded. If the crossing has been for floribundas, an important point which can be settled at this stage is whether the old flower 'shatters' (falls cleanly). Unless this happens one may be faced with an untidy head of flowers in old age, a most damaging factor for a floribunda. I have mentioned clarity of colour, and this is particularly important for the red colours. 'Muddy', pale, dull reds should be discarded ruthlessly. With cluster roses only one flower will appear on the head at this stage so that the size of the flower head will not be known until later.

On the amount of petalage necessary in a rose, less definite rules can be laid down. As a general rule, petalage will increase from the seedling stage. A variety with three rows of petals may well build up to a bloom of twenty-eight petals, quite enough for a decorative variety. The same factor at the end of the scale may be a warning. A very double variety in the seedling stage will not open outside. An 'ideal flower' in the seedling stage, growing in warmth and dry, may raise the hopes of a hybridist skyhigh. After a test in the open he may well wonder why he made such a hopeful forecast. Little can be said of the health or growth of the variety until grown outside.

If a preliminary sorting has taken place, the next stage is to bud these seedlings. It is not an easy matter to keep such seedlings alive if one tries to over-winter. Such thin wood needs smaller stocks and

3 to 5 millimetres should be the size planted for this purpose the previous winter.

When these budded seedlings begin to grow the following year their testing begins in earnest. Judgement should not be hasty, for some varieties, especially hybrid teas, may not develop good flowers until the second blooming period. Probably to save paper work a preliminary remark or sign may be placed on the wooden identity label. The parentage should be checked, and if the variety appears sufficiently promising, the identity number, the reason why it is considered good and such points as growth, colour and perfume should be noted. This may seem much trouble, but often a hybridist has to choose between two similar seedlings and some small advantage may place the chosen variety in the lead. During August a first selection may be made, and probably fifty buds of the best will be budded again for transplanting and other tests. Some important points may be overlooked in the first year, but an increased number of plants will show up the strength or weakness of the plants. An instance comes to mind. A seedling 'Karl Herbst' × 'Fandango' obtained a Trial Ground Certificate at the Royal National Rose Society's Trials. It had been propagated to seven hundred and fifty plants in the field and was due for distribution the following year. The season was a wet one and every bloom failed to open. The plants were burnt and the variety discarded. It is because of weather conditions that roses need testing in the open over a period of years before final decision and distribution take place. A commercial hybridist will distribute his varieties to agents in all parts of the world before these are put into commerce, and he will know that very few varieties can become international favourites. Climatic conditions can make or mar a rose, and demands and ideals vary greatly. Only those who do such work realize how much correspondence precedes the successful launching of a good rose, and only a very good rose is worth the trouble.

In some countries trained geneticists are seeking evidence to employ in the future building up of improved varieties. In some cases the raising of a hundred thousand seedlings a year is the objective.

One should not be deterred from 'having a go'. The delight of having raised a rose of one's own is very great, even if it is not a real winner. Not only are there the pleasures of anticipation, always more thrilling than realization, but there is the perennial hope of something better next time. 'Frensham', I believe, began very humbly from a selfed seedling crossed into a further generation, and the unknown may open a new approach, bringing fresh vigour and new strength to the future rose. It is not in the variety itself that all the inspiration lies. Some of it comes from the widened horizon and enlarged objectives of an increased hybridizing programme.

 CHAPTER XVI

Testing New Roses

The raising of the new rose itself is only a small part of what has to be done before the variety can be placed on the market.

Up to ten budding eyes of any varieties which promise possibilities are put on stocks the first season. During the following summer these full-sized rose trees are carefully checked and the opinion noted. A very few will show at their first flowering that they warrant further propagation; others will need growing on, perhaps through a second season. There will always be a few varieties promising some improvement other than in the flower itself. While of no commercial value, that may offer, by their growth, foliage, colour, or some distinct characteristic, some future improvement in the rose strain. These should be retained for more crossing and testing. Many great varieties have been raised from such parents because the breeder saw possibilities in what would have appeared to the average person a mediocre cultivar.

When a promising sort is spotted in the second year, this will be budded again in an increased quantity of fifty to a hundred stocks. While these are maturing, the original bushes will be divided up, part will go into the greenhouse and part into the trial bed. By year number 3, from the time of germination, some definite ideas will be formed, and there will be enough budding wood to raise up to five hundred plants, while the bushes of no. 3 crop will be distributed to agents abroad, and probably to a few reliable British rose friends in the trade for their opinion. If this opinion is favourable then the variety will be sent to trial grounds at home and abroad.

Different systems are in use and are, broadly speaking, of three kinds: a body of experts both amateur and professional, such as that of the Royal National Rose Society; a scheme run by professionals only as the All America Award and the British Association of Rose Breeders; and the Continental schemes, where an extended adjudication by experts is helped in assessing a final judgement given on a particular day at a *concours* by a wide variety of judges.

One must remember that various methods and standards applied differ because of local needs, climate and country. Few roses receive world-wide acceptance, as 'Peace', 'Super Star' and 'Allgold' have done. It is especially true of varieties which receive awards in extreme climates, for a rose growing in a warm dry country would be of a very different type to that receiving its award in the Scandinavian countries. Because a rose has won an award abroad it does not follow that it will be needed here. The reverse applies, the greatest differentiation being in the quantity and quality of the petal, for with the dull, wet and cold weather full roses and those with thin petals fail to open.

This is one reason why it is inadvisable to give undue attention to awards made in other countries. This is no reflection on the judging of the roses but is an acknowledgement that different climates and conditions demand other qualities than those which we require. The same applies in reverse, and a hybridist is well advised to acquire a knowledge of what is needed in other parts of the world if he is to make full use of the seedlings he raises. There is, of course, the further choosing of varieties for forcing, but these would rarely be acceptable for outside work and would usually be bred for the purpose of forcing only. This is a highly skilled professional matter where the testing is far more expensive and meticulous than the actual raising. The sort of things tested are colour which must be indicated from the tight bud; strength and length of flower stem and particularly the pedicle; type and quality of foliage with spray damage resistance; flower production which embraces quality, quantity, uniformity, ease and time taken to mature; above all its need for some greatly improved characteristics for which there is likely to be a real market demand, otherwise the expense of putting it into commerce would not be justified. Probably the greatest need is for attractive colour novelty. To list some of the requirements emphasizes afresh how exact, searching and expensive is the process of elimination and selection.

Other tests are needed for climbing and shrub roses and some time has to elapse before final results can be assessed. A good repeat climber would need to be grown for at least three years before its full flowering capacity could be ascertained. A compensation is that at the end of that time, one large specimen would yield many hundred budding eyes so that final distribution could be rapid.

For the British raiser his main trial ground will be that of the Royal National Rose Society which has its offices and trials under the judges' panel at St. Albans, Hertfordshire. Part of these grounds are a rose display garden of varieties which have already received awards, but the important work of the Society is adjudication on the new sorts. This trial is for any rose cultivar raised throughout the world and these may be submitted by amateurs or professionals or their agents, and while some raisers both amateur and professional may act as judges because of their specialist knowledge they are excluded from judging any rose in which they may have a professional interest. Because of the increasing number of entries each raiser is now limited to the number he may submit, although awards in prior years may add a bonus to the number allowed. A special part of the garden is set aside for these trials, and long beds, about 1·8 m wide, are prepared and planted with six specimens of a new hybrid tea or floribunda rose. Two climbers of a sort are submitted, and these are grown for three years. The first year they are not judged, although their general behaviour and especially their resistance to disease are watched. The second and third years they are eligible for judging and to compete for awards.

To judge these roses, a special panel of twenty members, with an amateur chairman, are elected annually by the Council (itself elected from seventy thousand members). From late June to September five members of this panel visit the trials each week by rota. Each member has his own book which is especially prepared with a page for each variety. Awards are based on a points system as follows:

Growth (vigour), 10 points
Habit of growth, 10 points
Freedom from disease, 20 points
Beauty of form and/or garden value, 10 points
Colour, 10 points   } 100 points
Freedom and continuity of flowering, 10 points
General effect, 10 points
Fragrance, 10 points
Novelty, 10 points

To qualify for the award of a Trial Ground Certificate, any variety must obtain a minimum of seventy points and 50 per cent under each heading, excluding fragrance. By this method a rose with some general weakness, such as proneness to disease, would be excluded. An alternative pointing, giving an aggregate of 1 to 10 based on the above system, is permitted. A set of rules has been drawn up for the judges, who attend the trials and mark their books separately.

During the period of judging all varieties will be seen at all stages by some judges. Every rose has its good days and 'off' periods. By this 'extended' judging, every rose gets a fair chance. Even with the utmost care, some varieties may present problems, and at a final meeting, all judges come together to make their final assessment and awards. Any doubt can be met by visiting the actual rose for a final decision.

The primary award is the 'Trial Ground Certificate'. This is a recommendation that the rose is a good reliable variety for the average garden. After this comes the 'Certificate of Merit' which is a guarantee that the rose has sufficient merit, as well as health, to warrant its introduction to the general public. The blue riband of the Society is the 'Gold Medal' which implies that the variety is outstanding in its class. The Gold Medal is actually of gold, beautifully engraved, on which the name of the rose, the raiser and the date on which the award is made, are added.

A coveted award is the 'Harry Edland Memorial Medal for Fragrance' given to the most fragrant rose of the year. A minimum award of Trial Ground Certificate is essential for the rose to compete. Beyond this lies the 'President's Trophy' award to the best rose of the year. The cultivar must receive a Gold Medal to be eligible. If no rose reaches this standard the award is withheld.

It is probably fair to say that this way of judging is as thorough as any method can be. All aspects of the rose from both amateur and professional viewpoint are considered. While no method is infallible, few really good roses submitted for trial are omitted from the awards list.

Once these awards have been made, and as soon as the plants are available commercially, they are distributed to centres throughout the British Isles. By this method local judgement may be made on how roses receiving National awards react to other parts of the British Isles. Also the new roses may be seen under conditions approaching those of the surrounding area without interested growers having to travel to St. Albans.

The British Association of Rose Breeders have united to form a scheme by which their own cultivars may be tested under professional field conditions to discover the best available for the home market. Each participant buds his own and other B.A.R.B. member varieties in a special position and adjudicates on them during the growing season. The pointing has a commercial bias in so far that ease of production in first-size plants, and selling qualities have a high rating. The collated results are submitted to the licencees with the object of promoting the best and eliminating the less useful, and the winning rose with highest marks is known as B.A.R.B. 'Rose of the Year'. The Association is not exclusive and is open to both professional and amateur raisers.

The All America Rose Selection is run by professionals to test the best varieties with the greatest commercial value. With such a vast country, having so many climates, one trial ground is totally inadequate, but as these trials are held at selected nurseries, separate trial grounds with separate staffs are not needed and they can be distributed evenly over the many states.

A high degree of cultivation is assured and expert attention at all times. Each variety is numbered, and the identity is not known during judging. A separate printed sheet is issued for each variety and is sufficient for the two seasons covered by the judging. This sheet is headed by its identity number, followed by the date when planted and number of trees. A note concerning the state of the plant when received, and the number of replacements, and their date of planting is also entered.

Four separate colours for the judging sheets are used to separate the four classes into which roses are divided: Tea Hybrid Roses; Floribunda–Polyantha Roses; Grandiflora Roses; Climber, Pillar–Rambler Roses. Thirteen characteristics receive points, except with the ramblers which are pointed on fifteen characteristics. Each of these is pointed according to its relative importance to the whole. A hybrid tea receives up to 7 for fragrance, a grandiflora a maximum of 4 for the same quality. In all cases 5 points are allowed for novelty. The maximum points given are 105 except for the fourth class which can rise to 110. Up to twelve separate pointings are allowed for each season, with a Spring Report and a Fall Report in the first year and a Spring Report and a Final Report in the second year.

All report sheets are sent in to the Secretary of the All America Rose Selection. These are collated, and the totals are made known. Awards are not necessarily made to those obtaining the top score. 'Potential Sales Possibility' receives the first consideration, and dictates the final awards made by the judges, who meet for this purpose. Primarily, then, the award is made with the objective of sales promotion, but the All America Award is given for good roses only, and these roses are very carefully assessed beforehand by real authorities who take their work very seriously. Roses for these awards have to be submitted through participating nurseries.

The third method, largely used in Europe, consists of a selected international team of experts leavened with local notables. The judging takes place on one day of the year, when the majority of rose trees are expected to bloom. Thus an early or late variety may fail to appeal to the panel. To offset this in part, some indication is given as to its general behaviour during the remainder of the season by those who have grown it. But, even so, a good rose out of bloom on the great day is unlikely to be considered.

Such *concours* have a social as well as a judging angle, also a considerable prestige pull for the city or country which sponsors them. Every effort is made to keep the identity of the variety anonymous, but professionals travelling from one *concours* to the other have a very good idea of the raiser and often the variety. In many cases participants in the Trials do not adjudicate at all. In others they may be appointed as judges, but are excluded from judging their own varieties.

A Rose Garden started by the Dutch under the auspices of The Hague is planted at Westbroekpark, The Hague, Holland. Here are roses in nearly four hundred varieties, eighty of a sort in separate beds. These are judged annually and over a period. The main test garden for the newest sorts has six bushes of varieties not yet in commerce. These are judged by experts who have detailed information as to the behaviour of the rose during its first year of growth. It is judged in its second season.

An excellent system of marking has been evolved, and the judging, which is done by individuals, not by a panel (which is more general at such *concours*) are collated and are ready for the final judgement and awards to be announced during the civic luncheon which follows the judging. In this instance awards are given first to new roses, second to the roses in commerce planted in the permanent beds which have excelled that year, and third to roses which, over a period, have been found consistently out-standing. This last, a Garden Merit Award, sets the seal on a good all-round variety.

France probably owed her earlier pre-eminence in the rose world to the Empress Josephine, who on her retirement to Mal-maison took up rose growing. I was informed recently that she was in correspondence with the British Museum, which at that time was also the Natural History Museum, about rose varieties; and William Paul states in 1847, 'The late Mr. Kennedy was provided with a passport to go and come as he pleased during the war, in order that he might superintend the formation of that garden.' As has been told elsewhere, it was the behaviour of naturally crossed species in producing unlikely seedlings, which led to artificial hybridizing by both amateur and professional rose growers in France.

Paris had the honour of producing the first international trial

ground at Bagatelle, but the group of nurserymen round Lyons
instituted a competitive award for new seedling roses about 1837,
so that to them belongs the honour of making the first awards to
new roses.

Many countries have their own trials for roses, the addresses of
some of which are:

Belgium   Responsible Technique de la Roseraie,
                   Chateau du Roeulx,
                   Roeulx (Mons).

         also   Internationale Rozentuin voor de
                       Noordzeelanden Kortrijk,
                   Secretariaat,
                   Leopold III, straat 16,
                   B–9002, Ledeberg/Gent.

Denmark   Copenhagen Municipality Test Gardens,
                   Valby Park, Copenhagen.

Holland   International Rose Competition,
                   Municipal Parks Department,
                   The Hague, Holland.

France   Direction des Affaires Domaniales
                       sous-direction des Parcs, Jardins et
                       Espaces Verts,
                   3 Avenue de la Porte d'Auteuil,
                   75016—Paris.

Germany   Internationale Rosenneuheiten–Wettbewerb,
                   757 Baden-Baden.
                   (Dip. Ing. Weigel-Gartenamtsleiter).

Switzerland   Service des Parcs et Promenades,
                   Rue de Lausanne 120, (Parc Moynier),
                   1202 Geneve, Switzerland.

Italy   Concorso Internazionate Al Premio
                       Di Roma,
                   Per Nouve Varieta Di Rose,
                   Rome, Italy.

New Zealand   New Zealand International Rose Trial Gardens,
               P.O. Box 1006,
               Palmerston North,
               New Zealand.

Japan   Nobuo Tanizawa,
               The Japan Rose Society,
               8–28–12 Okuzawa,
               Setagaya-ku, Tokyo.

There can be little doubt that the interest in the rose has been fostered by specialist societies throughout the world, and the Royal National Rose Society has the enviable position of being the largest plant specialist society in existence, the present membership being some seventy thousand. As explained in Chapter XI the Society began in 1876, but it was not until after the Second World War that membership increased so greatly. The large number of new houses, increased earnings and the innate love of the rose, have each contributed to the great success of this Queen of Flowers.

Any visitors to London should not fail to visit the Queen Mary Rose Garden at Regent's Park. This is not a trial ground, and many good varieties are missing, but for good cultivation, sheer beauty and interest this lovely garden should be seen. It is a revelation of what fine roses can be, cultivated in a difficult environment.

Whether it be the open admiration lavished on the rose, in the home, in parks, or at shows, or from whatever cause, the fact remains that the rose, by its inimitable adaptability, peerless beauty and gracious charm is enthroned in the hearts of thousands who, under its influence, have found a strong bond of fellowship spiced by friendly rivalry.

Raising new roses has become a highly technical and competitive business largely in the hands of a few raisers of world-wide reputation and experience. In addition there are many smaller raisers who have won an international reputation with a few choice new roses. It is probable that seven raisers between them produce two million seedlings annually and of those the number of good new roses of wide appeal would be ten or under while there would not be as many as one a year of outstanding roses of world choice. On the other hand requirements are so varied climatically and from the point of view of fashion that local demands may absorb many good sorts not universally required. The money invested in glasshouses for seed production, in land and rose stocks for testing, and above all in promotion, is extremely heavy. Because of this raisers rely more and more on the royalties they receive from their new kinds to continue in production. This has been recognized internationally as well as nationally and our Plant Varieties Rights Act gives some help in admitting the right of a raiser to obtain some recompense for the skill, labour and costs involved.

A 'Protected Variety' is registered with the Plant Varieties Rights Office on payment of a variable and increasing fee which if paid can keep the rights for fifteen years. In return the raiser may license others to grow his varieties on payment of a small fee. The actual royalty charge is not large, for profit can lie only in large sales with a small royalty, rather than small sales with a heavy payment. In Britain, B.A.R.B. acts as agent for the raisers and contacts the licencees for them, sharing the costs of collection.

The whole objective of testing roses is to ensure reliability, and protection should guarantee a higher standard. Exploitation of a gullible public is less likely, and the reputable grower will receive and give a fair deal to those to whom knowledge and experience have taught the value of the best at all times.

 CHAPTER XVII

Perfume in Roses

When one shows a new rose to a friend or inspects it oneself the first instinctive movement is to stoop and smell the blossom. Despite the historical fact that many roses have always had little perfume, we still tend to equate roses with that quality. Indeed, we fall into a greater fallacy by expecting a rose to have one type of perfume, when in reality there is a whole orchestra of lively notes in rose scent to play upon our sense of smell, conveying a delightful harmony, ever alive with variety, to appeal to each need and mood. While we associate perfume with blossom, a little reflection will remind us that many plants have strong odours in other parts as well. The rose itself has at least four parts which are perfumed. There is the scent of the leaves, especially in the sweet briers and their hybrids. This perfume is very strong and noticeable. All foliage of roses presents a definite if elusive scent, and this may well make it difficult to dissociate from the perfume of the flower, especially if in a confined place. On opening a box of cut roses this is very noticeable. It is also true of the growing roses in the greenhouse, which, long before the flowers appear, have a 'growing' smell.

The strong aromatic perfume of *R. primula* is emitted from its wood even more than from its leaves. The moss of the moss rose is noteworthy. It is in the blossom that the final and strongest perfume may be found. Generally speaking, evidence shows that the perfume is produced by growth substances, chloroplasts, in the green parts of the plant. Their manufacture is very closely associated with the chlorophyll (the green substance aiding the formation of starch by photosynthesis). It is a baffling fact that in

these tiny cells, highly complicated compounds are built up with the carbon dioxide from the air combining with the water in the plant. Thus the same elements which produce the starch, a simple and insoluble material which the plant changes to sugar when it is transferred elsewhere, also produce, possibly by the aid of some agent, a highly complicated chemical substance by way of dehydration (glucosides). These materials formed in the green part of the plant, largely the leaf, are odourless, but they may be readily broken down in any part of the plant, if the reagent producing the change is present. As we have seen this may occur in the wood, leaf, sepal, or in the hairy excrescences of the 'moss' rose, although generally speaking, the most noticeable scent-bearing part is the flower. These glucosides may be stored or transported in the sap or the petals. The part of the sepal and petal exposed to the light in the bud form is oxidized longer than the upper side of the petal, and in these more exposed cells tannin is formed. The inner side of the petal where the reaction with light takes place later, and oxidation is delayed, produces essential oil, the basis of perfume. During a warm sunny day activity is greatly increased, and if there is sufficient moisture to encourage chemical action more glucosides than usual are made by the chloroplast. These are more rapidly transported to the petals where they undergo a swift change. This has an important bearing on the increase of perfume, for the glucosides by reaction with water molecules (hydrolysis) are changed into glucose and alcohols, the first step in the building up of the perfumes. A further change takes place when the alcohols are changed to aldehydes, and in this form the perfume strength is increased enormously, in some cases multiplying the strength up to two hundred times.

What causes the glucosides to remain stable and then change? This is probably due to an enzyme or ferment, a medium which makes conditions favourable to further chemical change. The essential oil appears at once and begins to circulate. Sometimes this medium appears in wood, root, stem, or leaf but usually is most commonly found on the upper surface of the petal. The cells or structures where these essential oils are oxidized are known as papillae and are like blunt hairs or slight undulations on the surface

of the petal presenting the maximum area on which the sun and air can play. There is some doubt as to the method and place of storage of these substances, but it is suggested that these essential oils are also stored just below the outer skin of the petal and the first row of cells, and are thought to be stored there as glucosides (combinations of the sugar, glucose, with the rose alcohols).

Part of the difficulty of identification is the rapidity with which the changes take place and the possible difference between various types of plant families. It does seem that most of this storage takes place just below the 'skin' or cuticle of the plant and that at times these spaces may intrude upon cell space. Because of their nearness to the surface of the plant's tissues, the slightest bruising of the plant where this storage is found gives rise to the release of perfume.

In the rose, it can occur in the green sepals, and one may confuse the scent from the sepals (especially with moss roses) with the scent from the petals with which it mingles. The reaction of light on the colour of the petal may set up the necessary chemical change to produce a particular type of perfume. Enough has been said to show the extremely complicated processes which go to produce rose perfumes, but we may take it that the original unscented basic substances (glucosides) are produced in the plant cells by the action of chlorophyll, transported by the sap to the petals; and in the petals the glucosides are hydrolized into glucose and rose alcohols. These rose alcohols may then be oxidized into the petals to form aldehydes and oxides. Thus, degree of perfume and variety will depend upon weather conditions, soil conditions and the stage the flower has reached. With this brief and necessarily sketchy review of how scent is manufactured in roses we may now consider how perfume can be assessed. This is beset by difficulties, but should not lead to defeat. Rather is it a challenge to explore another delightful aspect of rose cultivation.

In the first place, smelling can be a trained sense and can be greatly improved by experiment and use. Just as ability to taste, discern colours, feel cloths, or distinguish musical notes is developed by intelligent use, so this sense of smell can be improved by comparison and employment.

'The odour strength of a compound depends to some extent on its volatility, but even more on the irritating properties on the nerves of the inner nose membranes which are above the roof of the mouth and between the eye sockets.' This fact points to the necessity for taking a deep sniff. To get the best results one should hold the severed bloom in cupped, warmed hands, expelling warm breath into the flower and then inhaling through the nose. Make sure hands are clean and soap free. Even so, experience shows that there is a very wide divergence in the power to smell and more, that individuals are highly selective in the odours which they can smell. The majority can smell the strong damask perfume, but other types of perfume appeal to a very varied selection of human beings. We are highly selective in what we 'notice' when we inhale. Judging perfume has always been a controversial issue, and the method used by the Royal National Rose Society of taking a majority vote of all judges assembled, gives a fair cross-section, and is probably as accurate as any. The difficulty is heightened by the fact that different roses have their optimum diffusion period for perfume. One half-open bloom in one variety will have more scent at that time than at any other stage, while another variety may have more perfume at full expansion.

I am told that one branch of the rose, the synstylae, where the stigmas are fused together, have their perfume in the anthers and not in the petals. This I have not proved but I do know that certain roses of this type lose their perfume as soon as the anthers begin to die and long before the petals show signs of degeneration.

A further important point is that the perfume of a rose can be seriously affected and diminished in a room, for there are too many background odours. Outside, the perfume is less seriously affected by surroundings, and ability to discern scent is stronger. 'In all things charity' should be the rule when judging for perfume and final judgement can only be accurate when it has been accumulated over a number of tests carried out at different times with differing stages of flower. Climatic conditions greatly affect the production and dissemination of perfume, so that all assessments can only be comparative.

Having said all this, what is the ideal time for testing a rose?

Probably on a damp morning, after a night's rain, when the sun has risen long enough to warm the earth, dry the petals and play upon them for a time. Needless to say, smelling a rose while holding a pipe or cigarette or chewing peppermints should be avoided! The best place to smell a rose is the natural surroundings of the garden.

Those who are blind find great pleasure in using their enhanced powers of smell, and can soon distinguish individual roses by the different perfumes they emit. In such cases, lighter pruning of the bushes has much to recommend it, so that their blooms may be brought more on a level with the person. This might well be achieved by interspacing standard and half-standard trees, which will not only raise the level of the flowers, but make identification of varieties more easy. Such being the case, the bushes should be planted wide enough not to jostle one another, so that their individual qualities may be appreciated and they may be grouped for perfumes. Strong-smelling plants such as thymes should not be planted near, so that the true scents may be more easily discerned. The beds should be simple but normal, to take not more than two rows of plants at 1 m (3½ ft) wide so that all rows can be reached easily from either side.

Before we consider the differing types of perfume some further explanation of the behaviour of this factor of scent is advisable. The availability of a perfume at any time depends on various circumstances. One of these is the vapour pressure. The more volatile the essence, the more readily it disperses; the less volatile the more slowly does it become discernible. Thus the variety 'Crimson Glory' passes from rose to clove scent. The damask rose perfume, being more volatile and so appearing first, diminishes with age, when the less volatile clove takes over. As we have seen some odours depend upon when the glucosides are changed, and this process may be delayed until the flower has fully developed.

The most powerful perfume is produced when the alcohols of the original processes are oxidized into aldehydes which are very much stronger in degree of scent. Another factor with perfume is that on dilution, the vapour as it loses intensity appears to change its character. The strong orris becomes violet with greater dilution.

I

Lest we grow disheartened over these complicated processes which give us such lovely perfumes, let me state here that as rose growers, we are concerned with our ability to appreciate and analyse these perfumes for our own pleasure. But knowledge should give edge to our experiment, and 'knowing why' may help us in our 'know how'.

We come now to the crux of the matter: seeking to define the actual perfumes. We cannot emphasize too often that rose perfumes seldom consist of one scent at any time, and certainly not of one scent all the time. The appearance and disappearance of perfumes may well depend upon their volatility. Trying to analyse the perfumes and give them names to recall perfumes we know in standard terms is useful but not as accurate as one could wish. The following have been chosen as possible guides to their identification: 'damask', 'orris-violet', 'apple', 'lemon' and 'clove'.

Damask. This is the strong, sweet, heady perfume which has been associated with roses as a whole. It is largely confined to reds and pinks with a magenta base. While the standard basis for this perfume may be considered to be *R. damascena* 'Kazanlik' it is at times difficult to flower this cultivar in our cooler climate. Transferring the character to present-day roses we would think of older roses such as 'Étoile de Hollande', 'Crimson Glory' (both obtainable in their climbing forms), with 'Ellen Mary', 'Maturity', 'Ernest H. Morse' and 'Alec's Red' in descending order of strength. For a long while it seemed certain that there was a special rose oil constituent having the rose odour which had not been isolated. Mr. Neville F. Miller tells me that this has now been done. This has been named at present 'rosenoxide' by its discoverers. This powerful rose constituent helps to explain why a single flower *R. damascena* 'Kazanlik' can be identified by its odour when the observer is twenty feet or more away from the plant. Mr. Miller continues, 'This new compound has sufficient volatility and the right kind of odour to account for this fact. It is my theory that this newly discovered compound is manufactured in the petals by action of the sunlight and by the catalytic action of the red or pink pigment in the petals. This would account for the damask or true rose odour being confined to red or pink roses.' It is possible that one may be more precise and suggest that the important colour factor is magenta found in both red and pink types, e.g. 'Crimson Glory'.

In my last edition the next type of perfume was called 'nasturtium'. We do not feel this to be an accurate description for present-day roses such as 'Pink Favourite'. While the scent is sweet one would prefer to call it lingering rather than intense, and with it is linked the green growing smell with a slight spiciness like peppercorns—a strange combination but recognizable once one has smelled it. A more recent and stronger perfume of the same type may be found in 'Peer Gynt'.

Orris-violet is a perfume obtained from the dried rhizomes of some iris. Diluted by the air, this gives an odour of violet and is present in a number of roses both as a predominant factor and in combination with the type called 'nasturtium'. Among those possessing an orris perfume it appears that the salmon colour in the petal acts as the catalyst. Because of the vast increase in the orange-salmon roses this has become a more usual although recent addition. It is a sharp lingering perfume often in combination. The strongest perfume may be found in 'Orange Sensation', while 'Salmon Sprite' and 'Elizabeth of Glamis' are good examples of this strong and penetrating perfume. Examples of damask-orris are 'My Choice' and 'Dearest', while the very fragrant 'Blue Moon' may be described as lemon-orris.

Apple. Many perfumes are described as 'fruity' which I feel is conducive to sloppy thinking, but it does provide for the multitude of roses which are perfumed but not comparable with known existing scents. Apple is probably a fair description for 'New Dawn' and 'Ellinor Le Grice'.

Lemon is a common perfume mostly in combination. I would prefer to think of it as lemon-scented verbena (*Lippia citriodora*). A rose with this perfume is 'Sutter's Gold', while 'City of Hereford', 'Harriny' and 'Ophelia' are a mixture of damask and lemon, the former being more evident in the younger flower.

Clove. There are some with a honey-like sweetness which is cloying. Of these 'Amberlight' is quite distinct reminding one of exotic honeys imported from Australia. The clove perfume is also alleged to be present in a number of roses such as *Rosa paulii*.

As usual there are the Awkward Squad refusing to be dragooned into uniform classifications. There are the so-called hybrid musks which despite their doubtful ancestry have a unique perfume: sweet, but overripe and musty at times. Nevertheless roses like 'Buff Beauty' have an added attraction in their distinct but unidentifiable perfume. A sweeter but less musty perfume is found in the delightful 'Lavender Lassie'.

These basic perfumes may be, and often are, in combination, when the one which vaporizes more easily will appear in the younger flower, and the less volatile will appear later, other factors already mentioned being taken into consideration.

Enough has been said to show what a wide and fascinating study this field of perfumes provides, but it also presents other difficult problems for the hybridist.

It may be said that the British raiser, at least, is showing considerable advance in producing perfumed varieties. This does not mean that raisers of other countries are producing all scentless flowers. It is, however, the popular opinion which creates the demand and it is the aim of the raiser to fulfil it. The Royal National Rose Society with its stress on perfume makes it almost impossible to obtain the coveted Gold Medal for a scentless variety of hybrid tea.

While perfume is more common, and is of a much greater variety in new roses than it was twenty years ago, the public have themselves to blame if fewer with damask perfume are appearing. Here we have a baffling linkage of genes. The highly prized red of 'Ena Harkness' is produced by two tones of red: a brilliant currant-red base overlaid by deep, almost blackish, maroon. This is the most popular colour in red roses, and the public demand the characteristic damask perfume with it. But the public also increasingly require a flower which remains upright both when growing and when cut. Unfortunately with this quality of colour goes a weak stem due to length and frailty of the flower stalk, an inherited character, and this linkage so far remains unbroken. It is possible to breed the perfume of 'Sutter's Gold' (a fruity perfume classed as 'lemon') into a red, but this gives a bright red with thin wiry upright stems and sparse foliage, which makes a poor bedding rose. It is possible to cross 'Ena Harkness' with an upright-stemmed pink such as 'Wellworth', and produce a strongly scented pink rose such as 'My Choice' or 'Lively', but crossing into a second generation (F.2), always leads to a weak stem if the red damask-scented flower reappears.

The best one can do is to produce a light flower of twenty petals or less, such as 'Josephine Bruce', whose weight can be supported by a weak stem, so that for most of its life it will appear upright.

While perfume is highly desirable, it is not a necessity, and one should consider it as an extra gift bountifully provided. Test this statement for yourself. The most vociferous exponent of perfume will forget this quality for the moment when face to face with an outstanding colour. Perfume is a gracious asset bestowed more frequently than we are apt to think and by training the faculty of smelling we shall view our roses from a different but very rewarding angle.

Few roses are without some perfume, and the faint fragrance produced by some varieties linger in one's memory long after it has wafted away, leaving a desire to renew the acquaintance whenever possible.

This chapter would be unfinished without reference to three ways in which the essence of the rose has been captured to release its fragrance when desired. The simplest and oldest is probably rose water, the actual result of distilling rose blooms in water and steaming out and catching their perfume in the cooled steam. At a later stage it was found that a concentrated oily substance came to the surface of the rose water in tiny quantities. This became known as 'attar of roses', and because of its strength and rarity was highly prized and priced. A more modern method is to trap the perfume in a solid base. Methods of distillation vary and until 1574 the rose 'Otto' or 'Attar' was unmentioned, although the distillation of roses probably began in Persia before the Christian era. Very great differences are observed in the quality and intensity of the perfume when made. This depends in part on the type of rose used, that of Bulgaria being described as having a sweeter, fuller and more honey-like bouquet than the French type. Much also depends upon the freshness of the roses when distilled, and also on the care during that process. As the flower heads are gathered as early in the morning as possible, many are wet with dew, and if they remain in bulk for any length of time, they will heat and spoil. It is usual to finish distilling the day's picking without delay and the stills are kept going until the early hours of the following morning, if necessary, to dispose of the day's picking. Bulgaria is famous for the rose perfume which comes from a comparatively small area, a valley some 130 km (80 miles) in length by 16 to 48 km (10 to 30 miles) wide, running from Klisura to Kazanlik. The valley is well protected by mountains, and climate and soil are ideal for rose production. Rose picking extends from mid May to mid June. The whole head of the flower with calyx is taken as soon as opened, and before the hot sun develops. This is the period of maximum perfume. The rose fields themselves are of *R. damascena* and the distinctive strain, which has already been mentioned, is known as 'Kazanlik'. This is pink in colour with thirty to forty petals. The bushes are high with just enough space between them for picking. There are 'boundary' hedges of *R. alba* and these, although less fragrant, are also used. Reliable figures are very hard to obtain. The following facts may be of interest: that thirty-two thousand roses weighing about 81 kg (180 lb) yield 28 g (1 oz) of rose oil; five million roses, weighing nearly 4,064 kg (4 tons), would make about 4·5 kg (10 lb) of attar of roses. This would be the daily production of a large distillery and would go on for four or five weeks. Bulgarian 'Otto' smells very sweet and quite sharp, but not much like a rose. It is used to add sweetness to many perfumes and is very expensive.

A second area of production is in Southern France in the Grasse area of Provence. This variety is known as the 'Rose de Mai', from its time of flowering, or 'Rose de Provence'. It has a semi-double flower of rose-pink, with at least two rows of petals. The flowers, which are small, 5 to 7·5 cm (2 to 3 in) across, are carried in trusses with at least ten flowers in a head. The bloom produces a perfume of outstanding delicacy and strength. This 'Rose de Mai' was a hybrid between *R. centifolia* (from Asia Minor) and 'Rose de Provins' (*R. gallica*) which is said to be indigenous, although it is believed that Theobault IV brought back from Damascus to Grasse a type of 'Rose de Provins' with a reddish purple flower.

There are two varieties, one with many thorns and one with few. The first is more suited to very dry areas without irrigation. It is more vigorous, with smaller flowers, although these are highly perfumed.

Propagation is done by budding on *R. indica major* or *R. canina*, which gives a more regular and abundant crop with fewer suckers and therefore fewer thorns. Canina is a more compatible stock, but the budding or grafting is more costly. The other method is to select healthy suckers at pruning time and after 'heeling in' to plant out in the spring. Planting is done in well-prepared soil which should be of a heavy rather than light texture. Bushes are placed about 40 cm (16 in) apart and with about 2 m (7 ft) between rows during March. Although irrigation is not essential, it improves yield. A good fertilizer, high in superphosphate, is used during planting. Pruning is done by removing all old and exhausted shoots: about four shoots to a plant are left, all young, vigorous and upright. By the process known as *'entortillage'* these are bent over and entwined by tying with their neighbours, so making a continuous fence which encourages the maximum of bloom in the easiest form for picking.

A note states that strong gloves are needed for this thorny operation! Feeding is on conventional lines with sulphate of ammonia, superphosphate, and sulphate of potash. In 1952 there were about 253 hectares (625 acres) in cultivation and the area was being increased. Production was about 1,000 kg (2,200 lb) of the concentrated perfume. Today the roses grown at Grasse are extracted with highly purified petroleum ether and even with butane which boils below room temperature. The butane extracts, called 'butaflors', are probably very close to the true rose odour. The evaporated petroleum ether extract, called 'Rose de Mai Concrete' is quite close to the original.

Since this was written an excellent article has appeared in the 1975 *Rose Annual* by Dr. A. S. Thomas in which his recent researches have shown that considerable changes have been made both in the varieties used and in the method of production. One great change appears to be that the 'Rose de Mai' has been replaced by more modern roses chief of which are 'Ulrich Brunner-fils', H.P. (A. Levet 1881), of doubtful origin, 'Louis van Houtte', H.P. (Lacharme 1869) and 'Marie van Houtte', T. (Ducher 1871) 'all of which are less troublesome and are very fragrant and give recurrent bloom'.

The rose-perfume industry of Morocco is confined to two centres, the Dades rose valley and the Oulmes area of North-West Morocco. History does not relate when and why the older enterprise of the Dades valley came into being. The rose-growing lands are 1,500 to 1,800 m (5,000 to 6,000 ft) above sea-level and high mountains shelter it and in fact almost encircle it. A small, swift stream provides sufficient water in a narrow, restricted belt for the raising of a limited supply of food crops and quantities of wild roses. These may have been introduced and cultivated at one time, but at present they are left to grow naturally in the valley without feeding, watering, or pruning. They cover an area about 96 km (60 miles) long and a few kilometres wide.

The rose crop is never fully utilized, because there are only two distillation plants and transport and related difficulties make complete exploitation almost impossible. Each bush yields from a hundred to a thousand buds, and the five-week picking period begins round about the last week in April. Picking begins at 1 a.m. and continues until 10 a.m., for during these hours the buds contain the strongest concentration of perfume. On arrival at the factory, the buds are spread out and turned over from time to time so that 'sweating' of dew-laden blooms shall not ruin the scent. With no delay, distillation follows. Roses are the only crop grown for perfume in this Dades region, so the factories are closed for the greater part of the year; however, the limited water supply and the difficulties already mentioned preclude extension of the season.

When Morocco was under the administration of France, modern methods of effective manufacture were introduced, so that in five days the plant in Morocco can treat as many rose blooms as are gathered in an entire season in France. Even so, half the available roses remain unused. The Dades rose area is of 1,294 hectares (3,200 acres): the variety of rose appears not to have been identified.

Around the Oulmes area of the north-west the industry is fairly recent, for in 1936 the 'Rose de Mai' of Grasse was introduced by the French, and about 970 hectares (2,400 acres) are devoted to roses. However, there is profit to be made here, for the most modern extraction methods are used and other perfumes such as jasmine, lavender, geranium and orange are distilled.

The 'Rose de Provins' is a special rose named after the town of Provins and has the peculiar chemical property of retaining its perfume when dried. In 1310 the trade was active, and roses were highly regarded for their medicinal qualities. Its popularity continued throughout six centuries and built up a major industry, including crystallized rose leaves as a confection.

The names 'Rose de Mai' and 'Rose de Provins' appear from recent research to be local names given to forms of *R. gallica* or closely related hybrids preserved for special purposes.

 CHAPTER XVIII

Some Old Garden and Shrub Roses

In no other class of roses is the demarcation line so thinly drawn and it would be most difficult to substantiate some of the claims made for choosing one home rather than another. (Nearly all the early cultivars have 28 chromosomes. A few of the later crosses have 21 and so are infertile.) This is not as foolish as it sounds for in the early days when many of these roses were first grown, a rose was a rose and demanded no classification. The need came later to satisfy the orderly mind of the botanist or to find a home for the rose in a competitive function. There is no reason why we should bother whether a rose is a fellow traveller with the gallicas or damask roses as long as we remember that the main object of this chapter is to suggest roses for your appreciation and enjoyment. It may well be useful to classify these sufficiently to enable us to know the main characteristics in order to plant them where they will be happiest.

When one remembers that roses of the old order were chance seedlings gathered at random from an heterogeneous mixture of seed pods, one cannot be surprised if the progeny produced had mingled characteristics taken from such sources. One might well feel that the gallica was seen in the growth of a particular sort and damask in the flower, and it was often a matter of chance which went where. Having said all this and allowed for the Awkward Squad of unsettled abode, there are certain dominant traits which decide the final choice but the last thing one must do is to be dogmatic about the resulting decision.

How shall we regard these subjects? The answer is as shrubs and very choice ones too. As shrubs we should not expect too much

266

from them all the time. There was excellent reason in the old days for placing the roses in the kitchen garden where they bloomed in a profusion few shrubs could equal for a short period and then quietly rested until the next summer. Not that flower was the only gift, for the rich perfume was often trapped and preserved in potpourri in a lingering but potent reminder of fleeting beauty, leaving a happy memory to gladden cold dark days.

There are exceptions where blooms linger long after summer is past, and also where fruits adorn autumn with another season of delight.

In this chapter the age of the variety will not be the decisive factor, but form and purpose will. Speaking broadly, the 'Old Garden Rose' types will be classified by parentage and form as guessed at by the inspired and informed knowledge of the specialist. The colours will be red and pink with magenta influencing these so that the reds and red-pinks may mature into grey and lilac, mauve and purple, with the pinks varying in shade from blush to lilac as time mellows the blossom. The whites will be paper-white, an almost transparent white, ivory and white with blush. To attempt basic descriptions shows one at once what a vast and exciting choice one may have, but as I have no poetic flight of imagination to offer, I will state the prosaic dominant colours and leave the reader to rhapsodize over the bewildering and varying shades these choice roses offer when they are grown.

Having raised the temperature of desire to boiling-point one should be prepared to reduce this ardour with a douche of cold fact. Not that I would try to cancel the wish to share these pleasures, but that we might by foresight continue to enjoy without regret. I cannot recommend these roses as trouble free, nor would it be wise or truthful to do so. I would expect to include shrub roses in an ordinary spraying programme against disease for at least two reasons. They deserve the best we can give, and although many cultivars are hardy they do need protection for their own and for their neighbour's sake. So I would urge that these shrubs be included in your rose spraying programme; you will never regret it.

Established bushes may not need such heavy feeding as other roses, for less wood is removed during the flowering season, and so their leaves produce the necessary autumn food for ripening wood, but they will respond to feeding on a less generous scale than more modern cultivars, if you cut down to a little nitrogen but are free with potash and generous on odd occasions with phosphates and magnesium. For pruning, remember that a shrub needs to have its worn wood cut out and long whippy shoots shortened to reduce wind damage, but every healthy shoot left is a potential flower bearer. A little support may be needed for long pendulous shoots but give this with discretion.

As I said, I cannot burble in ecstatic prose about the colours of these roses. They are extremely beautiful in their own way. They belong to an opulent past reminding one of the 'justice in fair round belly with good capon lined', or a nineteenth-century, opulent, well-dressed and well-upholstered lady of the better sort. The often huge, almost voluptuous beauties, loll against one another in a boundless rich plenty, spending their all of perfume and blossom with prodigal profusion in the early days of summer, so that even the light prolongs its hours to share the pleasures they offer with such abandon. Many blooms start as tight red buds, opening to cerise-pink, rose-pink, mauve-grey and purple, pouring out a heady perfume from the developed flower. Just as there are these huge and rather coarse beauties, so there are fragile retiring examples, antitheses of their neighbours, but living in harmony, even while by contrast they accentuate the charming divergence to be found in these many forms.

I will try to describe a few of the 'Old Garden Roses' even if some of them have actually been produced later than the main groups. I have chosen to list them according to their periods of introduction, for some are so buried in the mists of time that years stand still in the distance of antiquity.

In the following descriptive list the roses have been dealt with in their chronological order as far as their influence was felt in the rose world of their day. Readers are reminded that in many instances these roses used for hybridizing were in no sense the original wild varieties, but were 'tamed' forms which had been selected, some for at least a thousand years. They had been selected for special reasons, and specific purposes. In China their originals were climbers and once-flowering. In the course of many years' selection recessive factors had appeared and had been propagated so that dwarf, remontant and doubling factors had been encouraged by selection.

These are the principal sub-divisions dealt with:

Rosa gallica (R. rubra), page 269
Rosa damascena, page 272
Rosa alba, page 273
Rosa centifolia (The Cabbage Rose) including the Moss Roses, page 275
Bourbon Roses, page 277
Hybrid Musk Roses, page 280
Rugosa Roses, page 281
Hybrid Sweet Briers, page 283
Species Roses and Similar Hybrids, page 284

Rosa gallica (R. rubra)

Rosa rubra was the original name of the 'French Rose' later renamed *R. gallica*. This ancient rose covered a wide area in its wild state, stretching from Persia to France, and may be said to be the common ancestor of the gallicas, the damask, the Provence with its moss roses and the white roses. The original bushes were low-growing for that period, about 90 cm (3 ft) high. They suckered freely and in the wild type made a sprawling bush. The foliage has small, rounded, light green leaves, with few large thorns as these are more often present as bristles. The original is of little garden value, but there are many variations and hybrids. The flowers come in grouped inflorescences and were of 5 cm (2 in) diameter.

The colour is not an intense or clear red. Indeed most old roses of this type were either pink or light pinky red. *R. gallica* itself varied from a deep old rose-pink to light carmine or crimson. The magenta factor was strong in the pink, and later, where it dominated, the lilac and plum-coloured roses appeared among the gallicas. All these were tetraploids (7 × 4).

R. gallica has been grown from very ancient times; records go back to 1200 B.C. in Persia. Closely linked to religious observances, its cultivation spread through the centres of civilization, Greece, Rome and later, through the Arabs, to Spain. Of much interest is the 'Apothecary's Rose', the 'Rose de Provins', which, because of its quality of holding the perfume in its dried petals, retained an important place among roses from the twelfth century onwards.

Although the choice is limited to eight in this list the varieties are by no means so few, but these offer a selection which should give ample choice for a small garden.

'Belle de Crecy'. By general consent one of the best, with double flowers having tightly folded, short, incurved petals in the centre. The buds are cerise-pink with lilac. As the flowers open they turn to lavender-grey with purple shading. A rather relaxed grower, benefiting from the support of stronger and more upright neighbours. Intense perfume. About 1·20 m (4 ft).

'Cardinal de Richelieu'. A justly famous variety revealing a depth of rich vinous purple equalled by few. Like so many cultivars, the pink buds give little indication of the depth to be revealed when the flower opens fully, showing that exposure to light is needed to develop the deep rich shades of purple and mauve found in some of the gallicas. Each petal base of the fully double flowers is white, giving a distinctive character to the many blooms carried on green stems with deep green foliage. 1·20 to 1·50 m high (4 to 5 ft).

'Charles de Mills'. A compact shrub giving a colourful display. Its almost thornless wood and pale green, rounded leaves reveal its group. Very double flowers when fully expanded, having an even circular outline to the flat-petalled crowded surface. A varied colour from crimson-purple to lilac and vinous red. Height to 1·50 m (5 ft).

'Complicata'. A tall bush which may well thrust its strong shoots into the lower branches of a small tree if given an opportunity. Not much like the type, and is probably a hybrid. The very large, single, brilliant pink blooms flower over an extended period. 1·50 m (5 ft).

'Du Maître d'École'. Deep magenta-pink maturing to shades of purple, mauve and grey. The large, perfume-laden blooms are freely produced on stiff stems thrusting from an almost thornless sturdy bush of shorter growth than some, varying according to soil. 70 cm to 1·20 m (2½ to 4 ft).

'Officinalis' (*R. gallica maxima*). This is a form of the famous 'Apothecary's Rose' which was probably slightly smaller, and suckering freely produced the flowers from which preserves were made from the dried petals which retained their perfume, and from which the name 'Rose de Provins' was derived. The flowers are in small clusters of semi-double, 5 to 7·5 cm (2 to 3 in), light red blooms with golden anthers. One of the oldest roses, it was cultivated at least prior to 1300, although tradition says it was introduced by the crusaders from the East where it was grown by the Persians in 1200 B.C. It is the progenitor of many of our modern roses. We may be sure this is a selected form of the original which followed the monks as they spread their religion and their herbal remedies over Europe. Height about 90 cm to 1·20 m (3 to 4 ft) on good soil.

'Tuscany Superba'. A double flower of rich maroon-violet, almost purple tints. A sturdy variety making a good bush, normally 90 cm to 1·20 m (3 to 4 ft) high.

'Versicolor' (*R. mundi*). A sport from *R. gallica officinalis*. Of great beauty and must not be omitted from any list. Large 7·5- to 10-cm (3- to 4-in) flowers, striped, splashed and marked with pale pink or white on the original carmine background. A neat, compact and upright bush, producing a mass of multi-coloured blossoms and ideal for a low hedge of 90 cm to 1·20 m (3 to 4 ft) where the neat growth and pleasing foliage delight the eye. Golden anthers and rich heady perfume crown this charming rose.

Rosa damascena

R. damascena is a rose of very early origin. It was certainly grown and forced in its autumn flowering form during Roman times. This group has always been sure of a very warm spot in the hearts of gardeners and has come to represent a special type of colour and perfume. There is strong reason for believing that the damasks are hybrids with one parent strongly influencing their character. This parent is *R. gallica* and is common to both strains. The second parent in the summer-flowering strain is *R. phoenicea* (the 'Phoenician Rose'). The other parent in the autumn-flowering strain is *R. moschata* (the musk rose). Because these groups are hybrids, one cannot define their characteristics easily, but they may be said to have downy grey foliage, more thorny wood than the gallicas, and often weak flower stalks. Some varieties have their flowers in long bunches. They too have a very sweet perfume and are summer- and once-flowering except *R. damascena semperflorens* (known also as *bi-fera*) which, although it does give some autumn flower, is by no means free in flower at that time; but it was important as being the only variety known in Europe to give two crops of flower, until the arrival of the 'China' roses.

'Celsiana'. Very free-flowering with 10-cm (4-in) semi-double blossoms carried in clusters; warm dog-rose pink, fading to blush, with strong perfume. 1·50 m (5 ft) high.

'Ispahan'. A strong upright bush of up to 1·50 m (5 ft), with the longest flowering period of this group, beginning first and finishing last. Very double flowers of a rich warm pink, offset by shining foliage, unusual for this group. A useful variety for hedges.

'Mme Hardy' 1832. A beautiful white variety occasionally tinged with flesh-pink. The double flowers are frequently produced in large clusters, the outer petals reflexing, leaving a little green eye in the centre. If only one of the damask roses were to be grown this should be the one, although the foliage and type of flower are hardly characteristic. A strong erect shrub of 1·50 to 1·80 m (5 to 6 ft).

'**Rubrotincta**' (known better as 'Hebe's Lip'). Again a cross, this time with *R. alba* (?). Semi-double creamy white flowers with golden centre, stained with deep rose at the notch of the petal. 90 cm to 1·20 m (3 to 4 ft) high.

'**Trigintipetala**' ('Kazanlik'). This variety with its wonderful perfume is of commercial interest rather than garden worth, as it is the main source of Bulgarian 'attar of roses'. Spindly growth up to 1·80 m (6 ft), small flowers of soft pink with about thirty petals. My experience with this rose has been that it is slow to flower and possibly our cooler climate leaves the wood insufficiently ripened for full flower.

'**Versicolor**' (the 'York and Lancaster Rose'). A typical tall-growing damask with striped flowers of pale pink and white. The proportion of colouration varies greatly. Rather shy flowering. An ancient, historic rose about whose hoary head much apocryphal 'history' has gathered. 1·50 m (5 ft).

'**The Autumn Damask**' (*R. damascena semperflorens*, previously known as *bi-fera*, or 'Quatre Saisons'). Of great interest to hybridists. The flowers open from shapely buds and are of a clear pink with deeper centre. It apparently gave rise to the sport 'Blanc Mousseux', the only moss damask. 1·20 m (4 ft).

Rosa alba

R. alba (the 'White Rose of York'). One of the oldest known roses which Dr. Hurst, the prominent Cambridge geneticist, ascribes, giving many cogent reasons, to a hybrid between *R. damascena* and a white form of *canina*, probably *R. canina froebelii*. It has produced one of the hardiest and tallest forms of shrub roses, many of which are almost thornless although some hybrids are very thorny.

As Graham Thomas, the eminent authority on old roses, states: 'The white roses are supreme over all the other old races in vigour, health, longevity, foliage, delicacy of colour (for they embrace some exquisite pink varieties) and purity of scent.' In growth and vigour they take after their *canina* female parent. I shall mention six only by name:

'Celeste' (not to be confused with the damask rose 'Celsiana'). Semi-double flowers of soft, clear pink. The great leaves make the upright bush, which is 1·80 m (6 ft) high, a very handsome trouble-free shrub.

'Königin von Dänemarck' ('Queen of Denmark'). One of the loveliest hybrids with very full flowers. The opening flower is intense carmine paling to pale clear pink when fully expanded. It is tall, up to 1·80 m (6 ft) high and, like others of its type, has rather thin growth for its height.

'Maiden's Blush' (Great). Known for at least five hundred years. Widely grown here and on the Continent. Its hardiness and beauty contributed to its survival, and its ubiquity produced many charming local names. It has a large flower with rounded outline, very full, with exquisite perfume. It is a sturdy 1·80-m (6-ft) bush with greyish foliage. On opening, the bloom is a pleasing warm pink which fades to ivory, tinted pink, with more pronounced pink in the centre.

'Maiden's Blush' (Small). A less rampant form of the above with slightly smaller flowers and growth of 1·20 m (4 ft).

'Maxima'. A bold vigorous shrub up to 2·10 to 2·40 m (7 to 8 ft). A redoubtable rose of great age always healthy and vigorous. By shortening a few of the outer shoots and so encouraging growth at the base its rather gaunt appearance is hidden. Full flowers without much shape unfolding from white with blush-pink to milk-white flowers festoon the long branches and display its golden anther centre with charming effect.

'Semi-plena'. Probably the form of *R. alba* used for making attar of roses at Kazanlik where it forms the boundaries of the rose fields. Its semi-double milk-white flowers, and growth, make it a suitable shrub for grouping with other rose species. 1·5 to 1·8 m (5 to 6 ft).

Rosa centifolia (the Cabbage Rose), including the Moss Roses

Sometimes also called the 'Provence Rose', but I have omitted this name as it is apt to be confused with the 'Rose de Provins', a form of *R. gallica*. These are not good garden plants, most of the growth being open and rather sprawling. The flowers, too, droop very much, their heavy heads being too much for their slender stems. They have a beauty of their own and must be judged by other standards than those generally accepted today. They excel in their double flowers and rich fragrance. Usually making large bushes (1·50 to 1·80 m (5 to 6 ft) high, they flower in June and July and are richly scented. With these will be grouped the moss roses which probably first sported from a cabbage rose.

'Bullata'. A rose with the deep pink flowers of centifolia type, but with most unusual foliage. The leaves are large, crinkled and puckered. Noteworthy for this outstanding ornamental characteristic. 1·20 to 1·50 m (4 to 5 ft).

'Cristata' (Chapeau de Napoléon'). Technically Dr. Hurst does not consider this a moss rose. The 'mossing' is very remarkable on the calyx, covering the whole bud at this stage. For gardening purposes one may consider it a moss rose, and a very charming variety too, of a rich rose-pink. 1·20 to 1·50 m (4 to 5 ft).

'Fantin-Latour'. Although not a typical centifolia it has many similar characteristics, bearing very large 7-cm (2½-in) flowers of deep blush-pink fading on opening. The blooms are carried in clusters of three to twelve flowers. Strong, bold, deep green foliage

with green shining wood possessed of few thorns. Little perfume.
Height 1·50 m (5 ft) with graceful arching shoots.

'**La Noblesse**'. A more compact and better growth than most of
this class. The latest of this group to flower it produces numerous
blossoms of deep rose. Very sweetly scented. 1·50 m (5 ft).

'**Petite de Hollande**'. A shorter form with miniature flowers. The
leaves too, although true to this type, are smaller. The long arching
shoots are laden with pure rose-pink, double flowers, which deepen
in colour in their centres. Because of its growth, it is the most suitable variety if one wants an example of *R. centifolia* in a small
garden. 1·20 m (4 ft).

'**Tour de Malakoff**' 1856. This is included because of its great
variety of lilac-purple shades. Cupped flowers of light carmine-
pink in the bud, deepening on expansion to vivid magenta with
deeper veinings, fading to lilac-grey in the old flower. The tall
stems, up to 2·10 m (7 ft) on really good soil, need support. Because
of its height and size its use is strictly limited unless space is no
object. Up to 2·10 m (7 ft).

The moss roses are a type of *R. centifolia* which first appeared
as sports. The 'moss' is a curious mutation and varies in colour
from rich green to wine-red. It is caused by glandular projections
which cover the sepals. The 'moss' when pressed has a fragrance
of its own, which must not be confused with the scent of the flower.
A number of varieties were raised from seed after a single form had
appeared in 1807. Many of the hybrid moss roses lack the charm of
their older rivals, although a wider range of colour has been forth-
coming.

'**Blanche Moreau**' 1880. A beautiful white moss of vigorous but
rather slender growth. The buds are covered with dark red moss
and an occasional autumn flower may be found. 1·80 m (6 ft).

'**Gloire de Mousseux**' 1852. A sturdy shrub with light green leaves and moss. Enormous full flowers of shell-pink. Growth 1·20 m (4 ft).

'**Little Gem**' 1880. An attractive full flower, almost a miniature, in light crimson. Not as heavily mossed as some, but with shorter growth. 60 cm (2 ft).

'**Maréchal Davoust**' 1853. An excellent bush up to 1·20 to 1·50 m (4 to 5 ft). The buds have brownish moss, and open to intense carmine with paler reverse. The blooms, full and cup-shaped, are deep crimson-pink with paler reverse. Very free-flowering and effective.

'**Nuits d'Young**' (de Young) 1845. One of the most famous moss roses, having the distinction of unusual foliage and attractive colouring. The small, very double flowers are of intense maroon-purple and the bud is covered with dark brownish moss. Up to 1·50 m (5 ft).

'**William Lobb**' 1855. The heavily green mossed buds are borne in large clusters, on exceptionally strong shoots. The whole plant is extremely vigorous and thorny and can reach to 2·40 m (8 ft) on really good soil. The crimson buds open to fuchsia-purple with paler edges, fading to slate in the old flower. It may be treated as a semi-climber rose, as its tall shoots need some support.

Bourbon Roses

('Pink Autumn Damask' (*R. rubra* × *R. moschata*) × 'Parson's Pink China' (*R. chinensis* × *R. gigantea*))

We may consider these as one of the type of roses which led to the parting of the ways, from the old, full, heavily perfumed, weak-stemmed shrubs which, except for the chinas, usually flowered once only. We find the same process of evolution: first triploids with little fertility then tetraploids with compatibility. The chief characteristic was the autumn-flowering and, in the later progeny, the change in shape. Dr. Hurst tells us that the first generation of bourbons was a natural hybrid between 'Pink Autumn Damask' and 'Parson's Pink China', which was found growing with its parents in the French Île de Bourbon in 1817 by the Parisian botanist Bréon. As so often happens, it is the man with 'an eye to a plant' who discovers the new variety, which, but for his discernment, might never have been found. It was from seeds of this discovery that the first French bourbon rose was raised. This variety, called 'Le Rosier de l'Île Bourbon', was more compact in its growth, had a double dose of the china gene for continuous flowering, beauty of form and colour, nearly evergreen foliage and the delicious fragrance of its damask grandparent. Truly a segregation of commendable qualities which, combined with those of other parents, gave rise to other distinct types. Crossed with 'Hume's Blush Tea-Scented China', it helped to create our pink tea roses. It was the main source of the hybrid perpetual. One break led to the scarlet and crimson hybrid perpetuals with their rich damask perfume. Later came the bourbon-noisettes, adding purple. In 1842 'Souvenir de la Malmaison', a triploid and a very large double, strongly fragrant, often quartered, creamy flesh with rosy centre, was raised. It became the parent of the vigorous climbing tea rose 'Gloire de Dijon', a tetraploid. Thus the climbing form, while still appearing, had less and less influence, and the perpetual-flowering character became stronger and stronger.

Life is not long enough to describe all these roses, and the average garden of today cannot contain a representative sample of each. I have chosen seven, not necessarily of the best, but as far as possible the most representative of the group.

'Boule de Neige' 1867. A vigorous erect growth carrying small clusters of crimson tinted tight buds, opening to ivory-white, the outer petals of which turn back to form a rounded ball-like flower. Sweetly scented, the flowers are carried over a long period. 1·80 m (6 ft).

'Commandant Beaurepaire'. A striped rose with light carmine-pink base splashed with rose-madder, deep carmine, and purple.

The flowers are cupped. The growth is arching and very vigorous. Height about 1·50 m (5 ft).

'**Louis Odier**' 1857. Continuous flower from June to October. Full, flat flowers of a warm pink shaded with lilac. Vigorous, about 1·80 m (6 ft) tall.

'**Mme Isaac Pereire**' 1880. Huge double flowers, rose-madder, shaded magenta. Intermittent in flower with very strong fragrance. A large bush with matching bold foliage. From 1·80 to 2·40 m (6 to 8 ft) high. Some support is an advantage.

'**Mme Pierre Oger**' 1878. An old favourite sporting from the deeper pink 'La Reine Victoria'. A soft creamy pink with the pink intensifying as heat increases. The formation of the flower and petal presents the best in this type of old-fashioned rose. It throws some delightful late smaller flowers. 1·80 m (6 ft).

'**Variegata di Bologna**' 1909. Long upright shoots with comparatively thin foliage. Blush-tinted flowers, producing an early heavy crop followed by a few late summer and autumn flowers. The striking feature is the striping of the blooms with vivid crimson-purple. To give firmness to the bush in autumn gales the long shoots should be shortened to produce a more compact effect, otherwise it is too straggling. 2·40 m (8 ft).

'**Zéphirine Drouhin**' 1868. The force of the written and spoken word is proved by the popularity of this much publicized rose. It is thornless, sweetly scented and free-flowering. Really a climber, it can be used for many purposes. Its cerise-pink flowers borne in clusters are not easily matched to the more modern and clearer shades, and for best effect it needs to be placed carefully. Well-trained, it will make a vigorous and charming hedge. There is a paler pink form, slightly less vigorous but more amenable for colour grouping. This sport, known as 'Kathleen Harrop', occurred in 1919. Both are very liable to mildew and a dry or draughty position should be avoided. 2·40 m (8 ft).

Hybrid Musk Roses

The musk rose itself, *R. moschata*, is a very tall climbing rose
with great trailing stems up to 12 m (40 ft). The strong, all-pervad-
ing perfume of this variety is passed on in some degree to the
hybrids raised by the Revd. J. H. Pemberton, who used 'Trier'
(Paul Lambert). The large flowering hybrids raised by Herr Wilhelm Kordes from 'Eva' (1933) ('Robin Hood' × 'J. C. Thornton')
are included here, but the characteristic scent and small flowers in
great clusters have been superseded by size of flower and brilliancy
of colour.

'Berlin' 1949. Orange-scarlet single flowers with a large white eye
carried in clusters on a handsome bush about 1·50 m (5 ft) high.

'Bonn' 1950. Large 10-cm (4-in) double flowers, cerise-scarlet on
the reverse and cerise on the inner side of petal. Moderately
vigorous, a 1·50 m (5 ft) bush.

'Buff Beauty' 1922? The last and probably the best hybrid musk
raised by the Revd. J. H. Pemberton and shown posthumously.
The flowers are double, large for the class, 5 to 7·5 cm (2 to 3 in)
across, carried in large arching clusters on long stems. The colour
is unique, a lovely biscuit shade and the perfume is strong. A
strong bushy growth of 1·80 m (6 ft) but the terminal growths are
subject to some mildew.

'Cornelia' 1925. Pink with a flush of apricot in the centre of its
small 4-cm (1½-in) double flowers. Large clusters of flowers with
red-brown almost thornless wood. Very fragrant and vigorous.
1·50 m (5 ft).

'Felicia' 1928. Salmon-pink, semi-double with 7·5-cm (3-in)
fragrant flowers in large clusters, making a bush of 1·80 m
(6 ft).

'Kassel' 1958. Large corymbs of light red 10-cm (4-in) semi-double flowers. A tall strong bush bearing a profusion of flowers in late autumn. 1·80 m (6 ft).

'Pax' 1918. A large, creamy white, semi-double flower. Scented. A strong, tall 1·80-m (6-ft) bush.

'Will Scarlet'. A bright red sport of 'Wilhelm' producing a succession of flowers in large clusters. Moderately vigorous for this type, about 1·50 m (5 ft).

Rugosa Roses

The true 'rugosa' is one of the hardiest and most disease-resistant types which we possess. The growth is rounded, dense and very thorny. Its habit is to sucker very freely. For this reason, where control is essential, I strongly recommend budded plants, as otherwise the bushes can take over quite a wide area and defy all but the most drastic and costly eradication. It is a particularly useful shrub on the sea coast, and in its single white and red form is useful for massing or as a low hedge on the sea front. Its fruits are large, rounded and ornamental, distinguished by their large sepals. Better treated as an ornamental shrub than as material for floral decoration.

'Agnes' (*R. rugosa* × *R. foetida persiana*). A narrow upright bush of about 1·80 m (6 ft) height. The many flowers are very double, pale primrose yellow, sweetly scented and very beautiful for a short period. 1·80 m (6 ft).

'Blanc Double de Coubert' 1892. The first thing about this rose is its sweet scent; the second, the pleasing white buds slightly rolled and opening into loose semi-double pure white flowers. Of less vigour than some rugosas, it grows about 90 cm (3 ft) and may be improved by the complete removal of ageing shoots from the bush.

'Conrad F. Meyer' 1899. A tall, rather gawky growth. This should be treated as a semi-climber. It flowers in June and gives some flowers again in September. Large, full, deep pink, scent-drenched blossoms. Not a rose for small gardens and can be badly affected by black spot. 2·10 m (7 ft).

'F. J. Grootendorst' 1918. Light red, fringed small blooms. Not so distinctive as the pink form. 1·20 m (4 ft).

'Frau Dagmar Hartopp' 1914. A clear pink with lovely single flowers on a healthy plant of low compact habit. An added advantage are the bright red hips which follow. 75 cm (2 ft).

'Mrs. Anthony Waterer' 1898 (*R. rugosa* × 'Gen. Jacqueminot'). This is a great favourite of mine, although I would place it as a modern shrub despite its age, 1898. Pleasing semi-double flowers of deep crimson produced most abundantly with plenty of autumn flower. The tall bush is stiffly erect and grows 1·50 to 1·80 m (5 to 6 ft).

'Pink Grootendorst' 1923. An unusual fringed, deep clear pink, with short-stemmed flowers in small clusters, reminding one of a dianthus. Always in bloom, it is useful as a hardy hedge in cold windswept places. 1·20 m (4 ft).

'Roseraie de l'Hay' 1901. A very large, dense bush, up to 2·10 m high (7 ft), bearing a number of rich vinous red flowers. Sweetly scented and free in flower.

Rosa rugosa alba. A useful hardy shrub with many paper-white, single, scented blooms. Useful for a seaside hedge. 1·20 m (4 ft).

'Scabrosa'. A very large form in both its vinous red flowers, 13·5 cm (5½ in) across and its foliage. The creamy white anthers are a lovely foil for its deeply shaded petals. The bush is not too tall for the average garden. 1·80 m (6 ft).

'Schneezwerg' ('Snow Dwarf') 1912. A compact bush bearing a profusion of semi-single pure white flowers with yellow anthers and a rich sweet perfume. Later in the season the flowers nestle against the small orange-red hips formed from earlier blooms. A charming shrub. 90 cm (3 ft).

Hybrid Sweet Briers (Rosa rubiginosa)

This small-leaved low bush with its sweetly scented flowers and equally perfumed foliage is one of the most delightful plants in the warmth of a summer evening, especially after a shower. One should be careful not to expect too much. The foliage is poor as it grows mature, and the planting should be done with discretion. A hedge of sweet brier should be placed inconspicuously and should make its presence known by its perfume.

In 1894 and 1895 Lord Penzance sent out a number of hybrids which have become popular. Sharing the perfumed foliage of their sweet brier parent they are of much greater size and coarser, but are attractive under certain conditions. Of uncertain height depending on treatment. As climbers 3 m (10 ft) or as shrubs 2 m (about 7 ft) when the tops of the long shoots should be shortened.

A brief selection of these and other hybrids are:

'Amy Robsart' 1894. Deep rose, free-flowering, semi-single blooms.

'Lady Penzance' 1894. Single, pink with a yellow flush especially in the centre. Scented foliage (*R. rubiginosa* × *R. foetida bicolor*).

'Lord Penzance'. Single, pink predominates but with the yellow ground, salmon also appears in the composition of the colour (*R. rubiginosa* × 'Harrison's Yellow').

'Manning's Blush Sweet Brier'. A pleasing compact bush with small double flowers in blush-pink. Unknown origin. Bush 1·80 m (6 ft).

Species Roses and Similar Hybrids

A selective list of other roses follows, mostly species and older varieties suitable for shrubberies or specimen bushes. The only pruning needed in most cases is the removal of the whole branch when this becomes weakened and exhausted, besides the occasional shortening of a long whippy growth to prevent lashing and damage in winter gales.

Californica plena. A charming shrub with slightly doubled flowers in which the anthers are still prominent. A pleasing pink with a slight lavender shade. The foliage is characteristic, mat with rolled-back edges and prominent veining. The old wood is thin purple-brown with one pair of hooked thorns immediately beneath the leaves. The hips of the single form are red with conspicuous brown stipules. 1·80 to 2·40 m (6 to 8 ft).

'Canary Bird'. Of uncertain parentage, possibly *R. hugonis* × *R. xanthina*. This is the loveliest and most charming of all the species type. Its deep golden yellow flowers grow in spreading wreaths on arching shoots. The foliage is bright green, ferny, and the shape of the rounded bush, with its full outline broken by a few taller arching shoots, is ideal. An added advantage is the occasional odd flower carried on the twiggy growths throughout the season. A very fine hedge. One should not be afraid to remove old branches to promote better and more vigorous growth. 1·80 m (6 ft).

Canina andersonii. A wide arching bush bearing a deeper pink, larger brier flower. The perfection of the colouring lies in their clarity of shade. An excellent shrub for a wild garden. 1·80 m (6 ft).

Chinensis mutabilis. When one first sees this rose it appears to be an untamed 'Masquerade' with all the variety of colouring in its changeable flowers, but with the unfettered free growth of a wilding. Said to need protection of a sheltered position to be at its best, it is of much charm both in foliage, wood and flower, which changes from a brilliant orange bud through soft yellow to sunset-pink, continuing over a long period. 60 to 90 cm (2 to 3 ft).

Dupontii. A charming single pure white flower with golden anthers, the buds are stained pink, carried in bold masses on thick almost smooth stems. Foliage is large, pale dull green and closely spaced. The plant makes an upright vigorous shrub. The flowering period is an extended one. 2·40 m (8 ft).

Ecae. This Afghanistan species is unusual in its deep yellow single flowers, and its slender growths have prominent reddish thorns which almost overpower the small green fern-like leaves. Normally a short bush it is sometimes confused with the vigorous *R. primula*. 60 to 90 cm (2 to 3 ft).

Farreri persetosa. The 'Threepenny Bit Rose' so named from the size of its flowers which match its tiny leaves with their many leaflets. Quite charming for its dainty wood, hair-like thorns, tiny leaves and fragile flowers. 1·80 to 2·10 m (6 to 7 ft).

Fedtschenkoana. A difficult name for a distinguished and unusual rose. The cool pale grey-green leaves carried on almost horizontal branches which carry white, 5-cm (2-in) flowers for a long period in the summer. 2·40 m (8 ft).

'Golden Chersonese' (*R. ecae* × 'Canary Bird'). A very fine cross producing a rich mass of golden yellow single (five-petal) small blooms spaced throughout the whole upright vigorous shoot. The foliage is very plentiful, small, medium green, mat while the wood is reddish-brown. 1·80 to 2 m (6 to 7 ft).

Hugonis. Habit and foliage like 'Canary Bird' although the growth is less compact. The flower is quite different. Sulphur-yellow in colour, with the small flowers carried singly in profusion along the whole stem. These blooms appear half opened all the time. Attractive for decoration. 1·80 m (6 ft).

Hulthemosa hardii (*R. hardii*). Not for the average garden but a rose over which the hybridist may dream. A sterile hybrid with single 5-cm (2-in) flowers of a bright yellow. Its unique feature is the scarlet blotching at the base of each petal inherited from the specie plant, once known as *R. persica* now called *hulthemia persica*. It requires the warmth and controlled health check of the greenhouse, for it is a martyr to mildew. Given these conditions it flourishes as a 90-cm (3-ft) dense, thorny bush producing many flowers over a very extended period.

Macrophylla doncasterii. Clear deep pink blooms of large size with beautiful foliage and almost thornless wood. It excels in the masses of large urn-shaped fruits reminding one of *R. moyesii*. 2·40 m (8 ft).

Moyesii. This is a striking family, notable for the single flowers usually of orange-scarlet which are of perfect symmetrical outline enriched by prominent stamens and stigma. Such a flower could come only from China, and the long gaunt upright shoots with their short twigs adorned with leaves of eleven to thirteen leaflets have their crowning glory in their huge urn-like fruit. Interesting types are:

Moyesii fargesii. Deeper flowers, which being tetraploid, offer hybridizing possibilities. 2·40 m (8 ft).

Moyesii 'Geranium'. An excellent form raised at Wisley, more compact and therefore better for the average garden. 1·80 m (6 ft).

Moyesii 'Sealing Wax'. With pink flowers and very brilliant fruit, a shorter but more spreading bush. 1·80 m (6 ft).

Nitida. One of the shortest in growth, making excellent cover. The leaves are shining green with small bright pink flowers 2·5 to 5 cm (1 to 2 in) across, followed by red bristly hips. An excellent shrub for autumn colour. 90 cm (3 ft).

Primula, the 'Incense Rose'. The ferny foliage and shining red-brown wood of this large shrub have a very strong pervading perfume. It is worth growing for this characteristic alone, but the pale primrose-yellow of the flower loading the shoots is an added delight, while the leaves, with their many leaflets, add to the charms of this vigorous shrub. It will occupy and grace 3 square metres (10 square feet) and reach at least 1·80 to 2·10 m (6 to 7 ft) in height. A bush planted near the entrance of a house breathes a fragrant benediction on those who pass by. 2·40 to 3·00 m (8 to 10 ft).

× **pteragonis cantabrigiensis**. A rounded shrub of about 1·80 m (6 ft) with pale clear yellow flowers in early May. The fern-like foliage is brownish-green and ample. A useful shrub where a less deep yellow than 'Canary Bird' is desired. 1·80 m (6 ft).

Rubrifolia. Unique in its foliage which is a violaceous red, carried, well-spaced, on upright shoots with pendulous ends. The flowers are pinky white with small petals and are almost insignificant. The hips too, are small and in small clusters of about six purplish-brown fruit. A very useful foliage plant. Thinning old wood induces strong, young, healthier shoots, useful for cutting. The thorns are few and almost absent from the young growths. There are two distinct forms in commerce, one being deeper with smaller, more attractive growth and leaves. 1·80 to 2·10 m (6 to 7 ft).

Sericea pteracantha (sometimes known as *R. omeiensis pteracantha*). A massive bush with huge winged thorns subduing the small feathery leaves. When young, these thorns are bright translucent red, and on the young green wood tinged with brown are unique and highly decorative. To see this growth at its best one needs the setting sun which lights every thorn, until the bush is a ruddy lambent glow. In age the thorns are dim, dull greyish-brown. Another variety where one should remove the oldest branches year by year. The flowers, which are plentiful but very transient, are pure white and single. They appear in May. 1·80 to 2·40 m (6 to 8 ft).

'Stanwell Perpetual' 1838. An interesting hybrid with slightly double blush-pink flowers carried over a long period. Slightly pendulous growth, so making a graceful small-leaved shrub. 1·20 to 1·50 m (4 to 5 ft).

Virginiana. Like *R. nitida* is noted for its shining leaves and autumn colouring. A very handsome variety for its cerise-pink, 5-cm (2-in) wide flowers and later than most, flowering in June and July, to be followed by round red hips which persist until the spring. About 1·50 m (5 ft).

Villosa duplex ('Wolley-Dod's Rose'). A very ornamental fruit in a semi-double hybrid form of villosa. The large grey-green leaves make a charming display with the clear pink flowers. Many thorns, on a vigorous shoot and plant. 1·50 to 2·10 m (5 to 7 ft).

Webbiana. One of the more graceful shrubs with light twiggy brown shoots tinged with a purple sheen, and small fine leaves. The flowers are pale lilac-pink, 5 cm across (2 in), with a prominent ring of pale yellow stamens. These are followed by bright red fruits which persist. 1·50 to 1·80 m (5 to 6 ft).

Woodsii fendleri. Flowers up to 5 cm across (2 in) lilac-pink, solitary or in corymbs on very short stems. A graceful variety flowering in early May. A tall bush carrying a profusion of large red fruits hanging until late. 1·80 to 2·40 m (6 to 8 ft).

Willmottiae. Another of the charming, small, ferny-leaved thin-shooted varieties, with plum-coloured slender shoots bearing a multitude of lilac-pink flowers with a ring of creamy anthers clustered on short lateral branchlets. A thicket of slender shoots, its small orange-red hips are an added attraction. 1·80 m (6 ft).

 CHAPTER XIX

Modern Roses, a Selected Descriptive List

As one tries to write of modern roses one is immediately faced with their variety and multiplicity. No plant can present so wide a choice for so many purposes as I have discussed in the first chapter where I have tried to enumerate their many uses.

How can one define a modern rose? Possibly the turn of the century might be a convenient starting date but I may well be taken to task for placing the few teas and hybrid perpetuals in this 'modern' list. Yet these two types straddle the gap between old and new, and in both cases have cultivars which possess qualities belonging to both periods. To help the grower in his selection I have grouped the sections as follows:

Tea Roses, page 289
Hybrid Perpetual Roses, page 291
Hybrid Tea Roses (absorbing the Pernetianea), page 293
Floribunda Roses, page 307
Miniature Roses including Polyantha Roses (Poly-poms), page 321
Climbing and Rambler Roses, page 328
Modern Shrub Roses, page 334

Tea Roses

For a moment one must take a deep breath and gather courage before plunging into the vortex of mixed ancestry from which the hybrid tea of the present day emerged. Because older types were used in different proportions at various times, dates have little importance in marking the waves of progress and their periods of

recession. Progress may be considered as the segregation in extra
and effective proportion of desirable qualities such as continuous
flowering or remontancy, hardiness and bushy qualities and the
pointed reflex shape of the bloom. These advances first led to sterile
or near-sterile triploids. Then came the pause before the fresh
advance, when a tetraploid form made hybridizing easier. At times
these parents produced climbers, more often bushes, and later the
bushes became more dwarf and tractable.

There were different types of tea roses. They were produced by
crosses of the original china imports, 'Hume's Blush Tea-Scented
Chinas' and 'Park's Yellow Tea-Scented Chinas' on the one hand
with bourbons and noisettes on the other. The first pink tea, called
'Adam', was probably 'Hume's Blush Tea-Scented China' crossed
with the original bourbon (1833). The first yellow tea rose was
raised in England (again in 1833) and called 'Smith's Yellow'. This
was a cross between 'Blush Noisette' and 'Park's Yellow Tea-
Scented China'. Back crossing, and crossing, gave rise to many
exquisite varieties between 1840 and 1890. While their shape was
perfection and their colours had the exquisite gradations in the
shades of mother-of-pearl, they lacked the hardiness and vigour
necessary to survive easily under our weather conditions. Many
demanded the care and skilled attention of the professional
gardener to grow and give of their best. They were not fitted for
the harsh task of survival in a modern, look-after-yourself garden,
but they passed on many good qualities to the modern hybrid teas.
They lost the exquisite graces of the Victorian gentlewoman but
gained the vigour necessary for present-day contingencies. In
warmer climates they may still excel.

Parallel with the appearance and development of the tea roses
were the hybrid chinas, a mixture of the then known sources.
About 1830, four important varieties were bred which were used
in the production of the hybrid perpetual roses. While they carried
the gene for flowering more than once this was hidden, awaiting
the next generation, but they differed in one essential feature from
the early crosses, in that they were fertile tetraploids, not infertile
triploids.

'Lady Hillingdon' (*ss*)* 1910. One of the few surviving with lovely purple-red wood and semi-double flowers of deep apricot-yellow. Not over hardy and addicted to the scale insect. The climbing form is better. Bush form 60 to 75 cm (2 to 2½ ft).

Hybrid Perpetual Roses

The hybrid perpetuals were evolved by trial and error over a long period and were the results of crossing hybrid chinas with portlands, bourbons and noisettes. Beginning in 1816 with the French 'Rose du Roi' they passed from the small cluster type to the larger hybrid perpetuals, which began with 'Princess Hélène' bred by Laffay in 1837. In William Paul's *The Rose Garden* of 1863, five hundred and forty-nine varieties are listed and fifty and more varieties were added each succeeding year. Most of these earlier types were of the flat double type so that one should not consider the shape of the later 'Frau Karl Druschki' as typical of the majority. Probably 'Roger Lambelin' and 'Blue Boy' would be more typical in flower and growth. The flowers were judged not for their pointed bud but for the rounded outline of the full bloom as illustrated on page 292. Because of their ancestry, some of these hybrid perpetuals were not autumn flowering—it depended on the degree of remontancy caused by the doubling or otherwise of the free-flowering gene.

Some characteristic varieties showing the wide range in variation of shape in flower are on page 292.

'Blue Boy' 1958. A modern variety in purple shaded violet. The flat blooms are freely produced on the two-year-old shoots. Moderately vigorous but inclined to mildew in the autumn. A very sweet scent. 1·20 to 1·50 m (4 to 5 ft).

'Frau Karl Druschki' 1900. Possibly by parentage a hybrid tea, but in growth a true hybrid perpetual. A very vigorous bush with

* See page 102

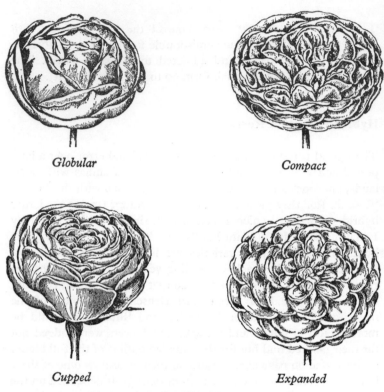

Globular	Compact
Cupped	Expanded

Ideal forms of Exhibition Roses about 1850

tall shoots with short whorls of leaves near the flower. The bloom is pointed and carried on a stiff stem in clusters and singly. The outer petals are stained pink, but the flower opens to a pure unshaded white. As with the majority of this type, the tall shoots should be pegged down, when the leaf buds in the axils of the leaf will develop into flowering stems the second year. Growth 1·20 to 1·50 m (4 to 5 ft).

'**George Dickson**' 1912. Dark vinous red with deeper maroon shading. A good specimen flower is high-pointed and very fragrant. Again sometimes classed as a hybrid tea, but a true hybrid perpetual in growth. The huge heavy blooms nod badly. 1·80 to 2·40 m (6 to 8 ft).

'**Hugh Dickson**' 1904. Grown as a pegged-down plant, a bed can produce a mass of bright crimson flowers. These are full and of exhibition size and standard if well grown. Very fragrant. 1·50 to 2·10 m (5 to 7 ft).

'**Mrs. John Laing**' 1887. A very full-cupped bloom of deep rose-pink with a lilac flush. Very free-flowering and constant in bloom. Growing up to 1·80 m (6 ft), it is vigorous and healthy, while the massive blooms are very heavily scented.

'**Roger Lambelin**' 1890. This needs good soil and treatment to give of its best. A sport from 'Fisher Holmes' (1865). The background colour of the flower is very rich dark blood-red, the petals are notched at the ends and streaked with white. A very satisfying and lovely variety of moderate vigour which flowers over quite a long period. 90 cm to 1·20 m (3 to 4 ft).

Mention should be made of 'Général Jacqueminot' (1853). With its crimson, fully double, very fragrant red flowers it was the forerunner and forebear of a vast number of famous red roses such as 'Liberty', 'Richmond', Étoile de Hollande', 'Crimson Glory' and 'Ena Harkness'.

Hybrid Tea Roses (absorbing the Pernetianas)

While the hybrid perpetual held pride of place until the turn of the century, another type was already acknowledged as its successor. These were the hybrid teas. The first of these was the favourite of many gardens for a generation or longer, 'La France'. Raised by Guillot in 1867 by crossing the hybrid perpetual 'Mme Victor Verdier' with the tea 'Mme Bravy', it was a silvery pink with shapely, very fragrant flower. As a class, these were not recognized until 1884. One of the most popular, for the longest period, was

'Mme Abel Chatenay'. Its small but exquisite reflexed bloom was of silvery pink with deeper shading on the reverse and very sweetly scented. One must remember when sighing for the passing of old friends that its growth was not very robust and the bush had the awkward habit of thrusting one shoot well above its more feeble companions. Otherwise, the exquisite shape of the flower might well be remembered and emulated in the present day. These early H.Ts. were chance seedlings. The true H.Ts. began with Bennett, see page 183. Before listing these varieties one ought to pause and consider the major breakthrough at the end of the century, when Pernet-Ducher, after long and persistent endeavour, combined the brilliant yellow of *R. foetida persiana* with the hybrid perpetual 'Antoine Ducher' obtaining a few seeds after thousands of infertile crosses. One seedling which showed traces of *foetida* in its growth was retained and crossed to produce the first yellow rose 'Soleil d'Or'. So distinct were the roses now raised that they became known as Pernet roses or pernetiana roses. They brought in not only yellow, but the brilliant orange-red shade, leading to a series of striking bicolours. Here was colour in abundance, but also a cupped bloom with split centre and a very thorny growth prone to die-back and black spot. Gradually, but surely, the hybrid tea and Pernet roses became merged, and in the modern list we shall consider, all will be termed hybrid teas. They will in many cases have the Pernet blood in their veins.

Before I make the selection, I should give readers a few rules and reasons for my choice. I have not tried to present a complete list of even the best hybrid teas. It is too bewildering, too controversial and too big a task. Also I would emphasize that the choice I have made is one for a British garden; it is very noticeable as one travels around the world that most countries have their own lists of rose varieties and only a few cultivars have world-wide appeal. So I have attempted to give a selection of good roses in varying colours whose special qualities are worthy of notice. The omission of a variety does not condemn it. The inclusion, however, does indicate that here is a variety meriting your attention because there are sufficient all-round qualities to ensure successful cultivation. In a number of cases the alternatives might pass as insufficiently distinct, but while colours may be alike, growth and purpose can be very different. This is particularly true of bedding versus exhibition blooms, and such differences will be noted.

The colour groups used will be taken from the most recent R.H.S. colour chart which uses group colours and numbers with letters for intensities of the same colour. I have found it extremely difficult to match these colour chart shades with the actual rose colour which so often combines a number of basic colours to produce the shade we see.

The colours have been divided as follows:

(i) *Red:* Light Red; Glowing Red; Dark Red
(ii) *Pink:* Rose Pink; Bicolour Pinks; Clear Pink; Salmon-Pink
(iii) *Orange:* Orange-Flame; Orange-Vermilion; Orange-Salmon; Orange-Yellow
(iv) *Yellow:* Golden Yellow; Canary-Yellow
(v) *White:* White and Tinted-White
(vi) *Polychromes*
(vii) *Lilac-Purple*

Some indication of the degree of perfume is given by the letter '*s*'.

The heights given in this section are relative as growth varies enormously with soil and cultivation. Approximations are S = short, 45 to 60 cm (1½ to 2 ft), M = moderate, 60 to 90 cm (2 to 3 ft), T = tall, 90 cm to 1·50 m (3 to 5 ft).

(i) RED

LIGHT RED (Red Group 50–3). This is the dominant colour in red and is usually associated with vigour and perfume. The colour of the blooms on opening or in dull weather is often a brilliant red, but in heat or with age, blooms lose their sparkle and fade to a duller tone.

'**Fragrant Cloud**' (*sss*) 1964. A good rose of variable colour; at times it can be orange-flame, at others smoky red. Full, very sweetly scented, carrying large candelabra of full-sized flowers in the autumn. Of medium height and upright growth. The health and foliage are good. S.

'**Red Lion**' (*ss*) 1966. One of the largest flowers I know, inclining to clumsiness at times. Growth a little spreading. Healthy in constitution, it should be grown for exhibition. In colour variable, deep cerise to light red. S.

'**Wendy Cussons**' (*sss*) 1959. Medium- to large-sized flowers are borne freely on sturdy thorny shoots. The foliage is healthy and the growth is dense. A rose for general cultivation. Easy to grow. M.

GLOWING RED (Red Group 42–5). This is the most popular shade in red and provides a number of good roses for all purposes.

'**Alec's Red**' (*sss*). A deservedly popular rose with large, full, almost globular flowers carried on strong stiff stems. The colour is dependable and the growth strong which may lead to coarseness in bloom and foliage if overfed. M.

'**Ena Harkness**' (*sss*). Probably one might dismiss this with a sigh as past history, but it is still capable of exceedingly high-class blooms which with their almost scarlet-red overlaid with maroon can produce a delightful bloom of exhibition quality. Its failing is the weak flower stalk and, by present standards, rather thorny and moderate growth. M.

'**Ernest H. Morse**' (*ss*) 1965. A vivid bright red blossom of perfect exhibition form. The growth is tall and upright with strong healthy foliage and the flowers are sufficient for a good bedding rose. One should bear in mind that some fading is likely in hot sun. I would prefer a cool position for one of our best roses. T.

'**National Trust**' 1970. Here is an excellent bedding cultivar. Compact, upright, healthy and plentiful if rather thorny growth producing full flowers in quantity, of a clear, pleasing, unfading red. M.

'**Red Devil**' (*ss*) 1967. This must be considered as an exhibition rose *par excellence*. It needs care and protection from wet to produce its prizewinning blooms of scarlet-red with paler reverse. Strong, upright growth. T.

DARK RED (Red Group 46–53; Red-Purple Group 60). This is the heartwarming red which pulsates with memory, and without which no rose collection is complete. Because some of this shade have magenta in their composition they may go a little blue in exceptional heat or as they fade.

'**Chrysler Imperial**' (*sss*) 1952. Cup-shaped blooms of rich dark red with deeper shading. The many flowers are carried upright on short sturdy shoots. The bush is compact, healthy and rather low. S.

'**Ellen Mary**' (*sss*) 1963. A very deep vinous red with pointed bud and shapely flower. The petals are very thick, long lasting and heavily perfumed with a rich damask perfume. The growth is upright, a little thin, but wiry and free. M.

'**John Waterer**' (*sss*) 1970. A good rose with full flower, healthy growth and vigour. A little shy but a thoroughly reliable rose of medium height. I would prefer this to 'Josephine Bruce' whose passing I deeply regret, but with it goes one source of mildew and black spot. M.

'**Papa Meilland**' (*sss*) 1963. Richly perfumed full flowers. The buds are almost black and open into full flowers of a brilliant currant-red, heavily flushed with maroon. Not a healthy bush in our climate and rather shy in flower, but under glass it can be superb. M.

(ii) PINK

If one had to depend upon the 'pinks' in the R.H.S. colour chart one would fail to perceive the latent charm of this lovely group which gathers so many beautiful graduations of shade from this one colour.

ROSE-PINK (Red Group 51). This shade could merge into light red at times according to the age of the bloom. On the whole it is slightly lighter and brighter, and has its separate place in the gradations of colour.

'**Maturity**' (*sss*) 1973. A large full flower on a vigorous upright bush itself clad in thick deep olive-green, disease-free foliage. Remarkable for its rich perfume. T.

'**Mullard Jubilee**' (*ss*) 1970. A rose with every good quality one feels. The shape and production of the deep pink blooms are very good, the foliage is free, plentiful and healthy. The bush is a little thorny, but dense, strong and free. Possibly the colour is not sufficiently glowing. At the moment it does not receive the recognition it deserves. M.

BICOLOUR PINKS (Red Group 55, 49, 38, 36).

'**My Choice**' (*sss*) 1958. The buds are gold, splashed crimson, but as the full, richly fragrant blooms expand, the colours change to a pleasing contrast of softer shades, pale carmine and peach within and straw-yellow on the reverse. It is tall, vigorous and free flowering, opening with the first hybrid teas of summer and producing many perfect flowers in October. An excellent bedding rose with full exhibition qualities, but the blooms should be cut on the young side for the latter purpose. T.

'**Pink Favourite**' (*ss*) 1956. One of the finest roses ever produced. Shell-pink on the inner side and deeper pink on the reverse. Nearly all the flower stems have three buds at the terminal and these should be reduced to one if the blooms are to be cut or exhibited. Tall, healthy with abundant deep green foliage it makes an ideal vigorous bedding rose, producing a mass of lovely flowers. A pale and pleasing sport is 'Honey Favourite'. T.

'Prima Ballerina' (*sss*) 1958. This is a wet-weather variety when it excels, opening bravely in all weathers. Of exquisite shape, the petals, which are about twenty in number and retain their colour, are deep pink. The open flower reveals a wealth of golden stamens. Free in growth and flower, this is a bedding rose of high quality. S.

'Rose Gaujard' 1957. A trouble-free rose with tall, strong, branching growth. The abundant, glossy, healthy foliage enhances the full bold flowers, which are strongly weather resistant. It is a bedding rose. The blossoms, deep pink with silvery reverse, are often quartered, although at times a good exhibition rose may be found. A variety to plant where roses are usually less easy to grow. T.

'Stella' (*s*) 1959. Strong, tall, upright growth well covered with glossy, large, tough and healthy foliage. The blooms are basically cream flushed pink with deeper carmine at the edge. The full, slightly globular flower, withstands wet and is ideal for exhibition. T.

CLEAR PINK (Red Group 55B, 51B, 50C, 38A, etc.).

'Gavotte' 1963. Predominantly deep clear pink although the reverse is slightly more silvery, the large blooms are carried very freely on rather thorny shoots which tend to make a large, slightly sprawling, growth. The foliage is semi-glossy, dark green. Disbudded, it is up to exhibition size. Produces well under glass. T.

'Lady Sylvia' (*sss*) 1926. This is the deepest of the 'Ophelia' sports and, like all such derivatives, it is excellent for growing under glass. By today's standards the blooms are thin and the growth slight and wiry, but it produces many first-class blooms for

cutting. The perfume is intense, slightly sharp and strongly penetrating. Grown in the open it is best in its autumn flowering. M.

'Royal Highness' (*ss*) 1962. The blooms are a pleasing soft pink,
very full and free flowering. The growth is vigorous and branching
with glossy, deep green leathery foliage. Suitable for exhibition
but needs weather protection. M.

'Silver Lining' (*sss*) 1958. Large very shapely flowers on a sturdy
bush of medium height. Equally good for exhibition or bedding. M.

SALMON-PINK (Red Group 38).

'Blessings'. This rose won my heart on a very wet day when it
remained unscathed amid many bedraggled companions. The
growth is tall, very free and upright. The strong wiry shoots support a lovely bloom ideal for bedding and excellent for cutting. S.

'Bonsoir' (*sss*) 1968. A very full, heavy bloom pre-eminently
suited to exhibition. Needs protection from wet. The growth is
vigorous, of medium height with strong foliage. S.

'Harriny' (*sss*). A seedling from 'Pink Favourite' with most of its
flower heads carrying three buds. A soft pleasing shade, the blooms
are better suited for bedding or cutting. The foliage is abundant
and healthy. Especially good in the autumn. T.

'Mala Rubenstein' (*sss*). Similar to 'Bonsoir', suitable for exhibition, of very vigorous growth. T.

'Sweet Promise'. Primarily a forcing rose but it is proving, under
the right conditions, to be an excellent bedding rose which can
produce an amazing number of small, shapely flowers for cutting.
M.

(iii) ORANGE

ORANGE-FLAME (Red Group 33 & 34).

'Mischief' 1960. Not an easy rose to put in the right colour group. As the bloom ages it might well be placed in the deep pinks, but in the early stages has a sparkling orange-flame shading. The small double flowers are carried upright on a medium-height bush, well covered with plentiful deep green foliage. It is a very good bedding rose even if the wood is a little more thorny than usual. M.

'Summer Holiday'. Very resistant to wet, the moderately full blooms are at times a deep orange-red. An ideal bedding rose with tall, upright growth, many flowers and healthy foliage. T.

'Violinista Costa' 1936. An excellent bedding rose somewhat pestered by mildew in the late autumn. The growth is thorny and covered with shining highly decorative foliage. Always in flower, the blooms are unsuited for exhibition but come in a spectacular mass through a long season. M.

ORANGE-VERMILION (Orange-Red Group 32, 33 & 35).

'Alexander' (*s*) 1973. The brightest colour of this group. Extremely tall and vigorous, one might well call it a shrub. Numerous pointed rather thin blooms (twenty-two petals) on long wiry stems, borne singly and several together. A good rose which should be planted in the right position. Very healthy, semi-glossy dark green foliage. T.

'Princess' 1964. A large globular bloom suitable for exhibition and very reliable. The growth is short, sturdy and upright. Trouble free. S.

'Super Star' (*ss*). This brilliant and popular rose has fallen from grace as mildew has taken charge of much of its growth especially in autumn. Well-sprayed it is still worthy of a place in the garden. T.

ORANGE SALMON (Orange-Red Group 34, 31, 30; Orange Group 29). This group has had many new varieties recently, and their colours vary from almost-red to golden-peach.

'Colour Wonder' (s). Full slightly globular blooms of orange-salmon with buttercup-yellow reverse, freely produced on short vigorous shoots clothed with glossy, dark green foliage. M.

'Diorama' (s) 1965. A long pointed bud of autumn tints, the blooms are fairly full and excellent for bedding or decoration as cut. The growth is medium-tall and healthy. A decorative and graceful plant. T.

'Duke of Windsor' (ss) 1968. Very brilliant flowers verging on the red side of orange-salmon, these are on the small side and very freely produced. The growth is short and compact. The main problem is health and this rose should be sprayed regularly for mildew and rust in some areas. S.

'Tenerife' (sss) 1973. The bloom which is very full and of exhibition shape and size combines peach, orange and creamy yellow influenced in part by the maturity of the flower and intensity of the light. The growth is healthy and vigorous. Probably not free enough or sufficiently weather resistant for bedding purposes. T.

'Troika' (ss) 1972. Orange-bronze with reddish shadings, the full, short-petalled flowers are very attractive. A healthy, tall, vigorous bush which promises to be a first-class bedding rose. T.

'Whisky Mac' (ss) 1961. An unusual combination of golden orange suffused tangerine which produces a very pleasing and striking effect. The flowers are a little small but very freely produced on a fairly healthy plant which is not easy to transplant. A colour one needs but of doubtful hardiness so one should try it out personally before a large planting is made. S.

ORANGE-YELLOW (Orange Group 26; Yellow Group 20).

'Beauté' 1954. A charming, graceful, pointed bloom on a short wiry bush of healthy growth. Highly decorative and useful as a low bedding rose. S.

'Dr. A. J. Verhage' (ss) 1960. Primarily a forcing rose but sufficiently satisfactory in performance to grow as a medium height, decorative bedder. The colour is a pleasing combination of soft yellow and fawny orange with sturdy upright growths covered with small, glossy deep green foliage. M.

'Fred Gibson' 1968. A very large exhibition bloom of high quality. The colour is pleasing amber-yellow to apricot. One of the best for a specimen flower. T.

'Just Joey' (ss) 1973. A different rose, medium to small in size, combining orange and copper, fading at the edges of the slightly serrated outer petals. The foliage makes a pleasing foil and is abundant and healthy. Early and late in bloom, excellent for bedding. M.

ORANGE-BROWN (Orange Group 24, 31).

'Fantan' (s) 1959. A most unusual combination of burnt orange to yellow-ochre, the blooms are full, short petalled, making it of unusual value for the floral artist. M.

(iv) YELLOW

GOLDEN YELLOW (Orange-Yellow Group 15–23).

'Ellinor Le Grice' (*ss*) 1950. Pure golden-yellow blooms with globular buds which are tinged with carmine. The large very double blooms are held erect on short stout stems. The foliage is glossy, deep green and healthy. The growth is robust. One of the best and most reliable bedding roses with a long record of consistency. A parent of the floribunda 'Allgold' ('Goldilocks' × 'Ellinor Le Grice'). S.

'King's Ransom' 1961. A pointed blossom of consistent clear deep yellow. The plant is of moderate height, upright, bushy and healthy. One could wish for a few more of these lovely colourful blooms which are still the best for general bedding. M.

'Spek's Yellow' 1947. An unusual variety in so far as the almost green buds give little indication of the opening flower which, although small, is well formed and of a deep intense yellow. The flowers are often carried many on a stem. The growth is tall, sparse of foliage and very free. T.

'Sutter's Gold' (*sss*) 1950. This choice variety differs from the others in this section in that the golden yellow is heavily overlaid and shaded with peach. The long elegant flowers are carried well above a healthy plant on strong wiry stems and are admirable for cutting. The rich 'fruity' perfume adds the crown to this excellent cultivar. T.

CANARY-YELLOW (Yellow Group 11–13; Orange-Yellow Group 14).

'Grandpa Dickson' 1966. The large ovoid buds are almost green but open to a full pale yellow flower of great size and classical outline. Usually carried one to a stem, the prolific healthy plant yields a great many flowers often of exhibition size. Deservedly much grown. M.

'Peace' 1945. So well known as to need little description. Its vigour and freedom leave little to desire. The large, almost coarse bloom is seen at its best when fully expanded and, grown as a specimen or a group of three, few shrubs can excel it in lasting effect. T.

'Peer Gynt' 1968. A vigorous bush full of growth and flower. Deep yellow up until old age when the red splashings found on the bud stain the ageing petals. A good bedding variety. M.

'Yellow Pages' (s) 1973. One of many newer 'yellow' roses which stain salmon with weathering. The growth is upright and free with glossy green foliage. Should be watched if a colour scheme is being considered. M.

(v) WHITE

WHITE

'Pascali' 1963. At the moment this rose stands so far above other whites that there is no comparison. It has the great advantage of healthy foliage. Its white buds on opening are slightly tinged fawn but open pure white. The plant is healthy and upright with strong deep green foliage. M.

TINTED WHITE

'Elizabeth Harkness' (sss) 1968. The full, shapely flowers are pale creamy buff, slightly tinted pink. Of exhibition size they do not like rain and therefore arc not really suited for bedding. M.

'Golden Melody' (sss) 1934. This lovely creamy tinted white rose with a hint of yellow at the base has long exquisite blooms very freely produced. The growth is somewhat spreading and low but despite this, a good rose. S.

'Golden Wings' (s) 1956. An unusual but lovely hybrid, more low shrub than bedding rose. The creamy white blossoms with golden base are massed on a vigorous, spreading, thorny bush. T.

(vi) POLYCHROMES

MANY COLOURS WITH RED AND GOLD PRE-DOMINATING

'Chicago Peace' 1962. This is an excellent more highly coloured 'Peace'. The cerise has been deepened until the whole bloom is suffused in some degree having a very colourful and attractive effect. An excellent, tall bedding rose. T.

'Piccadilly'. The blooms are scarlet with yellow reverse and, although of few petals, are long lasting and colourful, being exceptionally free in production. Of medium height with healthy growth and foliage, it is one of the finest roses ever produced for bedding. S.

(vii) LILAC-PURPLE

LILAC-PURPLE (Red-Purple Group 69; Purple Group 76).

'Blue Moon' (sss) 1964. This is the best of the lilac-lavender cultivars. Tall, upright and free growth producing a large number of good blooms which are found singly or in grouped inflorescences. T.

'Great News' 1974. The grouped full flowers might be placed among the floribundas for freedom of bloom. The growth is low and sturdy, of deep pansy purple with silver reverse. An important advance in colour. S.

'**Silver Star**' (*sss*). Very shapely flowers of greater clarity than most roses of this shade. Larger than 'Blue Moon' but a little less free. T.

Floribunda Roses

It is hard to realize how great a contribution this type has made to the decorative structure of gardens, parks and the landscape. I would like to stress that as much of this popularity lies in the variation of heights as in the multiplicity of the colourings. There are plants which may be measured in centimetres or in metres, yet each has a rich contribution to give to the general garden effect. What is a floribunda? I feel that the true definition must include three characteristics. The first is a multi-flowered head, a floribunda with a small head of two or three flowers is a negation of the name; the second feature is its readiness to flower again, and for this reason I consider a growth and flower buds should be developing in the axil of the first true leaf immediately below the flowering shoot before the previous flowers have faded. The third feature, and here there may be less universal agreement, is that a floribunda should be rapidly repetitive. I still believe that our ideal floribunda is 'Sarabande', i.e. one with unfading masses of continually repetitive bloom, of medium height and even growth. If constant repetition of flowering is essential then a five-petal flower takes less time to mature and a shorter growth takes less time to flower than a tall growth. Be that as it may, the justly heavy demand for variation in flower type and size as well as height means we must accept limitations to secure these wider aims.

The colours have been broken up in the following gradations:

Red (Red Group 42–8)
Scarlet-Red (Orange-Red Group 40–1)
Scarlet-Orange (Orange-Red Group 33)
Vermilion-Orange (Red Group 30)
Copper-to-Brown (no group colours)

Copper and Peach (Yellow-Orange Group 17; Orange Group 28; Orange-Red Group 30)
Mixtures
Yellow (Yellow-Orange Groups 17 and 18A)
Cream (Yellow-Orange Groups 18 and 19; Red Group 36)
Salmon-Pink (Red Group 38)
Clear Pink (Red Groups 55B, 51B, 50C, 38A, etc.)
Rose-Pink (Red Group 51)
White
Mauve and Purple (Red-Purple Group 69; Purple Group 76)

Where the individual flowers in the cluster are shaped like H.Ts. I have added (H.T. type) after the name and date of introduction of the cultivar, together with approximate heights and ratings for scent.

RED (Red Group 42–8).

'Dusky Maiden' (*ss*) 1947. A sweetly scented single or semi-single of dark maroon-crimson, enlightened by a circlet of golden-yellow anthers. Large healthy foliage, abundant flower. A fine bedding variety. Height 60 cm (2 ft).

'Europeana' (*s*) 1963. A great feature of this rose is the contrasting deep red almost blackish-red young foliage with the olive-green mature leaves. The large flower heads with full blossoms are weighed down with bloom, a weakness which can cause the plant growth to sprawl. For this reason close planting will provide the necessary support. Its weakness is mildew, and spraying is a necessary preventative. Height 75 cm (2½ ft).

'Lili Marlene' 1959. A most appealing flower, with large 8- to 10-cm (3½- to 4-in) flowers in large clusters held upright on stiff stems. The colour is a brilliant red with deeper shadings. The foliage is healthy, adequate in quantity and of a satisfying shade of dark green. A very colourful and effective bedding rose of top quality. Very free and resistant to sun and rain. Height 60 cm (2 ft).

'Marlena' 1964. This remarkable rose which is a bright deep red produces a mass of moderately full 5-cm (2-in) blooms singly and in trusses. The low branching foliage is dark green tinted bronze and is ideal for low coverage. Especially useful for the small garden or for low bedding beneath large deep windows. Height 45 cm (1½ ft).

'Red Sprite' 1974. This delightful very double bright red bloom when fully open shows bright golden-yellow anthers. Of similar height to 'Marlena' it is brighter and its light green foliage and erect growth make it excellent for similar purposes where a brighter shade is needed. Height 45 cm (1½ ft).

'Rosemary Rose' (ss) 1955. A double, rosy-red large flower in big clusters with lovely foliage. The young leaves are red, a perfect foil against the deep green mature foliage. Sweetly scented. A difficult rose at times to propagate. Unique for bedding. Height 60 to 75 cm (2 to 2½ ft).

'Stephen Langdon' 1969 (H.T. type). A tall upright growth with abundant deep green foliage. The flowers are full, of H.T. type and deep crimson. Very late to flower it is abundant in crop and may be useful where a cultivar is needed to be at its best in late July. A good rose. Height 90 cm to 1·20 m (3 to 4 ft).

SCARLET-RED (Orange-Red Group 40–1).

'City of Belfast' 1967. A very brilliant red with close compact heads of double flowers carried on short sturdy shoots. Excellent for bedding where a medium height is required. Height 60 cm (2 ft).

'Evelyn Fison' 1960. A tall upright growth on a stiff strong stem. The buds are shapely and open to semi-double flowers of a dazzling red of extreme purity. A really good bedding rose which weathers well. Height 90 cm (3 ft).

'Fervid' 1960. It is difficult to say what makes the unique appeal of this rose. It has vigour and health. It is tall enough to make a good hedge. It is extremely free-flowering especially in late autumn; its October blossoms are peerless. Its colour is deep red lit with an orange glow, which it keeps consistently, whether the flower be young or old, or the weather be hot or wet. The flowers are single and slightly crinkled, an added charm. Ideal for lighter soils. Height 1 m (3 ft).

'Korp' 1972 (H.T. type). The blooms are full, singal-red with scarlet reverse. The growth is upright and bushy with branching inflorescences with each flower on a short separate stem. The foliage is small, dark green and healthy, and red when young. Height 1 m (3 ft).

'Meteor' 1958. The flowers are short-petalled, full, about 6 to 7 cm (2½ in) carried on short stout shoots. The growth is dwarf and branching with abundant mid-green, semi-glossy foliage. Height 40 to 50 cm (1½ to 2 ft).

'Meipuma' 1974. Well-formed full blooms of scarlet-cerise with silvery reverse, borne in large clusters on a robust medium-height plant, the foliage of which is tough and bright green. An attractive and excellent bedding rose. Height 60 to 75 cm (2 to 2½ ft).

'Molly McGredy' 1969 (H.T. type). An aristocrat in looks and performance. The full, pointed, elegant blossoms are crimson-red with a silvery reverse. They are full petalled and borne profusely on strong stems decorated with large, handsome deep green, disease-free foliage. Height 60 to 90 cm (2 to 3 ft).

'**Rob Roy**' 1971 (H.T. type). Scarlet overlaid with deep crimson, large petals forming a high-pointed flower. The growth is strong and vigorous. Height 75 to 90 cm (2½ to 3 ft).

'**Sarabande**' 1957. Already described as an ideal type of true floribunda with its brilliant red, semi-double flowers carried in large trusses and flowering freely over a very long period. The mid-green healthy foliage completes the ideal qualities of this excellent bedding rose. Height 45 to 60 cm (1½ to 2 ft).

'**Scarlet Queen Elizabeth**' (H.T. type). This very tall variety needs special placing and is best treated as a shrub grouped three or more together or as a hedge. The brilliant red flowers are particularly free in the autumn. The individual flowers are rather loose but the overall effect is both striking and pleasing. Height 1·20 to 1·50 m (4 to 5 ft).

'**Topsi**' (s) 1973. A very brilliant semi-double bloom with dwarf, bushy, compact growth. The sturdy shoots usually carry four to five flowers and are well covered with large medium green tough leaves. A very good bedding rose where low growth is essential. Height 40 to 60 cm (15 to 24 in).

SCARLET-ORANGE (Orange-Red Group 33).

'**Bountiful**' 1972 (H.T. type). The full shapely flowers are borne in large clusters on a strong, erect, well-leaved, healthy shoot. A difficult colour to describe with more scarlet-red to the orange than usual in this group. A rose of individual character and charm. Height 75 to 90 cm (2½ to 3 ft).

'**Orangeade**' (s) 1959. The vivid semi-single blooms are carried in well-spaced large trusses. Of medium height it is ideal for illuminating a dull patch in the garden. The growth is robust and healthy and yields a large crop of first-class bedding-quality blooms. Height 60 to 75 cm (2 to 2½ ft).

'Orange Sensation' (*sss*) 1961 (H.T. type). Of similar colour to 'Orangeade' but a tall, vigorous growth beginning to produce its fuller blooms a little later and carrying through to late October. Where more height is needed such as a low hedge or a bed at some distance from the house this is ideal. Height 90 cm to 1·20 m (3 to 4 ft).

'Orange Silk'. Again of similar habit to 'Orangeade'. Almost superfluous unless one prefers a more double flower of similar height. A little less free-flowering but blooming spread throughout the season. Height 60 to 75 cm (2 to 2½ ft).

VERMILION-ORANGE (Red Group 30).

'Anna Wheatcroft' 1959. An excellent and attractive rose of soft vermilion producing large semi-single blooms on heads of variable size, some extremely large in the autumn. Height 60 to 75 cm (2 to 2½ ft).

'Anne Cocker' (*s*) (H.T. type). A most unusual habit of growth with the flower head produced on a thick robust shoot which terminates in a series of shorter stems of sufficient length to cut. The one terminal bloom on each shoot is very full and of brilliant colour. The flowers are long lasting and remain fresh for many days. A variety for flower arrangers. Abundant dark green foliage. Height 90 cm (3 ft).

COPPER TO BROWN. Colour chart colours to describe the many colour combinations are not available. From copper to bronze with pink and other shading. This is the section to widen the colour range for the flower arranger.

'**Amberlight**' (*sss*) 1962. A full flower of golden buff fading to creamy amber. The delightful blooms have much of the charm of some older garden roses but are unique in colour and rich honey fragrance. A real floral artist's treasure, it is sufficiently free and healthy for bedding, making an excellent foil or buffer between orthodox shades and the startling moderns. Height 60 to 90 cm (2 to 3 ft).

'**Brownie**' 1959. A full flower on a short sturdy plant. Another floral arranger's dream in blends of tan, copper, cream and pink. Height 60 to 75 cm (2 to 2½ ft).

'**Café**' (*ss*) 1956. An unusual blending of coffee with cream in the full flower. Again a floral arranger's choice. Height 45 to 60 cm (1½ to 2 ft).

'**Copper Delight**' (*sss*) 1956. Large, semi-single flowers in a delightful shade of copper burnished gold. A wonderful perfume enhances this delightful low-growing, free-flowering plant. The shining large foliage needs protection from black spot if it is to yield its heavy crop of choice flowers all season. Height 45 to 60 cm (1½ to 2 ft).

'**Copper Pot**' 1968 (H.T. type). A stately flower on a tall upright stem borne in small numbers on each stem. The colour is more buff than copper but is very pleasing. Height 75 to 90 cm (2½ to 3 ft).

'**Jocelyn**' 1972. A very unusual, indeed unique, cultivar both in foliage and colour. The bush is sturdy and healthy producing a crop of glossy deep green holly-like leaves, an attraction in themselves. The colour is completely new and best described as a full flower, mat mahogany-brown with purple shadings in the old flower. This is a flower arranger's dream and challenge. Height 60 cm (2 ft).

'**Vesper**' (*ss*) 1966. Another delightful rose which has excellent garden habits such as growth, vigour and freedom of flower with health, added to which is a clear pastel shade of orange-amber. A lovely foil for 'hot' shades. Height 90 cm (2 to 3 ft).

COPPER AND PEACH (Yellow-Orange Group 17; Orange Group 28; Orange-Red Group 30).

'Circus' 1955. A neat sturdy grower with large clusters of small H.T. type flowers in scarlet and maize with an overall impression of coppery orange. Very free flowering making an excellent bedding cultivar. Height 45 to 60 cm (1½ to 2 ft).

'Ester Ofarim' 1970. A strong robust growth with small neat olive-green foliage. The flower heads have a few fully double 5- to 7-cm (2- to 2½-in) flowers on each upright stem in strikingly contrasting colours, coppery peach within and golden yellow without. Height 45 to 60 cm (1½ to 2 ft).

'Superior' 1968. Full flowers of peach with reverse pale yellow, the growth is free and even, small, abundant, healthy foliage. The flower stems are rigid carrying large clusters of delightful blossoms. Height 60 to 75 cm (2 to 2½ ft).

MIXTURES. I have put these under a special heading, for while in many cases there is more than one colour, many roses have a predominant colour. The few listed here give a less definite predominance and can be useful for carrying over neighbouring colours which need a blending colour to harmonize.

'Masquerade' 1950. Perhaps this rose has been in commerce long enough to have an obituary notice rather than a description, but although there have been many newer roses they have disappeared while this cultivar persists. It is tall, very free flowering, colourful and still grows well despite a virus. Scarlet, orange, gold, all well mixed, the rather ragged flowers are massed in prodigious profusion. Height 90 cm to 1·20 m (3 to 4 ft).

'**Redgold**' 1967. The medium-sized double flowers are predominantly golden yellow flushed and edged scarlet. A little flashy but cheerful, it is pre-eminently for bedding. 45 to 75 cm (1½ to 2 ft).

'**Shepherd's Delight**'. A more dignified 'Masquerade' with more yellow in the flower which is of better substance and usually fewer seed pods are produced. Makes an excellent low and colourful hedge. Height 90 cm to 1·20 m (3 to 4 ft).

YELLOW (Yellow-Orange Group 17 & 18A).

'**Allgold**' (*s*) 1956. Few roses have stood the test of time so consistently and so deservedly for the brilliant, unfading, clear deep yellow has yet to be improved. The small flowers open a little thinly but effectively in all weathers. It is very early to flower and very late to finish. Of marked resistance to black spot it makes an excellent bedding rose with its glossy bright green foliage. It is wise to prune at least one shoot each year to one or two eyes to ensure that the basal growths develop, upon which strong growth depends. Height 60 to 75 cm (2 to 2½ ft).

'**Arthur Bell**' (*sss*) 1965 (H.T. type). The large, deep yellow buds like small H.Ts. open into full flat flowers which fade to cream. These are carried five to seven on a tight head produced on an upright stem well covered with abundant deep green foliage. Height 60 to 90 cm (2 to 3 ft).

'**Goldgleam**' (*ss*) 1966. The large golden yellow flowers develop from handsome buds, usually in small clusters, while the deep green glossy mature foliage contrasts with the bronze younger growth. An excellent rose for bedding giving a bolder flower than 'Allgold' but needing some protection from black spot. Height 60 to 90 cm (2 to 3 ft).

'**Golden Treasure**'. Deep golden, full, double flowers on a low bush with plentiful deep green foliage, the clusters can be quite large on the slightly open growth of the bush which appears at times to lack winter hardiness. Height 60 cm (2 ft).

CREAM (Yellow-Orange Group 18 & 19; Red Group 36).

'**Chanelle**' 1958 (H.T. type). This variety might well be placed in the yellows but the yellow is so pale and elusive, and the orange-salmon so slight and yet so distinct, that one can only consider this as a delightful and refreshing change from the more brilliant and restless colours so popular today. The strong deep green foliage is also a foil for the pale but distinct freshness of the colour. The large flowers are borne in well-spaced clusters on stiff upright stems. The growth is robust, strong and free. Height 45 to 60 cm (1½ to 2 ft).

'**Dairy Maid**' (*ss*) 1957. A very charming single, small flowered 5-cm (2-in) variety in large, sweetly scented clusters. The buds are creamy yellow, tinted carmine. As these unfurl, they open to white with yellow centres when one sees the lovely anthers to great advantage. Excellent for bedding and very decorative when cut. The blooms should be cut in the bud stage and allowed to open in water. Height 75 to 90 cm (2½ to 3 ft).

'**Moon Maiden**' (*ss*) 1970. Large flowers of pale primrose yellow with buff shading produced very freely over a long period. The growth is bushy and excellent for bedding. Makes a pleasing foil for 'News' as grown at the Royal National Rose Society's grounds.

'**Yellow Queen Elizabeth**' 1964 (H.T. type). A pale, straw-yellow sport of 'Queen Elizabeth' although the flowers have slightly less substance. Height 1 to 1·50 m (3½ to 5 ft).

SALMON-PINK (Red Group 38).

'**Dearest**' (*sss*) 1960 (H.T. type). Lovely H.T. type flowers of a soft glowing salmon carried in large trusses on sturdy shoots. The foliage is dark green and glossy. Like many of this type impatient of wet, when it pays to remove the 'crown' (centre) bud from the head. Height 60 to 90 cm (2 to 3 ft).

'**Elizabeth of Glamis**' (*sss*) 1964 (H.T. type). A delightful flower, many on a stem, a little more pink than salmon, with golden base. A robust, bushy plant, with good growth and health. Does not always transplant well, apparently enjoying a well-drained friable soil. 75 to 90 cm (2½ to 3 ft).

'**Salmon Sprite**' (*sss*) 1964. Deep salmon-pink, double H.T. type flowers carried singly and in small clusters on upright stems. Free-flowering and excellent for bedding. Height 60 to 90 cm (2 to 3 ft).

'**Tip Top**' (*s*) 1963. One of the new short type with robust growth; plentiful normal foliage with many fully double flowers. These are ideal for low bedding and excellent for the smaller modern garden with limited space. Height 45 cm (1½ ft).

CLEAR PINK (Red Groups 55B, 51B, 50C, 38A, etc.).

'**City of Leeds**' 1966. Clear, bright pink fairly large semi-double flowers borne in great profusion on large flower heads. The growth is vigorous and upright. The foliage is a little below what one would expect from such a plant being semi-glossy, medium green and rather small. Should be sprayed regularly. Height 75 to 90 cm (2½ to 3 ft).

'**Dainty Maid**' (*s*) 1938. Still unique among single roses for its satisfying yet subtle charm. Its colour has the dainty freshness of the dew-washed brier rose in early morning. Pale shining pink within with clear deep pink reverse. The five-petalled flowers are borne singly and in large clusters throughout the growing season, and are untroubled by rain and rough weather. A lovely bedding rose which contrasts with the dark glowing red of 'Dusky Maiden'. A very fine variety for a hedge. Both 'Dainty' and 'Dusky' should have their old flower heads removed to prevent seeding. Height 90 cm to 1 m (3 to 3½ ft).

'**Nathalie Nypels**' 1919. A rose of mixed parentage probably leaning more heavily toward polyantha than floribunda. A little, shrubby plant with continuous masses of pale pink blooms and small light green foliage. An excellent link between shrub roses and floribundas or a break from a formal planting to an informal background. Height about 60 cm (2 ft).

'**Pernille Poulsen**' (*s*) 1965. A delightful deep, clear pink flower which is large, semi-double and very early with its first blooming. A little late with its second heavy crop. An excellent, low-growing, compact habit. Height 60 to 75 cm (2 to 2½ ft).

'**Pink Parfait**' 1962 (H.T. type). Even now one of the finest vigorous bedding cultivars. The lovely individual blooms are two shaded, clear soft pink on a yellow base and are reproduced on strong upright many flowered stems. The foliage is semi-glossy, leathery and deep green. Beautiful as a cut flower. Height 90 cm to 1·20 m (3 to 4 ft).

'**Sea Pearl**' (*s*) 1964 (H.T. type). Overall deep pink although the colour is made up of pale orange and pink with a yellow reverse. The foliage is glossy medium green, large and abundant. A tall, vigorous, upright growth suited to a large bed or specimen group. At its best in a dry autumn when the blooms attain a depth of colour and perfection of shape known to few varieties. Impatient of wet conditions. Height 90 cm to 1·20 m (3 to 4 ft).

'**Vera Dalton**' (*ss*) 1961 (H.T. type). Large, double, cupped, fragrant blooms in soft clear pink. The foliage is dark green and glossy while the plant is bushy, vigorous and healthy. Always in flower, it is an excellent bedding variety. Height about 90 cm (3 ft).

ROSE-PINK (Red Group 51).

'Paddy McGredy' (*s*) 1961 (H.T. type). A very full, almost globular, bloom in carmine with lighter reverse, which are often of small H.T. size. The low bushes are crowded with these large blooms and then have a resting period before another similar crop. Quite distinct in type but the foliage, which is semi-glossy, dark green and small, needs protection from disease. Height about 60 cm (2 ft).

'Plentiful' 1961. A most unusual very double, short-petalled cultivar, reminding one of an old garden rose in the flower but the growth is typical of the best and most free-flowering floribundas. The tight rounded buds open into 8-cm (3½-in) flowers borne in huge, well-spaced clusters. The foliage is bright green and the robust bush carried many shoots springing from the base. Height 60 cm (2 ft).

'Posy' 1951. This little charmer is too big in flower and leaf for a miniature but it is a small floribunda carrying strong clusters of 5-cm (2-in) very double pink blooms with a slightly mauve tint. The growth is erect and plants should be spaced at 37 cm (15 in).

'Queen Elizabeth' 1954 (H.T. type). A cultivar which has made itself an almost unique position. Its double, clear pink flowers of H.T. size and type are produced singly and in clusters on long stems springing from very vigorous upright growths. The best rose for a tall hedge but requiring care to prevent all the flowers appearing on the top of the plant so that up to 1·20 m (4 ft) may be without colour. It is advised very strongly to cut at least two shoots on each plant each year pruning these to about 10 cm (4 in) from the base. This will encourage a lower growth and flower. Height 1·20 to 1·80 m (4 to 6 ft).

WHITE

'Iceberg' (*ss*) 1958. One of the great roses of all time. The small well-formed flowers are produced in unmatched profusion on light green almost thornless wood with glossy light green foliage. Pure white most of the time it can stain pink with age or in rain. Useful for large beds and excellent for hedges. Height 90 cm to 1·50 m (3 to 5 ft).

'Snowline' 1971. Pure white well-shaped flowers borne very freely on short upright growths. A very useful plant for bedding where a low-growing rose is needed. Height about 60 cm (2 ft).

PURPLE AND MAUVE (Red-Purple Group 69; Purple Group 76).

'Escapade' (*ss*). Semi-double flowers of magenta rose showing a white 'eye' when fully developed. An unusual and charming cultivar equally at home as a bedding rose or with old garden roses. Extremely free flowering and very healthy. A dainty 'picture' rose which may be combined with excellent effect with many colour combinations. Height 75 to 90 cm (2½ to 3 ft).

'News' 1969. A complete break in colour: a rich claret. The semi-double flowers have bright golden anthers which serve to illuminate the whole 10-cm (4-in) flower. The growth is extremely free. Early to flower it continues until late in the season offering a constant succession of blooms throughout the growing season. In practice one finds that this colour blends or contrasts pleasantly with all rose colours and offers a new dimension for the rose garden. Height 60 to 75 cm (2 to 2½ ft).

'Ripples' (*sss*). An unusual, unfading mauve-lilac flower of H.T. shape with an intriguing waving of the petal. The cultivar is extremely free in flower with plentiful light green foliage and compact upright habit. Its one weakness is a tendency to mildew in the autumn and spraying should be carried out regularly. A very beautiful variety worth the extra care. Height about 60 cm (2 ft).

HAND-PAINTED ROSES. Basically these remarkable roses are in three shades or intensities of colours from red to pink. Raised by McGredy IV they are distinct and will undoubtedly improve and vary even more with continued experiment.

'Eye paint' 1975. This is really quite a tall shrub with innumerable red and pink edged 5- to 7·5-cm (2- to 3-in) flowers on a white ground with a distinct white 'eye'. It appears to be very healthy and always in flower. This will be quite a feature among shrub roses. Height 90 cm to 1·20 m (3 to 4 ft).

'Matangi' (ss) 1974. The semi-double flowers of orange-vermilion are shaded silver on the reverse, and are produced in large striking trusses on a very healthy plant. A great advance in size and substance of flower and colour. Height 60 to 90 cm (2 to 3 ft).

'Old Master' 1974. A novel maroon and white with silvery-white reverse. The semi-single open flowers are most striking while the upright bush with unusual pointed dark green foliage is completely healthy. Height 75 to 90 cm (2½ to 3 ft).

'Picasso' 1971. This was the first of the 'hand-painted' series and at its most distinct is very intriguing. The cream-white background is flushed and edged deep pink to crimson giving three distinct circular zones of colour. Growth is short, branching and free. Height 60 cm (2 ft).

Miniature Roses Including Polyantha Roses (Poly-poms)

Having dealt with the two principle modern types of bedding roses
L

we come to a class which is becoming increasingly popular. This is the miniature group. We will deal with its history later but it is well to realize that an increasing number of ardent rose and plant lovers are compelled by circumstances to live where they cannot possess gardens. What remains? They may visit parks, flower shows or read gardening papers or visit more fortunate friends at week-ends but what can they do? Even a small flat can possess a window-box or sufficient room for a flower box or soil receptacle of some kind. Here small flowers and bulbs may be grown with much pleasure and good effect if drainage, soil and watering are attended to as required. There are few better or more rewarding plants to culti-vate under such circumstances than miniature roses although I believe a modicum of sun some part of most days is essential. They have the great advantage of flowering frequently throughout the season and besides adorning the position in which they are growing can also provide small floral decorations of great beauty and charm for the home.

There is now an added incentive, for miniature roses have classes provided for them at the Royal National Rose Society's Shows so that one may pit ones skill against others and share the delight of friendly competition. Miniature roses, especially in the United States, have a wide publicity at the rose shows and in number of entries may be up to 25 per cent of the total exhibits staged. They are always a focus of attention and while we have everything to learn about their presentation at British shows they give an opportunity for a wider public to take an active part in the Rose Society's activities and, because they take up little space, are easy to transport.

My own experience has been that the major part of the growth of miniatures is taken up by the inflorescence, so that the removal of the dead flower stem reduces the growth to two or three basal eyes. In practice, where a quantity of plants have been involved, I have found trimming all the shoots to within an inch of the ground, using a sharp instrument to ensure a clean cut is quite sufficient pruning.

The history of this type of rose is somewhat obscure. Its origin lies with the dwarf form of the 'China' or 'Bengal' rose *R. chinensis minima*. It is a well-known fact among rose hybridists that a dwarfing factor lies within the genes of this type of rose and it is not unusual for this to appear in dwarf forms of floribunda roses. When these factors are doubled the dwarf form usually breeds nearly true and the dwarfing effect acts as a dominating factor, so that on its being crossed, many of the progeny are equally small in habit. This is true of the form now under discussion. It is possible to raise seedlings which flower as annuals and are known as 'Fairy Roses' but many of their pleasing characteristics disappear if they are kept longer. Their single flowers, mostly an insipid pink, grow from a bush which loses the charm of its low bushy character after the first year. Some forms were certainly present in the early 1800s. Fresh interest was aroused by the discovery by Dr. Roulet in Switzerland in 1922 of a small rose in a window-box which was named after him. Dr. G. D. Rowley identifies this with the old 'Pompom de Paris' 1839 but in the description of the latter in *Modern Roses, VII* the flowers are described as brighter pink and more double than *R. rouletii*. It is unlikely that the single flowered type called *R. lawranceana* is actually that rose. Be that as it may, *R. rouletii* caused a new interest, and with the advent of a variant of *R. chinensis minima* in 'Oakington Ruby', material was available to invite crossing. It is probable that we owe the beginning of interest to Mr. John de Vink of Boskoop, Holland, and soon others were involved. Each raiser seems to have had his special 'stud' but in most cases *rouletii*, 'Oakington Ruby' or near descendants, carrying the gifts of these parents, were used. Unfortunately, there has been a considerable drift away from the true crosses with *R. chinensis minima* and although many have retained the small leaf and flower there has been an increasing tendency to produce a more vigorous bush until a so-called 'miniature' outstrips some of the dwarf floribunda roses in size, with the result that the dainty features of the true miniature have been coarsened out of recognition.

Two distinct types of propagation are used. The first, which ensures a dwarf plant, is that produced on its own roots. The drawback is that such plants have a less strong root system and can be more susceptible to local conditions and suffer more quickly from water shortage, either by the failure to water or other plants poaching the supply. The second method of propagation produces a strong plant, some may consider too strong, but by grafting or budding on to a stronger brier the resulting plant will have a better drought resistance and if taller can always be pruned a little harder. Many new cultivars are coming on the market and I have had to choose from many of equal worth. Many of those mentioned have had other names disguising them but the names given are those registered. Certain characteristics are general to most miniatures and for this reason the term 'very free flowering' is omitted. 'Small' flowers are about 4 cm (1½ in), 'very small' under that size.

'Baby Bunting' (*ss*) 1953. Very small, double, light magenta flowers with prominent stamens. Height 25 to 30 cm (9 to 12 in).

'Baby Darling' 1964. A pointed bud with small double orange to orange-pink flowers. The growth is dwarf and bushy. Height about 30 cm (12 in).

'Baby Faurex' (*ss*) 1924. Really a dwarf polyantha, similar to a vigorous miniature with quite large clusters of violet flowers. Height 30 to 40 cm (12 to 18 in).

'Baby Gold Star' (*s*) 1940. A pointed bud opening into semi-double open flower, golden-yellow fading with age. The foliage is small and soft on a rather large bush. Height 45 cm (1½ ft).

'Baby Masquerade' 1956. A very small double flower in varying colours from lemon-chrome with degrees of rose-red shading. The plant is large and loose in growth being tall for the class. Height 45 to 60 cm (1½ to 2 ft).

'Cinderella' (*s*) 1953. Very small, fully double (forty-five to sixty petals) satiny-white tinged with pink. The growth is bushy, upright and thornless. A charming flower on a typical miniature plant. Height 30 cm (12 in).

'**Colibri**' (*s*) 1958. The ovoid buds open into a small, double, bright orange flower. The foliage is glossy, the growth very vigorous bearing a mass of bloom on a 45-cm (18-in) bush.

'**Cri-Cri**' 1958. Small double flowers in salmon shaded coral. The growth is dwarf and bushy with tough leathery foliage. Height 30 cm (12 in).

'**Darling Flame**' 1971. A small compact bush with double flowers of a very brilliant red turning to vermilion-red with yellow reverse on opening. Abundant and healthy foliage. Height 30 cm (12 in).

'**Dwarf King**' 1957. A small flower with double (twenty to thirty petals) cupped carmine flowers opening flat, produced singly and in clusters. The foliage is glossy and growth compact. 20 to 25 cm (8 to 10 in).

'**Easter Morning**' 1960. A pleasing change. A small double flower with many petals (sixty to seventy). The ivory-white flowers are improved by their leathery glossy foliage. Height 30 to 40 cm (12 to 15 in).

'**Eleanor**' 1960. Very small flowers of twenty to thirty petals in coral pink deepening with age. Glossy foliage. Growth upright, bushy and dwarf. Height 30 cm (12 in).

'**Fire Princess**' (*ss*) 1969. Small double (forty-five to fifty) short-petalled flowers with large sepals. Very vigorous. Height 45 cm (1½ ft).

'**Gold Coin**' (*s*) 1967. Small double flowers of buttercup yellow, fully opened they show golden anthers within the crowded short petals. The growth is vigorous and abundant. Height 30 to 45 cm (12 to 18 in).

'**Gold Pin**' (*s*) 1974. A vigorous bushy little plant with masses of bright yellow flowers carried few or many on the stems. Height 45 to 60 cm (1½ to 2 ft).

'**Judy Fischer**' 1968. A pointed bud opening into a small double rose-pink flower. The foliage is dark green, bronzed and leathery. The plant is low, bushy yet vigorous. Height 30 cm (12 in).

'**Lavender Lace**' 1968. Small double high-centred lavender flowers. Foliage is small and glossy with a dwarf bushy growth. Height 30 cm (12 in).

'**Little Flirt**' (*s*) 1961. The small pointed bud opens into a very double (thirty-five to fifty petals) flower of unusual colouring being bright orange-red with golden reverse. The foliage is light green on a vigorous bushy plant. Height 30 to 35 cm (12 to 14 in).

'**Mr. Bluebird**' 1960. An oval bud opening to a small semi-double lavender flower. The plant is bushy and compact with dark green foliage. Height 25 to 35 cm (10 to 14 in).

'**New Penny**' (*s*) 1962. The bud is short and pointed, developing into a small semi-double flower of orange-red to coral-pink. The foliage is leathery and glossy. The plant is bushy and dwarf. Height 25 cm (10 in).

'**Perla de Alacanada**' 1944. A small bud opening into semi-double open carmine blooms. An excellent really dwarf habit of the early miniature with dark glossy foliage. Height 15 to 25 cm (6 to 10 in).

'**Perla de Montserrat**' 1945. A small, semi-double flower which opens to reveal its stamens. The colour is clear pink edged pearl. The flowers are carried in clusters on a dwarf very compact bush. Both 'Perla's are deservedly popular.

'Pixie' 1940. A small very double (forty to forty-five petals) flower with white with blush centre. The dwarf compact bush has very small foliage. Height 25 cm (9 in).

'Pour Toi' ('Para Ti') 1946. The flower is semi-double (fifteen petals) white with yellow tinted base. A very bushy plant with glossy foliage. Height 15 to 20 cm (6 to 8 in).

'Prince Charming' 1953. Very small, double, bright crimson flowers. The deep green foliage is tinted red. Height 15 to 20 cm (6 to 8 in).

'Red Imp' 1951. Flower very small 2 to 2·5 cm ($\frac{3}{4}$ to 1 in), double (forty-five to sixty petals), deep crimson opening very flat. Upright, bushy and dwarf. Height 22 cm (9 in).

'Rosina' (s) 1951. Small, semi-double (sixteen petals) open sun-flower-yellow, fading. The foliage is glossy and light green. Height 30 cm (12 in).

'Starina' 1965. Small, double, orange-scarlet flowers. The foliage is glossy and the growth robust but short. 30 to 45 cm (1 to 1$\frac{1}{2}$ ft).

'Sweet Fairy' (ss) 1946. Very small, double (fifty to sixty-five petals) cupped apple-blossom pink flowers. A vigorous but dwarf growth, 15 to 20 cm (6 to 8 in). Foliage is small and dark.

'Tinker Bell' 1954. Bud ovoid, flower small and double (fifty-five to sixty-five petals) cupped and bright rose pink. The foliage is small and leathery on a bushy dwarf plant. Height 20 cm (8 in).

'Toy Clown' 1966. Small semi-double open flower in white with red edge. Foliage is small and leathery on a short strong bush. Height 23 to 30 cm (9 to 12 in).

'Twinkles' 1954. Pink bud opening to a small double (forty to forty-five petals) white flower. Growth dwarf 20 cm (8 in) and compact.

'Wee Man' 1974. A bushy little plant with semi-single bright red flowers showing golden anthers. Height 45 to 60 cm (1½ to 2 ft).

'Yellow Doll' 1962. Small very double blooms (fifty to sixty narrow petals) yellow to cream. Vigorous and bushy. Height 30 cm (12 in).

A number of the above varieties have climbing sports similar in all ways except for their greater vigour and flowering on the mature growths. There are a few much older roses which have similar tiny flowers but their growth is more branching and taller. Of these one should mention:

'Cecile Brunner' (*ss*) 1881 (Poly.). Clear pink on a yellow ground in large clusters. The foliage is sparse and soft on brownish wood. It produces an incredible number of perfect blooms on the climbing form where the winters are sufficiently kind. A much more vigorous but similar rose 'Bloomfield Abundance' is sometimes confused with it but differs in its extremely long fimbriated sepals, often three times the length of the flower bud. Height 60 to 75 cm (2 to 2½ ft).

'Perle d'Or' (*ss*) 1884 (Poly.). Very double small mother-of-pearl flowers in spaced clusters. The foliage is rich green and soft.

Climbing and Rambler Roses

In few groups have there been so great changes as here. This will account for the almost complete disappearance of the old rambler rose. Those that have been kept owe their survival to the fact that their pendulous habit makes them essential for satisfactory weeping standards. The advance has been in the production of climbers which flower more or less throughout the season, many with quite large flowers. One must remember that if the flowering period is to be prolonged one cannot have the spectacular mass of the once-flowering ramblers which are unequalled in their brief burst of flower for such a purpose.

R = rambler; K = *kordesii*, intermittent flowering rambler; C = intermittent flowering climber.

'Albertine' (*ss*) 1921. R. Handsome foliage, with a vigorous plant producing masses of clustered coppery-peach buds opening into pink shaded gold inner petals, with a deeper reverse. A comparatively short burst of flower but the persistent foliage which is deep green and glossy with young reddish shoots makes it a good plant or wall cover for a long period.

'Altissimo' (*s*) 1966. C. One of the most spectacular of all climbers. The huge single brilliant red, with darker shade blooms are enhanced by deep golden-brown anthers. Many flowers over a long period with strong deep green foliage as an excellent foil.

'Allgold' (*s*) 1960. C. This climbing sport should be planted only in a south or south-west position with ample space for growth. It must be allowed to grow without restriction or pruning for the first three years after which having obtained its blooming rhythm it will flower freely both in early summer and autumn.

'Autumn Sunlight' (*s*) 1965. C. The double blooms are of medium size, globular and of bright orange-vermilion. A strong growth with many flowers. A change in colour.

'Bantry Bay' (*s*) 1967. C. A large 10 cm (4 in) open bright pink flower coming in clusters freely borne on strong growths.

'Casino' (*s*) 1963. C. Well-formed primrose-yellow flowers on medium growths. Not so free as some varieties but useful in its colour as a low wall coverage.

'Compassion' (*ss*) 1974. Apricot-pink, double (thirty-nine petals) flowers carried singly or in clusters. Very vigorous and upright growth with glossy dark green foliage.

'Copenhagen' (*ss*) 1964. C. Large full 12½ cm (5 in) double, brilliant red blooms on a strong vigorous plant. The foliage is bronze green and very healthy.

'Coral Dawn' (*s*) 1952. C. The bud is ovoid opening into a large, double (thirty to thirty-five petals) bloom of rose pink. The growth is very vigorous with strong, healthy, leathery foliage.

'Crimson Showers' (*s*) 1951. R. A small double pom-pom type flower in large corymbs of deep clear crimson. The foliage is glossy light green and healthy. Flowering a month later than most ramblers it makes an excellent weeping standard.

'Danse du Feu' 1953. C. Bearing many medium-size double (thirty to thirty-five petal) flowers, opening cupped to flat in small and large clusters carried on vigorous plentiful shoots and flowering throughout the season. The colour is a brilliant orange red. A very good cultivar.

'Danse des Sylphes' 1959. C. Best described as a free and long flowering 'Paul's Scarlet Climber' to which it is in every way superior. Bright red 5-cm (2-in) flowers in great cheerful clusters.

'Étoile de Hollande' (*sss*) 1931. A once-flowering sport of the dwarf form of this old richly scented, smoky-red variety. An ideal plant for a tall wall on an old cottage where its pendant, perfume-laden flowers are a delight, filled with old memories.

'Excelsa' 1909. R. Similar to 'Crimson Showers' which see, but a lighter red and flowering earlier.

'Galway Bay' (*s*) 1966. C. Large well-formed flowers of deep salmon pink borne in clusters. The growth is strong, hardy and free.

'**Golden Showers**' (*ss*) 1956. C. A long pointed bud developing into a large 10-cm (4-in) flower carried singly and in clusters on a strong stem. The growth is moderately vigorous and very free, bearing many flowers over a long period.

'**Guinée**' (*sss*) 1938. C. A very full tight almost black bud opening into a full rather flat very dark red flower which is carried singly and in clusters on strong upright much branched stems, well covered with strong leathery foliage. Unique in its depth of colour and very free flowering.

'**Hamburger Phoenix**' (*s*) 1954. K. Rich red, double large, rambler-type flowers with very vigorous trailer growths with dark glossy foliage. Recurrent flowering like all of this type.

'**Handel**' 1965. C. A most delightful and charming colour blending ivory-white and cream with a deep rose-pink edge on its large, double flowers carried singly and in clusters on moderately tall shoots clothed with deep olive-green foliage.

'**Leverkusen**' (*s*) 1954. K. A very double, large, for rambler-type flower, in long sprays of primrose yellow. The foliage is glossy and light green on long trailing shoots. A very good cultivar.

'**Maigold**' (*ss*) 1953. C. This is sometimes classed as a shrub although the shoots, especially the side growths are better for some support. Quite unusual and pleasing but because of the thorny wood it should be kept away from paths. An unusual flower, semi-double, rather flat on opening, but an unusual bronze yellow. The foliage is glossy and although a first heavy crop, it does give some flower in the autumn on established plants.

'**Mermaid**' 1918. C. A unique breeding, with large blossoms like a white water-lily with some sulphur-yellow staining. The unusual glossy green foliage is supported by long very thorny brittle shoots. Very recurrent with many autumn flowers in short-stalked branches. Individual flowers are very transient. Better on a west wall where it is one of our loveliest roses.

'Minnehaha' (*s*) 1905. R. A typical rambler with very double deep pink blooms in huge corymbs. The leaves are deep green and glossy and both foliage and vigorous growths are stronger and larger than the average.

'Mme Alfred Carrière' (*sss*) 1879 noisette. An old but lovely climbing rose bearing large very full globular flowers of blush white. It flowers freely giving some autumn flower and seems at home in a north aspect.

'Mme Gregoire Staechelin' ('Spanish Beauty') (*sss*) 1927. C. A vigorous trailing growth with abundant deep green foliage. Smothered with clear pink ruffled flowers, each outer petal and reverse is stained crimson. Once-flowering but what a flowering!

'Mrs. Sam McGredy' (*s*) 1937. C. A climbing form which flowers once only. The colour, coppery orange flushed scarlet fading peach and salmon, is unusual while the growths of tremendous vigour are bronze in the early stage deepening to olive green. Once the growth matures, and it may take three years by which time it will extend at least 3 to 4 m (10 to 14 ft), it is capable of carrying three hundred and more flowers in its avalanche of perfect blossoms.

'New Dawn' (*sss*) 1930. C. This should be called a perpetual rambler. The flowers are small like tiny H.Ts. in a clear soft pink. The short growths have both terminal and side growths full of flowers which bloom over a very long period. It makes a delightful low hedge if supported, or covers a low wall or fence. A noted parent of many of the new perpetual climbers.

'Nazomi' 1970. C. Not an easy rose to place. It is really a once-flowering cover plant with a prostrate habit making an excellent carpet of off-white to pearl-pink blooms. Suitable as a low-wall cover also. Possibly a forerunner of cover plants. See also 'Temple Bells'.

'**Parade**' (*ss*) 1956. C. One of the best and most sturdy cultivars bearing large H.T. type deep bright pink blooms very freely over a long period. The foliage is handsome, deep green and healthy.

'**Ritter Von Barmstede**' 1959. K. Small 5-cm (2-in) semi-double flowers, which open to show their stamens set in rich velvety red petals. Very free with its blooms and vigorous growths suitable for considerable coverage 3 to 4·50 m (10 to 15 ft).

Rosa banksiae 1796. C. An old rose of unique habit largely once flowering. The small double deep yellow flowers are crowded in festoons of long pliant shoots. Must be planted where there is abundant warmth and sunshine. Almost evergreen covers at least 6 m (20 ft) when happy.

Rosa filipes Kifsgate (*ss*) 1954. C. This really belongs to species but it is worth a reminder. Once flowering, the massed racemes of pure white flowers crowd the branches. Ideal for covering a high tree stump or wandering in the boughs of a lightly foliaged plant. A wonderful sight as the white froth of blossoms cascade from the branches of the tree.

'**Royal Gold**' (*ss*) 1957. C. Large 10-cm (4-in) double (thirty to forty petals) cupped blossoms of clear shining gold, carried singly or in small clusters. The foliage is glossy and of medium coverage. Height 1·5 to 2 m (5 to 7 ft).

'**Santa Catalina**' 1968. C. An extremely free-flowering tall specimen or low climber in clear pink deepening in the centre petals with their golden petal base. Long pointed healthy growth.

'**Schoolgirl**' (*sss*) 1964. C. This colour is unique in climbers being a burnt orange shaded peach. The flowers are large of H.T. shape and size while the foliage is strong and healthy. Flowering freely over a long period.

'**Snowflake**' (*sss*) 1922. R. A typical rambler in pure white. Flowering once it makes an excellent weeping standard with ornamental shining bright green foliage.

'**Soldier Boy**' 1953. C. One of the most free-flowering of all climbers beginning before most and finishing when checked by frost. The large, single, scarlet-red flowers are carried in clusters on healthy vigorous growths.

'**Swan Lake**' (*s*) 1968. C. Very large rather globular fully double flowers, white with the centres tinged pink. Strong in growth and free in flower.

'**Sympathie**' (*sss*) 1964. K. Well formed velvety red flowers on a very vigorous plant with dark glossy foliage.

'**Temple Bells**' 1974. R. I have classed this as a rambler but it is a plant on its own with tiny glossy foliage of *wichuriana* type. It is primarily a ground-cover plant of exceptional merit which flowers in mid season, once only.

'**White Cockade**' (*s*) 1969. C. A small H.T. shaped full white flower on a plant of medium height. A charming plant suitable for a large specimen or low pillar.

Modern Shrub Roses

(R = repeat flowering, otherwise once only)

'**Ballerina**' 1937. R. A delightful low shrub 90 cm to 1·20 m (3 to 4 ft) bearing large corymbs of single pink blooms with a white eye over a long period. The foliage is light green, small and abundant.

'**Berlin**' 1949. R. A strong shrub carrying large heads of orange-scarlet single flowers with golden anthers on a healthy bush with plentiful light green foliage. Height 1·5 to 1·8 m (5 to 6 ft).

'Canary Bird', scc page 284.

'Cocktail' 1957. R. Numerous single crimson flowers with primrose centre fading to white in large clusters freely produced over a long period. The foliage is small, glossy, green tinted bronze.

'Constance Spry' (*sss*) 1960. R. A clear full pink with an 'Old Garden' type flower and bush. An attractive perfumed flower 1·5 to 1·8 m (5 to 6 ft).

'Chinatown' 1963. R. A vigorous shrub with the terminal growth carrying a large cluster of double yellow flowers. Hardy but a great deal of wood for the proportion of flower. Height 1·2 to 1·8 m (4 to 6 ft).

'Dorothy Wheatcroft' (*s*) 1960. R. Large semi-double brilliant deep red blossoms in large heads. The growth is strong, upright and free with bright green foliagc. Height 1·2 to 1·5 m (4 to 5 ft).

'First Choice' 1958. R. A gay flower in scarlet and gold, almost five-petalled, carried on a handsome shrub constantly in bloom, 11 cm (4½ in) across. Height 1·2 to 1·5 m (4 to 5 ft).

'Fountain' 1972. R. A free and long flowering shrub covered with exquisite blood-red flowers borne in clusters. Height 1·2 to 1·5 m (4 to 5 ft).

'Fred Loads' 1967. R. Large corymbs of brilliant vermilion-orange single blossoms carried on stout upright stems well covered with large and healthy foliage. A small group is the ideal way to plant this eye-catching shrub. Height 1·2 m (4 ft).

'Fritz Nobis' (*sss*) 1940. Most attractive bearing many large salmon-pink flowers. Although it has one flowering season, this is prolonged giving a really grand display. Height 1·8 m (6 ft).

'Frühlingsgold' ('Spring gold') 1937. A true Kordes' hybrid. Tall growth with slightly pendulous ends to the shoots. Flowering, like 'Frühlingsmorgen' and others of its fellows, but once, its beauty remains a treasured memory throughout the year. The very large sulphur-yellow flowers crowd the branches, jostling each other in prodigal profusion during mid and late May. Should be considered and planted as a highly ornamental shrub. Height 2·4 m (8 ft).

'Frühlingsmorgen' ('Spring morning') 1942. The same again, a little firmer flower but with a rosy hue over the pale yellow. Height 2·4 m (8 ft).

'Heidelberg' 1958. Well formed double crimson-scarlet flowers borne very freely on strong dense growths well covered with glossy leathery foliage. Height 1·5 to 1·8 m (5 to 6 ft).

'Joseph's Coat' (*s*) 1964. R. A large perpetual shrub or semi-climber of unusual colouring bearing a profusion of multi-coloured flowers in reds, pinks and yellows. Good throughout the season with dark green, glossy foliage. Height 1·2 to 1·5 m (4 to 5 ft).

'Kiese' 1910. Large semi-single bright red blooms on a spreading bush carrying a profusion of large, long-lasting hips. Height 1·5 to 1·8 m (5 to 6 ft).

'Lady Sonia' 1960. R. Deep yellow full flowers; the buds splashed crimson. Growth is medium but vigorous and healthy, about 1·2 m (4 ft).

'Lavender Lassie' (*sss*) 1959. Fragrance unlimited. Very double rosette flowers 5 to 6 cm (2 to 2½ in) across borne in great corymbs of lilac-pink flowers. Not over-tall for this type but very charming and quite different. Height 1·2 m (4 ft).

'Marguerite Hilling' 1959. R. A far superior sport of 'Nevada' with much more freedom and a clear delightful pink; otherwise as its parent.

'Max Graf' 1919. Medium-sized flower in bright pink with golden centre. The foliage is glossy and most attractive. Very vigorous, bushy and trailing, it is admirable for pegging down for ground cover, but its thorny wood demands careful handling.

'Nevada' 1927. R. Pale off-white with slightly more lemon in the flower centre. Semi-single, very large and striking flowers, loosely formed. Very delightful. After a first heavier flowering, other blooms appear throughout the season. A fine and pleasing shrub. Height 2·5 m (8 ft).

'Nymphenburgh' (ss) 1954. R. A lovely shrub of hybrid musk ancestry. The flowers are large, semi-double, flat salmon-pink shaded orange. The growth is upright with large glossy foliage. Height 1·5 to 1·8 m (4 to 5 ft).

'Scharlachglut' ('Scarlet Fire') 1952. Bright scarlet large single flowers with golden stamens. Many short-stemmed clusters on long arching branches carrying big pear-shaped hips in great profusion. The foliage is dull, matt grey-green. 1·8 × 1·8 m (6 × 6 ft).

'Sparrieshoop' (ss) 1953. R. Large, light pink blooms on a very upright vigorous and healthy bush. Height 1·5 m (5 ft).

'Uncle Walter' 1963. R. A very good H.T. type flower carried on very tall shoots, well-covered with leathery coppery foliage. A most effective plant for a small group. Height 1·5 m (5 ft).

'Will Scarlet' 1948. R. Semi-double scarlet flowers in trusses on a tall upright bush which grows freely and is well covered with dark bronze foliage. Height 1·5 m (5 ft).

It is possible to grow many of the most vigorous H.Ts. and

M

floribundas as specimens. Among these 'Chicago Peace', 'Pink Favourite', 'My Choice', 'Alexander', 'Queen Elizabeth', 'Fervid' and 'Troika' are good examples. If these are used, prune more lightly but always prune at least one shoot extra hard to renew basal growth. So treated these bushes will reach 1·8 to 2·1 m (6 to 7 ft).

 APPENDIX A

Selection of Roses for Special Purposes

Twelve Old Garden

'Blanche Moreau'	(*R. centifolia*)
'Cristata'	(*R. centifolia*)
'Maiden's Blush' (small)	(*R. alba*)
'Mme Hardy'	(*R. damascena*)
'Mme Pierre Oger'	(Bourbon)
'Mrs. John Laing'	(Hybrid Perpetual)
'Petite de Hollande'	(*R. centifolia*)
'Roger Lambelin'	(Hybrid Perpetual)
'Rubrotincta'	(*R. damascena*)
'Tuscany Superba'	(*R. rubra*)
'Variegata de Bologna'	(Bourbon)
'Versicolor'	(*R. mundi*) (*R. rubra*)

Hybrid Teas

Twelve medium height, about 60 to 75 cm (2 to $2\frac{1}{2}$ ft)

'Alec's Red'	'National Trust'
'Dr. A. J. Verhage'	'Peer Gynt'
'Fragrant Cloud'	'Piccadilly'
'Just Joey'	'Prima Ballerina'
'King's Ransom'	'Princess'
'Mischief'	'Stella'

Twelve tall, about 75 to 90 cm ($2\frac{1}{2}$ to 3 ft)

'Blessings'	'Pascali'
'Chicago Peace'	'Pink Favourite'

'Diorama'   'Red Devil'
'Ernest H. Morse'   'Rose Gaujard'
'Grandpa Dickson'   'Summer Holiday'
'My Choice'   'Troika'

Floribundas

Six short, about 30 to 60 cm (1 to 2 ft)

'Copper Delight'   'Red Sprite'
'Marlena'   'Tip Top'
'Posy'   'Topsi'

Six medium tall about 60 to 75 cm (2 to 2½ ft)

'Allgold'   'News'
'Chanelle'   'Orangeade'
'City of Belfast'   'Sarabande'

Six tall, about 75 to 90 cm (2½ to 3 ft)

'Arthur Bell'   'Orange Sensation'
'Dainty Maid'   'Pink Parfait'
'Iceberg'   'Vesper'

Hedges

Short, up to 1·5 m (5 ft)

'Alexander'   'Fred Loads'
'Chinatown'   'Iceberg'
'Dainty Maid'   'Scarlet Queen Elizabeth'

Tall, over 1·5 m (5 ft)

'Berlin'   'First Choice'
'Canary Bird'   'Queen Elizabeth'
'Golden Showers'   'Zéphirine Drouhin'

APPENDIX B

Unusual Colours in Roses

(Reproduced from *The Rose Annual*, 1969, pp. 124–7, by kind permission of the Royal National Rose Society, a paper given by the author at the International Rose Conference in London in 1968.)

In ten minutes I must leave far more unsaid than spoken and I can assure you that many fruitless sorties were made before the final field of discussion was settled. For those who wish to pursue the more technical side a few of the books and papers which I read are listed as being considered the more useful.

In *Colour Technology* F. A. Taylor asks what is colour? A property of light rather than of bodies. 'Lightwaves', differing in lengths according to the colour, reacting on the brain. To seek to build the colours of a rose from the artist's palette is not possible and no satisfactory solution can be found by applying a general rule to colour in a particular form.

Professor J. B. Harborne now of Liverpool University, in a reprint from *Colour and Life* speaking on chemical colours in plants, states that 'the colours of plants are due to the presence in the plastids or cell vacuoles of pigments which are capable of absorbing, transmitting and reflecting white light'. A relatively small number of pigments account for the majority of plant colours but these may be modified in a number of ways, such as mixtures of pigments occurring together, resulting in the brown and purple colours of certain primulas and wallflowers. Trace metals in petals may alter flower colours: the blue of the cornflower begins with cyanidin, a substance found in most roses—but a magnesium and iron complex turns the magenta to blue. Other ways in which variations

341

in the pigments occur is in their concentration or in the variation of the pH of the cell sap. I continue to quote from Professor Harborne on 'Chemical Colours in Plants': 'It is important to bear these colour modifying factors in mind when considering the production of new flower colour varieties. Many attempts have been made to breed a blue rose. The chemical evidence indicates that one source of blueness—the purple pigment, delphinidin—is absent from the *Rosaceae*, so that there is no chance of raising a blue-petalled rose by this means. Blueness, however, can also be produced by either metal-complexing or co-pigmentation and breeders might consider using varieties with this metal ion or high flavone concentrations in their petals. Co-pigmentation of the crimson rose pigment, cyanidin, by unidentified flavone materials is certainly responsible for the mauve and purple shades now available (in, for example, the variety "Reine de Violette").' Again to summarize it can be said that our knowledge of plant colours is fairly complete. By contrast our knowledge of the form in which pigments occur in living cells is still very superficial and much remains to be learnt about the distribution and function of plant pigments. In other words we know the chemical constitution of the colours but we don't know what makes them tick.

For these reasons alone it would be useless for a layman to enter this field with any anticipation of progress along these lines, but one may tackle this question from the experimental side and by analysing the measure of success already obtained seek to follow the paths indicated.

One finds at least four strains of the magenta-lavender-brown roses and one will find that they all appear to have common factors. The first and most important strain more frequently used than any other is the 'Grey Pearl'–'Pinocchio Cross' by Boerner who perceived the possibilities of an unusual colour break. The resulting 'Lavender Pinocchio' released a wave of experiment. Of over thirty cultivars listed in these colours, thirteen owe their existence to 'Lavender Pinocchio' and its parent 'Grey Pearl'.

'Grey Pearl' reveals a remarkable diversity within parentage both in colour and variety. 'Mrs. Charles Lamplough' white: 'Sir D. Davis' red, 'Southport' which in its parentage varies from the purple-red of 'George Dickson' to bicolour from *R. foetida persiana*, a parent of 'Soleil d'Or'. For reasons which I will refer to later I think the chain might well be completed by the un-named seedling in its pedigree being 'Chas. P. Kilham' or a similar derivative of McGredy's breeding. In other words we find a complete admixture of colour with a considerable bias towards bicolours which derive originally from *R. foetida persiana* as employed by Pernet Ducher.

Then there is what I would call the 'Meilland' strain based on 'Chas. P. Kilham' and *R. foetida bicolor*. Unfortunately the McGredy rose 'Chas. P. Kilham' has no declared parentage. Al-though we find the key in 'Prelude' a cross between 'Fantastique' × 'Ampere' × ('C. P. Kilham' × 'Capucine Chambard'). Here 'Ampere' has ('C. P. Kilham' × 'Condesa de Sastago') and 'Fantastique' contains ('Ampere' × 'C. P. Kilham' × 'Capucine Chambard'). Again we find this strong admixture of colours with bicolours and *R. foetida persiana* playing an important part.

The third strain again deriving through Meilland I would call the 'Peace' strain where a cross with 'Peace' has resulted in the violent purple-violet of 'Purpurine'. Here we have ('Peace' × seedling) × 'Fashion' which is ('Pinocchio' × 'Crimson Glory'). In 'Peace' we find 'Joanna Hill' × ('C. P. Kilham' × *R. foetida bicolor*) × ('C. P. Kilham' × 'Margaret McGredy'). Here we have the same pattern of parents bringing the same results. This same result through 'Peace' has been experienced by other raisers.

Even when some unlikely stray appears, a little detective work brings the same results and in 'Lilac Time' ('Golden Dawn' × 'Luis Brinas') we find the strong admixture with white and the *R. foetida persiana* background.

In my own case a cross between Tantau's 'Surprise' and 'Marjorie Le Grice' resulted in a mauve seedling the ancestry giving the same results.

The major part of this paper is largely the history of the mauves, lilacs and purples but the brown are intimately related but much more loosely held together. Let me explain: Blue × Blue, say 'Blue Moon' × 'Heure Mauve' gives many selfs in these colours. Purple crosses largely give reds. Browns intercrossed with salmons give wide variations in red, pink, yellow and white. In other words building up of colours to their peak give the so-called blues and purples but browns are caused by the partial break-up of those colours. In conclusion I would give the results of a few experiments for which you may find some explanation. 'Rosenresli' crossed with 'Blue Moon' gives whites in some cases heavily greyed like 'Grey Pearl' 'Blue Moon' crossed with yellow gives whites with pink tints. *R. californica* crossed with whites gave light browns and mauves and further crosses with lavenders gave bicolour browns with characteristic dominant slender but short growth and frequent bunched flowerings. This cross appears to give some stability in the browns. My latest break has come by crossing 'Lilac Charm' with 'Tuscany' which has resulted in purple floribundas of which 'News' was the first but an earlier unnamed seedling × 'Lavender Pinocchio' crossed with 'Marcel Bourgouin' gave the Egyptian buff 'Amberlight'.

Here we must leave this fascinating subject which owes its possibility to those wizards of hybridizing McGredy II and Pernet Ducher who leave us to perfect that which they so ably begun.

PARENTAGE OF THE MODERN LAVENDER AND LILAC ROSES

Early ancestors of 'Lavender Pinocchio' (taken from *Modern Roses, VI*). ('Grey Pearl' × 'Pinocchio') ('Pinocchio' = 'Eva' × 'Golden Rapture').

'Grey Pearl' (H.T.) McGredy intro. J. & P. 1945. 'Mrs. Charles Lamplough' × seedling × ('Sir D. Davis' × 'Southport')

'Southport'—('George Dickson' × 'Crimson Queen') × 'Souvenir de George Beckwith'.

'George Dickson' (parents unknown). 'Crimson Queen' ('Liberty' × 'Richmond') × 'General MacArthur'.

'Souvenir de George Beckwith' unnamed variety × 'Lyon Rose'.

'Lyon Rose'—'Melanie Soupert' × direct descendant of 'Soleil d'Or'.

'Soleil d'Or'—'Antoine Ducher' × *R. foetida persiana*.

Above contain a mixture of colours, red, yellow, white, pink with *R. foetida persiana*, which is true in all 'blues' and lavenders.

One parent being 'Grey Pearl' giving lavender, brown and lilac.

'Simone' 1957; 'Lavender Garnet' 1958; 'Lilac Tan' 1961; 'Heure Mauve' 1962; 'Intermezzo' 1963.

One parent being 'Lavender Pinocchio'.

'Lavender Lady' 1956; 'Café' 1956; 'Brown Eyes' 1959; 'Lavender Princess' 1959; 'Overture' 1960; 'Lilac Charm' 1962; 'Pigmy Lavender' 1963; 'Lavender Charm' 1964; 'Lilac Dawn' 1964.

Foundation and other parents of Meilland strain.

'Ampere' 1937 ('C. P. Kilham' × 'Condesa de Sastago')—scarlet red, yellow reverse.

'Fantastique' H.T. 1943 (brownish yellow, flushed carmine). 'Ampere' × ('C. P. Kilham' × 'Capucine Chambard'). N.B. 'Campucine Chambard'—unissued seedling of *R. foetida bicolor*.

'Pigalle' 1951; 'Prelude' 1954; 'Lavender Girl' 1958; 'Lila Vidri' 1958.

'Fantan' 1959; 'Violette Dot' 1960; 'Heure Mauve' 1962.

Other 'blues' and 'browns' owing their colour to 'Peace', 'Mrs. S. McGredy' or similar parentage.

'Royal Tan' 1955; 'Purpurine'; 'Sterling Silver' 1957; 'Blue Diamond' 1963; 'Blue Moon' ('Mainzer Fastnacht' or 'Sissi') 1964.

'Amberlight' 1961 (seedling × 'Lavender Pinocchio') × 'Marcel Bourgouin'.

'Tom Brown' 1966 unnamed seedling (from *R. californica*) × 'Amberlight'; 'News' 1969 'Lilac Charm' × 'Tuscany'

From the foregoing paper it will appear that mauves, lilac and brown colours appear only when a bicolour with red inner petal and golden reverse is used at least once in the crossing.

Recently I have found that with similar parents but with the bicolour changed from red and yellow to red with silver reverse, the result is vinous red to purple. The cross, 'City of Hereford' ×

'Rose Gaujard' gave 'Great News'. So far further experiments have yet to be completed for final confirmation.

Books etc., for further information:

Colour Technology, F. A. Taylor, Oxford University Press.

Journal of Genetics, 32 pp. 117–70, 'A bio-chemical survey of Mendelian factors for flower colour', Scott-Moncrieff.

The Genetics of Garden Plants by M. B. Crane and W. J. C. Lawrence, especially Chapter 3, Main floral pigmentation due to anthocyanins which may be:

(1) Pelargonidin in new vivid orange—no blue.

(2) Cyanidin usual in roses some purple-red can be made blue under some mineral complexes.

(3) Delphinidin, not present in roses producing vivid blues and purples.

These three may be modified by anthoxanthins, yellow and ivory will influence the other pigments or by insoluble plastic pigments making a background producing greater depth of colour.

Also 'The Anthocyanins of Roses, Occurrence of Peonin' by J. B. Harborne, reprint from *Colour and Life* (The Institute of Biology, 41 Queens Gate, London, S.W. 7).

Chemical Colours in Plants by J. B. Harborne.

Bibliography

* marks books most frequently consulted

(a) Earlier books

Andrews, Henry, *Roses* (with coloured figures of all the known species), 1805–28.

*Blondel, Dr. R., *Les Produits Odorants des Rosiers* (Octave Doin), 1899.

*Bradley, Richard, *New Improvements of Planting and Gardening*, 1717.

The Flower Garden Displayed, 1730.

*Camerius, R. J., *De Sexus Plantarum Epistola*, 1694.

Choix des plus belles Roses, Paris, 1845–54.

Curtis, Henry, *Beauties of the Rose* (38 hand-coloured lithographs), 1850–3.

Gore, Mrs., *The Rose Fanciers Manual*, 1838.

*Grew, Nathaniel, *The Anatomy of Flowers*, 1676.

*Hole, S. Reynolds, *A Book about Roses* (Edward Arnold), 1870.

Jamain, Hippolyte, and Forney, Eugène, *Les Roses*, 1893.

Lawrance, Mary, *A Collection of Roses from Nature* (90 hand-coloured etchings), 1799.

Lebl, M. (ed.), *Illustrierte Rosengarten*, 1879.

Les plus belles roses au début du 20ème siècle (Société Nationale d'Horticulture de France), 1886.

Parkinson, John, *Paradisi in Sole Paradisus Terrestris*, 1629.

*Paul, William, *The Rose Garden*, Kent & Co. (15 hand-coloured lithographs), 1848, 1872 and up to 1890.

Paxton, Joseph, *Botanical Dictionary* (Andrews & Orr), 1840 (with interesting list of dates of introduction and references to 'violet' and 'purple').

347

Redouté, P. J., *Les Roses*, 1817–24.

*Rivers, T., *The Rose Amateur's Guide*, 1837, 1877.

Roessig, C. G., *Les Roses* (60 hand-coloured engraved plates), 1802–20.

Singer, Max, *Dictionnaire des Roses*, 1885.

Sweet, Robert, *The British Flower Garden* (7 vols.), 1823–38 (300 hand-coloured plates).

Wallich, Nathaniel, *Plantae Asiaticae Rariores*, vol. 2, 1831.

(b) *Rose growing, and related themes: some books of this century*

Allen, H. H., *Roses: Growing for Exhibiting* (Van Nostrand), 1962.

Allen, R. C., *Roses for Every Garden* (Barrows), 1948.

Anderson, B., Fish, M., and others, *Oxford Book of Garden Flowers* (Oxford University Press), 1963.

Anstiss, L. A., and others, *Roses* (Abelard-Schuman), 1962.

*Arctander, S., *Perfume Oil Production in Morocco*.

Beaumont, A., *Diseases of Garden Plants* (Collingridge), 1956.

Berrisford, Judith M., *Gardening on Lime* (Faber and Faber), 1963.

Billington, F. H., and Easey, Ben, *Compost: for Garden Plot or Thousand-Acre Farm* (Faber and Faber), 1950.

Bois, E., and Trechslin, A. M., trans. J. W. Little, *Roses* (Nelson), 1962.

Brown, S. A., *Compost Flower Growing* (W. Foulsham & Co. Ltd.), 1960.

Bunyard, Edward A., *Old Garden Roses*, 1936.

Champneys, H. P. (ed.), *Encyclopaedia of Roses* (C. A. Pearson Ltd.) (new edn. revised), 1964.

Clements, Julia, *My Roses* (Collingridge), 1958.

Coats, P., *Roses* (Weidenfeld & Nicolson), 1962.

Crane, H. H., *Gardening on Clay* (Collingridge), 1963.

*Crane, M. B., and Lawrence, W. J. C., *Genetics of Garden Plants* (Macmillan), 1952. (*See also* Lawrence.)

Easey, Ben, *Practical Organic Farming* (Faber and Faber), 1955.

Edland, H., *Roses* (Collingridge), 1953.

Roses in Colour (Batsford), 1962.

The Batsford Colour Book for Roses (Batsford), 1962.

The Pocket Encyclopaedia of Roses in Colour (Blandford Press), 1963.

*Edwards, Gordon, *Roses for Enjoyment* (Collingridge), 1962.

Evinson, J. R. B., *Gardening for Display* (Collingridge), 1958.

*Fairbrother, F., *Roses* (Penguin), 1958; (Geoffrey Bles), 1962 (prepared in conjunction with the Royal Horticultural Society).

Fletcher, H. L. V. (ed.), *The Rose Anthology* (Newnes), 1963.

Gault, S. Millar, and Syuge, Patrick M., *Dictionary of Roses in Colour* (Ebury Press and Michael Joseph), 1971.

Genders, Roy, *Bedding Plants* (John Gifford Ltd.), 1956.

Pruning Roses (Gifford), 1959; (Foyle), 1960.

Miniature Roses (Blandford Press), 1960.

*Gothard, S. A., *Mechanized Municipal Composting*.

Grow Beautiful Roses (Muller) (How To books), 1960.

Hampton, F. A., *The Scent of Flowers and Leaves*, 1925.

Hariot, Paul, *Le Livre d'Or des Roses*, 1904.

Harvey, N. P., *Roses in Britain* (Souvenir Press Ltd.), 1951.

Also Kordes, Wilhelm (trans. by N. P. Harvey), *Roses*.

Hellyer, A. G. L., *Simple Rose Growing* (Collingridge), 3rd edn., 1962.

Hollis, L., *Roses* (Collingridge), 2nd edn., 1974.

**Insecticide and Fungicide Handbook* (Blackwell), 1963.

Jäger, August, *Rosenlexikon*, 1960.

Jarosy (ed.), *Redouté's Roses* (12 illustrations) (O. Wolff), 1960.

*Jekyll, G., and Mawley, E., *Roses for English Gardens*.

Jennings, O. E., and Avinoff, Audrey, *Wild Flowers of Western Pennsylvania*, 1953.

King, F. C., *Gardening with Compost* (Faber and Faber), 1944.

Kordes, Wilhelm, *see* Harvey.

*Lawrence, W. J. C., *Practical Plant Breeding* (Allen & Unwin), 1951.

*Lowson, J. M., *Text Book of Botany* (University Tutorial Press), 1956.

Mannering, E., *Best of Redouté Roses* (Ariel Press), 1959.

Maunsell, J. E. B., *Natural Gardening* (Faber and Faber), 1958.

McFarland, J. H., *How to Grow Roses* (Macmillan), 1948.

*McQuown, F. R., *Intelligent Gardening* (Transatlantic), 1959.
Plant Breeding for Gardens (Collingridge).

Milton, John, *Rose Growing Simplified* (Hearthside Press, New York).

*Norman, A., *Successful Rose Growing* (Collingridge), 3rd edn., 1962.

Park, B., *Collins' Guide to Roses* (Collins), 1956.
The World of Roses (Harrap), 1962.
Roses: the Cultivation of the Rose (National Rose Society).

*Pemberton, J. H., *Roses, their History, Development and Cultivation* (Longmans & Co.).

Poulsen, Svend, *Poulsen on the Rose* (trans. by C. C. McCallum) (Macgibbon & Kee), 1955.

Rayner, M. C., and Neilson-Jones, W., *Problems in Tree Nutrition* (Faber and Faber). (The reader's attention is called to the Bibliography.)

Rehder, Alfred, *Manual of Cultivated Trees and Shrubs, in North America* (Macmillan, N.Y.), 1947.

*Rolet, Antoine, *Plantes à Parfums et Plantes Aromatiques* (J. B. Ballière et fils), Paris.

*Seifert, Alwin, *Compost* (Faber and Faber), 1962.

Shepherd, Roy E., *History of the Rose* (Macmillan), 1954.
Roses, 1954.

Shewell-Cooper, W. E., *The A.B.C. of Roses* (English Universities Press), 1957.

Simon, Léon, and Cochet, Pierre, *Nomenclature des Roses*, 1906.

Sitwell, S., *Album de Redouté* (Collins), 1954.

Sitwell, S., and Blunt, Wilfrid, *Great Flower Books 1700 to 1900* (Collins), 1956.

Sitwell, S., and Russell, James, *Old Garden Roses* (Rainbird: Collins Bot.), 1955.

*Smith, A. M. (revised by): Sir A. D. Halls, *Fertilizers and Manures* (J. Murray), 1955.

Tergit, Gabriele, *Flowers through the Ages* (Oswald Wolff), 1961.

Thomas, A., *Better Roses: Rose Growing for Everyone* (Angus and Robertson), 1950.

Thomas, A. S., *Better Roses* (Angus and Robertson), 1954.

Thomas, D. Gourlay, *Simple, Practical Hybridizing for Beginners* (John Gifford Ltd.), 1957.

Thomas, G. C., *The Practical Book of Outdoor Rose Growing*, 1920.

*Thomas, Graham Stuart, *The Old Shrub Roses* (Phoenix House), 4th imp. rev., 1961.

    The Manual of Shrub Roses (Sunningdale Nurseries, Windlesham, Surrey), 1957 and after.

    Shrub Roses of Today (J. M. Dent & Sons Ltd.), new edition 1974.

Thomson, R., *Old Roses for Modern Gardens* (Van Nostrand), 1959.

Thomson, R., and Wilson, H. V. P., *Roses for Pleasure* (Van Nostrand), 1957.

Van den Berg, C., and Langen, F., *Rozen* (Van Dishoeck, Holland), 1964.

Van Konynenburg, J., and Lawfield, W. N., *The Encyclopaedia of Garden Pests and Diseases* (Collingridge), 1958.

Wescott, C., *Anyone Can Grow Roses* (Macmillan), 1952.

    Garden Enemies (Van Nostrand), 1953.

Whitehead, S. B., *Garden Roses* (Foyle), 1955.

Whiting, J. R., *How You Can Grow Beautiful Roses* (Arco), 1960.

Whitsitt, Edna, *Roses and Home Flower Arranging* (Greystone Press, New York).

Wickenden, Leonard, *Gardening with Nature* (Faber and Faber), 1956.

*Williams, Watkins, *Genetical Principles and Plant Breeding* (Blackwell Scientific Pub.), 1963.

Willmott, Ellen, *The Genus Rose*, 1910–14.

Wilson, Helen Van Pelt, *Climbing Roses* (Barrows), 1955.

Wright, R. C. M., *Roses* (Ward Lock), 1957.

Zirkle, Conway, *The Beginning of Hybridising* (U. of Pa.), 1959.

(c) *Journals, annuals*

Journals of the Royal Horticultural Society.

*Ministry of Agriculture *Bulletin*, No. 97: 'Pests of Flowers and Shrubs'.

    No. 36, 'Manures and Fertilizers Handbook'.

Modern Roses VII, The McFarlane Company, U.S.A., 1969.

Rosarian's Year Book,

★The Rose Annual, 1964 (Hon. ed. L. Hollis), National Rose Society of Great Britain, Bone Hill, Chiswell Green, Herts. (To members only 8s. 6d.), 1964.

★The Rose Annual (yearly since 1907) and *Select List* (National Rose Society of Great Britain).

★Rose Annual, American Rose Society (ed. L. G. McLean), 4048 Roselea Place, Columbus 14, Ohio, U.S.A.

★Rosenjahrbuch (Verein Deutscher Rosenfreunde), ev. (24b) Barmstedt, Düsterlohe, Selbstverlag.

★The Canadian Rose Annual, The Canadian Rose Society, Toronto, Canada, Publications: Mr. O. G. Bowles, 22 Cameron Crescent, Leaside, Toronto 17, Ontario.

★The New Zealand Rose Annual, ed. Mervyn Evans, 64 Sefton Street, Wellington, New Zealand.

Wallace, T., *Mineral Deficiencies in Plants by Visual Symptoms*, H.M.S.O.

Index

1. Rose Varieties

353

2. Rosa, references to

3. General Themes